D0267989

A LOCAL HABITATION

By the same author

Auden: An Introductory Essay
The Uses of Literacy
Speaking to Each Other:
Volume 1: About Society
Volume 2: About Literature
Only Connect – On Culture and Communication:
The BBC Reith Lectures 1971
An Idea and Its Servants: UNESCO from Within
An English Temper
An Idea of Europe
(with Douglas Johnson)

A LOCAL HABITATION

(Life and Times, Volume I: 1918–40)

RICHARD HOGGART

Chatto & Windus
LONDON

Published in 1988 by
Chatto & Windus Ltd,
30 Bedford Square
London WC1B 3Rp

A CIP catalogue record for this book is available from the British Library

ISBN 0 7011 3305 8

Photoset and printed by
Redwood Burn Limited, Trowbridge, Wiltshire

CONTENTS

To the memory of
our father, mother and grandmother

ACKNOWLEDGMENTS

For advice on the text, of many kinds, I am deeply indebted to: Geoffrey Goodman, Stephen Hearst, Jean and Arthur Humphreys, Graham Martin, John Miller, Michael Orrom, Bernard Schilling and Gwen and Roy Shaw.

For practical help, also of many kinds, I am very grateful to: N. K. Robinson (Headmaster of Cockburn High School), Mark Le Fanu, Jean Orba, the Local History Librarian at Leeds Central Library, the Registrar's Secretary at the University of Leeds, the West Yorkshire Archive Service and Jeremy Lewis, Kathy Zuckerman and all the supporting services at Chatto and Windus.

My debt to Catharine Carver is, as so often, enormous. Her editing, both detailed and imaginative, is irreplaceable.

Once more also, I owe members of my family a large debt of gratitude for guidance, encouragement and support: my brother Tom, our children and, above all, my wife.

The author and publishers would like to thank the following for permission to include copyright material: Professor Miriam Allott: 'Exodus' by Kenneth Allott; A. D. Peters Ltd: 'The Garden Party' by Hilaire Belloc; Faber and Faber Ltd: 'In Praise of Limestone' by W. H. Auden, 'East Coker' and 'Little Gidding' by T. S. Eliot, 'An Arundel Tomb' by Philip Larkin, 'The Combat' by Edwin Muir, and 'The Lake Isle' by Ezra Pound; Chatto & Windus Ltd: 'Missing Dates' by William Empson; Edward Arnold, Ltd: *Aspects of the Novel* and *Howards End* by E. M. Forster; Sidgwick & Jackson Ltd: *Waste* by Harley Granville-Barker; Tony Harrison: 'Cremation'; the Estate of the Late Sonia Brownell Orwell and Secker & Warburg: *The Road to Wigan Pier* by George Orwell; and Michael

B. Yeats and Macmillan London Ltd: 'The Tower', 'The Circus Animals' Desertion' and 'Lapis Lazuli' by W. B. Yeats.

PREFACE

This is an attempt to make, out of a personal story, a sense rather more than the personal. It cannot use the devices of fiction or drama: the shape, if any, has to emerge; and there can be no aesthetic distancing. Not that most fiction or drama can properly be called impersonal, entirely removed from the writer. I like Samuel Butler: 'Every man's work, whether it be literature or music or pictures or architecture or anything else, is always a portrait of himself.'

The motto from *Eminent Victorians* is a graphic image to describe the way one tries to tap memory. I have played with many others: it's like draining a glass tube inserted somewhere in the back of your head; it's a psychospeleological exploration; it's panning for gold – and there is never much of that.

How do you recognise gold anyway? The fact that memory clings to this incident and refuses against all evidence to agree to the recovery of that, may tell you little about the representational value of any incident, a lot about your own inhibitions.

In case anyone feels embarrassed merely by being mentioned in a book, and some people may no matter how friendly or neutral the reference, I have changed all names except those it would be pedantic to alter.

In *The Uses of Literacy* I also used some personal incidents for their general illustrative value. Some of them I could not omit here; they are also part of the personal story. But because the purposes of the two books are different, these few incidents have usually been described from different angles.

On the same reasoning I have used, again in altered form, elements of three pieces published elsewhere. The only one of substantial length comes from a memoir on Bonamy Dobrée and that is now taken up to his death.

RICHARD HOGGART

Home is where one starts from.

T. S. ELIOT

He will row out over that great ocean of material and lower down into it, here and there, a little bucket, which will bring up to the light of day some characteristic specimen, from these far depths, to be examined with a careful curiosity.

LYTTON STRACHEY

We feel in one world, we think and name in another. Between the two we can set up a system of references, but we cannot fill the gap.

MARCEL PROUST

CHAPTER 1

ST JAMES'S

My Aunt Annie is dying in St James's Hospital.

To someone not from the North that curt opening sentence might seem an attempt to capture sentimental attention. To someone from, for instance, the Leeds working class such a statement has had for decades a simple force. The possessive – 'my' or, when you are speaking from within the body of the family, 'our' – belongs to the fabric of your life; to start: 'Aunt Annie is dying . . .' would evoke a different world. St James's is where many of the poor of Leeds have gone to die for generations. 'She got real bad in the night, so they've tekken 'er to St James's.' There was fatality in the way that was said. It was accepted that this was what 'They' did at that moment. Not long after, you would probably hear that she'd 'gone'. The two most favoured words in the immediate prologue to and aftermath of a funeral were 'gone' and 'went' ('Ah, she went last week') rather than 'died'. For more genteel use, the favourites were 'passed away' and 'gone to a better place'.

It had to be St James's, that spreadeagled pile up in Burmantofts about a mile past the huge roundabout, on the edge of which Quarry Hill – a vast, Viennese-inspired, workers' apartment complex – used to stand. Promoted by a reforming and, with other projects, effective chairman of the Leeds Housing Committee, the Rev. Charles Jenkinson, that was. But English working-class people like horizontal urban villages, not European-style high-rise flats. By the Seventies Quarry Hill had become a noxious slum and is now knocked down.

Two monuments: one to the turn-of-the-century Board of Guardians' grim-brick era, the other to well-meant but culturally insensitive pre-war Socialism. (One of the earliest pieces I ever wrote – it was for the Leeds University students' magazine – was about the

Rev. Jenkinson's dream-block. Did I compare it with the back-to-backs of Hunslet? If so, in what sense? I cannot remember.)

St James's is still, in its central bulk, a great loveless and graceless-looking mass, though now it has some large modern additions whose architecture says 'function' rather than 'public charity'. The second biggest hospital in Europe, a registrar told me; in number of beds, I guess. By all sorts of large acts and small touches it's been made to seem more powerful and important yet less to be dreaded, less a patronage for the poor, brighter. The large sign outside now describes it as 'St James's University Hospital' and the blocks have been given conventionally and locally imposing names: 'The Princess Royal Wing' (that's the Harewood connection, their seat is a few miles up the road, into the country); and 'The Chancellor's Wing' (presumably in honour of the Duchess of Kent, a Yorkshire landowner's daughter and the present Chancellor of the University).

The National Health Service has poured money into the place, into its facilities and into trying to 'humanise' it. What a word of the times. Sometimes a manipulative word, a word which assumes people are to be handled, given some imitation of the familiar so as to keep them happy or quiet. Build some vast contraption devoted to your technocratic purpose, remember that it will have to be 'humanised', and so add a few inorganic touches, like the small whorl of confectioner's custard on each of a thousand mass-produced, synthetic buns.

Not that St James's is like that. It's too ad hoc, too make-do-and-mend, for real humanity to be squeezed out. For example, the funny little attempts to transform the long, high Victorian wards. The improvers start by painting the walls in a way which brings down the eye-line. They renovate the sitting-up areas with chintzy easy chairs (mass-produced, not middle-class quality, but inviting), television, vases of flowers brought by visitors and then donated by patients, prints of a sort well within the known range as defined by the chain-stores, cheerful curtains. The higher reaches of the ward are in semi-darkness so those sitting areas look like displaced sitting-rooms from a semi, or a rehearsal set for a Priestley play in a large high studio. Or, if your eye sweeps out to the massive public brickwork and back again, you are reminded of a cartoon elephant in a frou-frou.

The ward Aunt Annie is in has been given a name too. Strange the assumed power of names, no matter how obviously imposed, invented to suggest 'personalisation'; another trick and its concomitant word wholly of the late twentieth century. Perhaps, with 'humanise', it indicates that the more we are treated as parts of a mass in our public lives, and the more we withdraw to the small and familial in our private lives, the more the great public agents try to demonstrate that they too recognise the importance of the 'human' and personal. And not only the great public agents. Those who do insist on the value of the personal and small-scale fall into the same linguistic marsh by, for example, their addiction to the word 'community', as though simply to say: 'the Afro-Caribbean community', 'the ethnic community' 'the gay community', 'the lesbian community', 'the caring community' will create a unity and togetherness where, they fear underneath, there is no more than a disparate collection. The chief loss in all this, paradoxically, may be in the sense of the properly public.

It is fashionable to say that words have little meaning for most people today and have been replaced by visual images. Yet the power of the 'ise' words – not only –'humanise' and 'personalise' but 'privatise' and 'customise' and all the others which point towards a humanity which is felt to be slipping from us – their force suggests that we are denying the power of language far too soon. Words worry us because life worries us, and we worry at language so as to still the worry of life; usually by linguistic evasion. We hate to say 'out of work' so we invent 'unwaged', as though it will be nicer to the unemployed to hide them in a blanket category which also includes children and old-age pensioners. We hate to say 'retired' or, even more, 'old', so some smoothie invents the patronage of 'senior citizens'. Sophisticated people adopt the French *'troisième âge'*, but 'the Third Age' is an only slightly better evasion and irresistibly echoes 'the Third World' . . . the undeveloped and now rarely to be developed territories of the old.

So words still dominate. But yes, visual images, successive images, play an enormous part in our lives today, larger than ever before. Those images can show the same insecure inventiveness as do our manipulations of words.

Travelling almost anywhere in the developed world, moving from hotel to restaurant to airport lounge to hotel to bar and so on, you soon acquire the sense that the different settings you are moving through are just that: theatrical creations, settings or sets, something other than the building within whose shell they have been constructed.

Professional observers have labelled this 'life as spectacle' but the phrase is too one-sided and external. These are nostalgic gestures towards something important, 'meaningful', which is felt to be slipping away, a world of human contacts rooted in certainties. But the apparent memories are themselves largely artificial, second-hand, having been first mediated by television, the cinema, romantic novels. We have never known these things and places; we have known only the pictures of them which others have offered us, and to which the interior designers have given a further kind of artificial life. Even our dreams are made up for us.

Auden liked to tell this story about friends in New York. The husband died after a long illness in which he had been nursed by his wife. The wife telephoned the undertaker and went to sit beside the body. Surprisingly quickly, the undertaker rang the bell. 'Oh,' said the widow, 'I wasn't expecting you quite so soon. I was hoping for a last few quiet minutes with my husband.' 'Lady,' said the undertaker, 'I'm a busy man. Can we get on?'

Sitting at Annie's hospital bedside and thinking, now increasingly often, of the death of family and of friends, I realised more sharply than ever before that the sense of ageing and of the nearness of death comes to us at markedly different times. Some begin to show it, not physically but in temperament, before they are out of their forties; others in their fifties and yet others only in their sixties, when their own friends begin to go from the scene.

There can easily be a sentimental rhetorical attraction in recalling 'The death of friends, or death / Of every brilliant eye / That made a catch in the breath'. Tempted in that direction, I find Groddeck's puzzling, gentle observation a corrective: 'And even now it is not the death of friends which awakens sorrow in my heart but rather other occasions not usually much regarded, and this makes me a little sceptical at times about the mourning of others.' Yet one of the many telling epigrammatic judgments in *Aspects of the Novel* is, in its turn, a counter-corrective. Forster says Arnold Bennett's *The Old Wives' Tale* is 'strong, sincere, sad ...' and that 'Time is the real hero'. I have always thought Forster may have had in mind, in particular, Sophia's overwhelming experience on seeing Gerald again, thirty-six years after he had deserted her, now dead, in Deansgate, Manchester:

'She saw, in the pale gloom, the face of an aged man peering out from under a white sheet on a naked mattress . . . a general expression of final fatigue, of tragic and acute exhaustion . . . all the time she kept thinking to herself horribly: "Oh! how tired he must have been!" . . . The whole of her huge and bitter grievance against him fell to pieces and crumbled . . . "Yet a little while," she thought, "and I shall be lying on a bed like that! And what shall I have lived for? What is the meaning of it?" The riddle of life itself was killing her, and she seemed to drown in a sea of inexpressible sorrow.'

Forster comments: 'Of course we grow old. But a great book must rest on something more than "of course", and *The Old Wives' Tale* . . . misses greatness.' Perhaps. But one cannot ask Bennett or anyone else to deny his sense of the strong, sincere, sad and fatalistic stoicism of Sophia's (and his own, one imagines) sense of Time and its overwhelming final meaninglessness or riddlingness.

That interpolation about language, reality and the sense of death was prompted by the touching and uncynical efforts of St James's Hospital to soften the outlines of the hard and puzzling reality of which it has to be professionally fully aware. Whatever its given name, Aunt Annie's ward is in fact one in a group for geriatrics; number 45. The number is retained and is probably the way the ward is shown on official documents. Inside, the atmosphere gives a new and better than usual meaning to the word 'cheerleader'; a determined cheerfulness, a sustained feat of walking on the emotional water – since to do otherwise would be to give way to grief and that is unthinkable – pervades the room and is handed on from shift to shift. As we always say, and mean it, the staff do their best for all. Is it a mask which is taken off when the shift ends and they meet their husbands and boy-friends? In a way and not necessarily a discreditable way, this must be so. The tone inside the wards is probably as good as can be arrived at, given the range and severity of the problems every day. No one could keep up through all the waking hours this counterpointing of an ever so slightly hectic yet patient and relaxed jollying with the complaining, the incontinent, the slightly gaga and the violent.

There is one old woman who now and again bursts into obscenities and wild scratchings at whatever faces she can reach. And there's the usual petty theft of chocolates, handkerchiefs, Lucozade.

It's a closed world of its own where the senile, the confused and the doddering have been washed up for the last few months of their lives, a bourne from which hardly any return.

Some have regular visits from relatives, some seem quite alone in the world, one has clearly had a hard going on in the very basic working class. Another is the ward Queen Mother, visited with some style by three generations from the fairly comfortable lower middle class and aware of the difference. All are looked after with that professional, but not hard, unremitting cheerfulness. They must be given courses in sustained good cheer, those slim little trainee nurses who look about sixteen years old, and the hefty West Indian staff nurse. They have learnt too the language of hospital gentility, which is also reminiscent of semi-detached culture: 'How's your tummy today, Annie?' and, 'How are the waterworks, love?' Much more agreeable than: 'How are your bowel movements' (or 'your functions'), 'Mrs Birtle?'

I had a long talk with the doctor in charge of her case. He said he was interested to meet me after hearing so much about me: 'She's very proud of you and very fond. I expect you know.' I did, but my eyes filled at the thought of fifty-odd years of increasingly uncomprehending pride and constant affection since the day that boy, newly orphaned and freshly separated from his brother and sister, walked over her mother's threshold. At times such as that I think I know and believe what Larkin's haunting line is saying, 'What will survive of us is love.' At other times I don't believe it but wish I could.

Aunt Annie's file was extensive and detailed and so was the doctor's knowledge. They had found all sorts of things wrong and, short of going in for surgery, had been to great lengths to set her up; all, at first, on the assumption that they would be able to get her fit enough to go back home in a few weeks. Because that is what doctors do. But you were bound to think: what an extraordinary effort and expense for someone in her late eighties and so obviously breaking up. The principle that all possible efforts must be made to save the life until the very end seems absolute.

All the changes large and small in the hospital itself, from the major new equipment in the new and old operating theatres to the contrived suburban air within the cavernous wards, are gains. But the smell still takes you right back, instantly. Institutional polish, institutional cooking, disinfectant, antiseptic, the smell of bedsheets and bed-pans, phlegm on handkerchiefs, a touch of urine and the overall staleness which continuing sickness, individual or of a whole group, always creates. That compound whiff is as much a part of the active life of a hospital as sweat to a long-distance runner.

If I had ever thought of a way I would have liked Aunt Annie to end, I'd have wished her to be found, without warning, dead in her 'protected maisonette' (better planning there than in the Rev. Charles Jenkinson's blocks). That would have been preferable for and to her, no matter what the hospital's kindness. But she fell out of bed there and cut her head and the Warden came and called for another service they've been used to for decades in those parts, what they call 'sending for the ambulance men'. At first Annie hardly knew where she was, then thanked everybody for finding her and then, after a few weeks, began to alternate between saying how badly she wanted to go home and settling back into an increasingly helpless, institutionalised acceptance whilst also growing more and more confused.

When she has one of her urges to go home, though they have become rarer as the weeks have passed, she can rage and accuse the staff of ill-treatment. They've been trained to take that too, to deflect it. From one death to another, we tend to forget that consistently mild people, people who have been, year after year, apparently patient and quite unrancorous, can suddenly, at the end, open up a volcano of resentment and anger, capped for forty or fifty or sixty years. A friend's wife was always remarkably sweet-natured towards him, her family and all she met. She died prematurely of cancer. It was, he said, best not to think of her last few weeks. I remember an unmarried daughter who for years looked after her parents. As she neared death, long after the parents were dead, a stream of obscenities came from a mouth which had never before been known to utter a swear-word. It would be easy to think of reach-me-down psychological explanations for such events and no doubt some would be accurate. But even if the reality, the basic 'truth' about the character, were that last anger and hatred rather than the years of apparent gentleness, there is a kind of triumph in that the more loving side was fought for, retained and persuasive all those years.

When she is in a clearer and milder mood, Aunt Annie's habitual character asserts itself; sometimes in surprising ways. She asks me worriedly how much she should tip a certain nurse or orderly. I had not heard or thought of that before, not in Britain, though in at least one Eastern European country a local dry joke advises you to have your pockets well-lined if you want good surgery, or even reasonable nursing care, within the monopolistic state system. Here, Aunt Annie may well have thought of it entirely by herself. I don't think she was out to buy privileges; that would not have occurred to her. She was a great one for barter, especially during and just after the last war, and never asked questions about things which had fallen off the backs of lorries; almost no one in the world she inhabited at that time did. Yet she didn't seek to ingratiate or bribe. I suppose she may have been, in her helpless state, over-anxious to be on the right side of one or two recognisable people. But she had always been generous and I think the main impulse behind the question about a tip was simple gratitude to one nurse she mentions who is particularly kind and 'always has a nice word' and to a cleaner who stops to pass the time of day. That is true to her character and style in a way that rage is not and true to the complexities of her book of cultural rules.

When Aunt Annie dies there will be no one left of that generation on the Hoggart side. 'We'll be in the front line then,' my brother Tom said, showing a sharper sense of the march of generations than I have. Aunt Annie is the last of our direct uncles and aunts, our father's sister, the second youngest of ten. Ten seemed to be a very common number among those late-Victorian working-class families. Did the husband and wife, or more likely the wife, then say enough is enough? And what did they do about contraception, since they would hardly have been likely to use sheaths? Refusals, coitus interruptus, a few frightened lettings go? All of them messily unsatisfactory. Or was the wife often, after those ten kids, into her forties and more or less safe?

The ten in my father's family died out of chronological order, though not markedly so, given the usual pattern. A daughter went early, in her twenties, I think; inevitably she was remembered as the best-looking and nicest. Our father went early too, I guess in his forties. For all I know he died in St James's too; I shan't look it up. Nor where our mother was when she died only a few years later, though it is very likely that she was in St James's. It brooded on its hill, though then surrounded by jerry-built brick terraces not high-rise blocks, about a mile down the road roughly towards town from the damp, cockroach-ridden stone cottage in which Mother looked after the three of us. But all in all with that generation, the age-sex pattern of dying held. The women lasted longer, no matter how many children they had borne, often into their eighties and nineties.

When I went to live at Grandma's, on our mother's death, I was seven or eight. There were three in the Newport Street house already: Grandma, Annie and brother Walter; soon five, when Aunt Ethel came back from working in Huddersfield, about sixteen miles away up towards the Pennines; and then six, when a cousin arrived from Sheffield. I do not remember feeling cramped, though downstairs there was only a living-room; it seemed sizeable enough then; it opened directly off the street. There was a slit of a scullery at the back which gave on to a small yard with, on its far side, a couple of shared earth, or night-soil, closets and a 'rubbish 'ole'. Since ours was the end house in a terrace of only six, the yard had been made L-shaped and had a broken-down wooden double gate, opening to the street at the side of the house. There Grandad had kept his handcart; by the time I arrived he had been dead a few years.

Handcarts were as much a part of the furniture of the streets as gas lamps, horse-manure and the rag-and-bone man. They were the station-wagons or estate-cars, the compact pantechnicons of the working-class areas, indispensable for moonlight flits and for carrying odd pieces of furniture, some of them surprisingly large, across a few streets. I once saw a coffin on one. They were the first of the non-pedestrian welders-together of the neighbourhood, and did not often move out of their known servicing-areas. They're gone, but succeeded by their lineal descendants, the smallish Hire-and-Drive vans which now buzz around most towns, especially at weekends. Their hirers travel farther nowadays. It was predictable that today's working-class men would take to them; they are small, manageable, cheap and very convenient.

Upstairs at No. 33 there was a bedroom over the living-room and one over the scullery. Those cheap Victorian builders were symmetrical and economical. We also had an attic which went over the whole area of the house. That, like the little backyards and the fact that ours were 'through houses', marked us off from the back-to-backs opposite. Houses in our row were worth a bob or two more in rent. Our house, with its extra side-yard, was even more superior and the rent was nine shillings a week; I do not remember it changing. I suppose our small terrace had been put among the cheaper houses for renting by charge-hands, foremen and the like; Grandfather had been a boiler-maker, much above an unskilled labourer. And proud of it. A family story had him throwing up a good job in a Loughborough boot-and-shoe-machinery factory because an insecure boss criticised his work. 'Get back to t' cobbler', he is said to have replied, and walked out.

I slept in the attic with Uncle Walter, first in a big double bed, then in a small one of my own with a flock mattress. The attic looked over the backyard and the concrete playground of St Joseph's Roman Catholic School for Boys. Its glory, the house's chief distinction, was the bath, the only 'hot and cold' (mains connected) bath in the street and therefore one of the very few for some way around. It was cold iron, roughly painted white inside and out – one layer of paint on top of another without any preparation; like a ship's side when you look closely at it; and it had scrolly legs. A clothes-horse, pasted all over with riotously flowery lengths of spare wallpaper so as to make it into a screen, shielded the bather from the eyes of others, even when only the bather was there. More importantly, it kept out the draughts and that attic was bitterly cold in winter. It is the rituals one most clearly remembers, always; the rituals of the bath indicated its status. On certain occasions a mother from our terrace, rarely from farther afield, would knock on the door and ask if her daughter could have a bath since she was getting wed the next day. We were, though poor, clearly very much of the respectable working class.

In the living-room was Grandma, always in black though her daughters sometimes persuaded her to let them titivate her a bit for a special occasion – relatives we did not see often, for Sunday tea – with a white, lacy neckpiece. Like the widowed peasant women still to be seen in many parts of rural Europe, and she was a country-woman, she had probably worn black since the day her husband died. I remember her in no other hue, except for the occasional white touches. The high-backed chair, to the left of the fireplace and its black-leaded range, was hers. Hers too was the emotional undersea swell in the house, a quiet, worried, concerned swell.

What memories did Grandmother have of her own people in Boston Spa, of her grandparents who had known the later stages of the Napoleonic Wars and the troubles of the 1830s? She had no sense of historical perspective; how could she have? All the evidence was what was contained in the odd corners of the memories of her generation. Working-class people have virtually no sense of their own history except the oral and that is usually scrappy, confused and soon lost as they reach back to those unrecorded years. So when your hear the wife of a colleague say, for the first time: 'Ah yes, that writing desk; it was my mother's and her mother's,' you feel time shift horizontally back in a way you have never known yourself. For working-class people three generations or at the most four, alive and on the ground, an occasional conjuring up of a face (that lovely aunt who died young), a few small objects, an anecdote or two: that is usually all.

Such historical memory as my grandmother had would have been mediated to her through sensationalist news-sheets at second or third hand until she learned to read herself, or through the very prescriptive frames of reference deployed from the pulpit, or simply from gossip. The relief of Mafeking was one of the great remembered moments of her life, Kruger one of the great villains. Kaiser Bill followed him. Dramatically, it was a sub-Kiplingesque world.

She had a respect for learning, not so much as a way to wealth, though in part as a way to power and authority, but chiefly for the pure idea of learning as a liberation for the person. This may have had something to do with my own readiness, years after she had died and I had served in the Second World War, to go into university adult education; that would have been instantly comprehensible to her, and sympathetic.

Since she had been born and remained a country-woman, and became many times a grandmother and several times a great-grandmother, she had a family sense which overrode other senses. This had obliterated any personal ambition so completely that one never thought of such a quality in connection with her, and had kept well in the background any sense of a larger community other than the immediately neighbourly; and towards that she had established early her own terms.

There has long been in some older working-class women a family sense which takes the form of knowing when every member of the family was born and died over several generations, which continuously and accurately locates people, recalls weddings, illnesses, movements, spells in the armed forces. These are the family historians. My grandmother's family commitment was not of that kind. One of her daughters, Aunt Jenny, a congenital muller-over of family news, eventually assumed that role. Comparing the 'and then and then' way her mind dealt with her material with that of her mother, I realised how temperamentally different and special my grandmother had been even in comparison with her own daughters. She had no gossip and little small talk. Her mind could have coped with larger issues and with principles but had been given no opportunity. Nor did it occur to her to kick against the pricks. In another time and other circumstances, she might have become a don or a doctor.

But there she was, immensely be-family'ised. The family rootedness, above the level of trivial day-by-day talk, cooperated with her hazy but sure sense of a larger intellectual and imaginative world outside, to produce the only occasions on which she could appear to boast. The formulations were intriguing and sounded more Welsh than Yorkshire. She would say from time to time, when something touched that pocket of her mind, that 'Poet Longfellow' was one of our early Boston Spa relatives but that part of the family had gone to America where the poet was born. The eldest Hoggart boy in our branch of the family has had for some generations 'Longfellow' as a middle name. My father had it, my brother has it. My brother broke the line with his son since he did not want to burden the boy with so unusual a name.

The other artistic connection she claimed, if prompted, was with 'Painter Hogarth' who, she said, was originally 'Hoggart' but had changed his name to the smarter-sounding version on the prompting of his second wife, when he began to be well known in London. This sounds more far-fetched than the Longfellow claim. What is true is that 'Hōgarth' with a long 'o' is still felt to be more proper than the flat-backed 'Hoggart'. Not only in Britain but in Canada, Australia, New Zealand and the United States, if I give my name unmistakably as 'Hoggart' to a telephonist I will meet the response 'Thank you Mr. Hōgarth' with the long 'o' as though they must amend and gentrify my own name even to me. Those two fragments, both of which may be inaccurate, are the only intimations of early family history which I have heard.

Grandmother had a corrective concern that I should grow up to 'do right'; but above all she gave me unself-seeking love; and I returned it. Perhaps she too saw in me something of what she believed to be the talents of Walter together with a will not to squander them. Certainly she loved the fact that I was 'making my way' and above all that I could handle words well and, bit by bit, speak well.

In most of my visual memories of her, she is sitting at the side of the fireplace or, increasingly slowly, putting together a simple meal, a stew, a pie, fried fish. Her range of cooking was of course limited but, like most in her generation, she could turn even the cheapest food into a meal which was not only nourishing but appetising. So could all her daughters. It was many years before I realised that some people simply do not have that knack, or interest or sense of taste, and so produce stews which just don't come together; and can muck up any other dish, even those with much more expensive ingredients.

I have one chief memory of my grandmother outside the house. Quite early in my time at Newport Street, when I was about nine or ten and she in her early seventies, we went away together for a week's stay with one of her sons who was married but childless. That was a regular custom among our kind of people; you could not afford holidays at the seaside, even of the kind in which you paid only for rooms and the cooking of your own food. You had to have a good regular male wage-earner to afford that. Instead you went to a relative's, from Leeds to Sheffield or vice-versa; it was a change; the trams were different and the big shops for gazing in and the public parks.

The uncle we visited had worked in a draper's serving the middle class of Harrogate and was sacked for entirely commercial reasons. Grandma and I had a bleak week in their cheapish semi; they were skimping to buy it. I suppose it had cost not much more than two hundred pounds. His wife was said by the Hoggarts to have 'little idea how to make a home'; and, worse, suspected of 'not looking after him properly'. The judgment was in some respects too harsh. She seemed to be unseeing, to have no probes out, which would register how other people did this and that to make their homes cosy; nor to be able to take a message from the difference between the way other people's food tasted and that which she cooked; she simply did not notice such things and seemed to have hardly an interest in them. So her sitting-room said nothing, did not suggest warmth, or welcome, or calm. That it was untidy and cluttered was beside the point. Other people have untidy rooms, but may know by the placing of a cushion or a lamp how to make a room have a centre.

She was a skilled dressmaker and had no shortage of customers wanting dresses and suchlike to be altered or made from scratch; she could even make wedding dresses. No doubt the middle-class wives of Harrogate referred to her as 'the clever little woman who does my dresses' or 'runs things up for me'. Her earnings probably went above all to paying the mortgage. After the husband was kicked out of his job she stepped up the amount of work she took in and gradually the roles of husband and wife were fully reversed. He was a soft-hearted and now crushed man and sank into a sad secondary role, until the start of the Second World War brought him work as a temporary civil servant. Worry and the shock of losing an occupation which had been his passport to an identity had caused all his hair to fall out quite soon and suddenly, so that he appeared in public in an awful, crimped, gingery wig.

The wife's sewing operations had taken over the front or sitting-room of the house, small like the other rooms but with a bit of a bay. It could not be used at any time for sitting in and had what Orwell called 'that defiled impermanent look of rooms that are not serving their rightful purpose'. There remained only the back- or dining-room which was even smaller, but did look on to the matchbox garden. That room too was graceless. There was a fire that never had more than a few nuggets of coal in it and gave off little heat, which was largely kept from the humans by a small, spoilt and unresponsive fox terrier, the only creature on which affection was lavished in that house. The food was meagre and not very appetising: two qualities I had not met before in any relative's cooking.

By the second day, my grandmother decided to announce that she and the lad would go out for a breath of air after dinner (lunch) and so it was each day after that. We both wanted to be out of the cheerless house, to get some circulation going; and she wanted to buy me something more to eat, an apple for a penny or a bun. Those walks remain some of the most peaceful I have ever taken. What we talked about I do not remember. I expect I chattered almost non-stop and that she made suitably encouraging noises. We certainly did not discuss the inadequacies of our hosts; that would have been unthinkable. But we both knew we knew without having to enter into critical analysis. Much more important, we were bound together by unspoken affection and, in my case, by an emotional dependence I felt for no one else. It was a cardinal lesson in human relationships, in the power of love.

*

The Newport Street house was dominated emotionally by Aunt Ethel, the eldest daughter. Since our mother had been the only adult in our cottage and was, all the time I was aware of her, overborne and ill, I had never met full, physically charged, emotional rage until I lived in the same house as Ethel. It was an awful revelation and even now, if I hear a woman raise her voice along certain scales or registers, I want to be out of the way quickly.

Towards men Aunt Ethel was deeply ambiguous. She was much of the time bitterly scornful, as though she was talking about some aberration of the Creator, or randy dogs. But one of her favourite epithets was 'manly' and to that word she could give a vibrant force. She sometimes remarked on how much she liked 'the smell of a good cigar' though she cannot have smelled many good cigars in her life. She occasionally said it was a good thing to 'have a man about the house' and didn't seem to mean only that he would be useful at odd jobs; there was a suggestion that he might have some kind of charisma. At such times her voice took on a deeper note. Her ideal man appeared to be a capon or gelding who could smell of tobacco but not of sex. I never heard of her being betrayed or in any other way done ill by a man.

She did have a violent temper and a tongue to match. It is unlikely that she had been at any time good-looking. The Hoggart family tend to have one of two kinds of noses, the putty-like snubby and the large-hooky, and she had the second. Still, the most surprisingly unattractive-looking men and women get mates so long as something shines through: tenderness or shared wariness, cynicism, mutual greed, submissiveness or a similar funny-bone. An older member of the family once suggested that Aunt Ethel would have put off any man who might have been thinking of wooing her by the sheer power of her will and the tongue that went with it. One sees those capacities in some wives as in some husbands but they tend to come out most forcefully after the bloom of youth has faded. Perhaps Aunt Ethel showed them even as a young woman. Yet again, she was of the generation that grew up just about the time of the First World War, after which some women had difficulty in finding available men, so perhaps she had simply been unlucky. Or perhaps at bottom she really did not want to marry, in defiance of all the mores. At any rate she would realise eventually that it was now too late, that she was, in the phrase which then had dire force, 'on the shelf', and unlikely to be taken down. If she had, underneath, always wanted to marry, it was perhaps at that point that she began to insist, with increasing scorn and contempt, that she did not want what it was by now plain she was not going to have. She developed a dozen different ways of dismissing the other sex by inflections of the single word: 'Men!'

Annie was about ten years younger and Walter the baby of the family. He was thought, at the start of my time there, to be doing very well because he was 'a three-pound-a-week man'. Since most men round there earned anything from thirty bob to two pounds a week, he was in a different league. He was a salesman in a cheap furniture shop near the city centre and would certainly have been persuasive with young working-class couples anxiously looking for their first three-piece suite; he had a pleasant manner which only became ingratiating when he began to go to the dogs. A basic wage plus commission, though whether the three pounds included the commission I don't know. It was thought likely that he would eventually become 'a five-pound-a-week man' and no doubt migrate to the other side of town on marrying.

Being a five-pound-a-week man was the tempting goal offered to me once I had got to grammar school; by the family not by the school. The school would not have talked in figures. The top of their sights showed boys like me as possible teachers; who would not, I guess, have earned more than five pounds a week; but the school pointed to a profession, not a wage. At home the goals offered and the rubrics that went with them were always precise, tailored to the likely horizons, and metaphoric. So you wouldn't become a five-pound-a-week man unless you had 'a good hand', which meant copperplate. That was proposed to me by the uncle who had spent all his working life as a salesman in a posh drapery store, saying boo to no goose, in black jacket and pin-striped trousers, the perfect victim, until he was unceremoniously and without compensation sacked after a merger. The 'copperplate' phrase painfully illustrated the limits of his pride and the depth of his subservience. It partnered the insistence on the need to be 'well turned out' or, worse because more bitten in, 'properly turned out'. Those men, as they climbed out of the labouring working class so desperately, soon met a new ceiling and one just as ruthlessly sustained; hinds and hands of a different sort.

Cousin Winnie from Sheffield came to Newport Street not very long after I did, to get work in one of the big wholesale clothing factories. Her mother, Aunt Madge, was the oldest of all the daughters and had married a railwayman, by then one-legged because he had been kicked by a drayhorse, so they gave him sedentary work, gatekeeping or something like that. He was from Lincolnshire farm-labouring stock and did not change; pulled in as the expanding railways sought in the countryside men who could handle horses. They had eleven children, and twelve when they took in Tom on Mother's death. Winnie was a fugitive from the Means Test Inspectors which must have meant that someone in that Sheffield household was out of work and drawing the dole. If she had stayed at home and worked, the dole would have been stopped or reduced. Of all the rules which bore on the unemployed in the Twenties and Thirties that was the most hated, since it led people to act against a primary belief, that families should not be broken up.

Members of large families tend to take up one of two extreme positions: either they can hardly wait to get away from the noise and clutter or, like Winnie, they can hardly bear to be out of the crowded nest. She got herself the thirty-odd miles back home to Pitsmoor by the cheapest possible route every weekend she could and that, until she started courting, meant almost every weekend. She couldn't really abide Leeds; it was a foreign country. Nor could her mother. On her occasional visits to us in Hunslet, sitting massive and brooding and rumbling at the other side of the fire from Grandma, Aunt Madge almost always said at some point: 'Eh, it's a sinful city, is Leeds!' Had she, crossing City Square in the early evening through a swirling fog on the way from the railway station to the Hunslet tram, seen whores in tight skirts or men making propositions or couples necking near the Black Prince?

As I have said, the house was dominated, indeed oppressed, by Ethel and her moods which were often black. I do not know why she came home from Huddersfield; perhaps the job folded so that she had to head back to Leeds and get work in a clothing factory. It may be she felt she was needed at home, with her ageing mother. She did have a strong sense of family duty, but once she had obeyed it, often against the pricks, she made the lives of those around her miserable because of her sacrifice. If that was why she came back, she was misguided; they were managing in their own way, though it was a way of which she disapproved since it was ungenteel.

But she came back and, since she was the eldest of the siblings, we had to alter the sleeping arrangements. I cannot remember for how long after that Winnie was with us; until her marriage, I expect. For that period there would have been Grandma, Aunt Annie and Winnie in the 'big' front bedroom, Aunt Ethel in the small back bedroom on that floor (it took what was called a 'small double bed' which presumably meant one four feet wide, not four feet six).

Once home, Ethel was trapped and she knew it, though would not have acknowledged it. Trapped with not only her mother but with a sister and brother to whom she would be all her life emotionally connected, whose respect and affection she wanted, but of whom she did not approve; she was trapped in those shabby streets among those 'common' people; and she hated it all. Huddersfield had been an embodiment of a dream she never quite lost and in one part of her later life fulfilled. A dream of semis, of colourful curtains which pulled across rather than lace curtains which stayed permanently in place across the bottom half of the sash window and a plain roller blind for the evening; and an inside 'toilet' with a matching U-shaped rug and cover over the seat, a bathroom, some garden at front and rear and nicely spoken neighbours. She did not, could not, look higher or at any other model, and when she met, much later, the studied untidiness and unsmartness of the academic middle class she was shocked. Hers is not in itself an ignoble dream since it pays its tribute to the quieter, more obscure and unaggressive household gods. I had a colleague in the war, from Manchester, an insurance salesman. Sitting in the remote cork-treed hills of Algeria or on the beautiful tawny and blue Tunisian coast his eyes would mist over with memories of the ride back with his wife from Market Street on Saturday evenings to their semi up on one of the cheaper fringes; high tea, the wireless and – the unexpected part – exotic love-making practices. A favourite was when he pretended to be a sheikh and she his swooning white captive.

Ethel spent alternate weekends at Huddersfield and Hunslet. To us the Huddersfield weekends were a relief, until the sky began to darken again as Sunday evening approached. The Hunslet weekends were almost always thunderously unpleasant, do what we would. Winnie would go courting, Annie would go to a respectable pub or club with two or three spinster mates, Grandma would stare unhappily at the fire, at a difficult past, a miserable present and no sign of relief in such future as she might have. I would keep my head down on homework or perhaps get to the 'pictures' in the early evening of Saturday at least. So it was, until the storm broke and then no one escaped.

This usually happened when Walter came in smelling of beer. He was the first adult of some talent and promise whom I had seen casting himself downhill rapidly; not primarily because of drink, smoking, women, but through them; they were the symptoms and the agents, not the causes. The cause was weakness of will, the wish to be liked in a hail-fellow-well-met way even more than to be admired, or to be admired only if it came easy. Companionable at a casual, pub-bar level, he had an agreeable manner and I have no memories of his being vicious or mean. To me he was from the start not much of an uncle; yet he was kindly, if ineffectual. Later, as he sank downhill and saw me going the other way, he would advise me sententiously not to make a fool of myself as he had done; but he was never jealous or cruel towards me. He was, as Aunt Ethel said witheringly, 'unable to carry corn', his own worst enemy.

He had some minor talents. Once he showed me some short stories modelled on the sort of thing the cheaper weekly magazines of the time such as *Answers* and *Titbits* used to carry. They were not accepted, perhaps because they were handwritten or no better than stuff the publishers could get from known hacks in as much quantity as they needed. But they were quite competent and far more literate than anything other men in the streets around could have produced.

Whenever I come, in Auden's 'In Praise of Limestone', to the passage about the gregarious, self-indulgent, male layabouts, mothers' darlings and mother-exploiters, I think of Uncle Walter. The line about ruining 'a fine tenor voice/For effects that bring down the house' fits exactly. He did have a good tenor voice and before he began to slide was much in demand on the Leeds chapels' oratorio circuit, especially for productions of *Messiah* and *Judas Maccabaeus*. His mother and sisters were immensely proud, which made their disappointment and distress all the greater when he fell.

Drink was the known curse of the working classes and never to be condoned in excess; but to succumb to it when you were in a white collar job and the pride of your family was very much harder for them to bear. Walter had found drinking companions among other salesmen in the shops around, for the odd pint at lunchtime and then, more and more, for longer and longer sessions each evening. The congregations in those slightly raffish city centre bars ('raffish' here means given to snap-brim trilbies and three-piece suits which for their first few months have a superficial smartness but then fray and become shiny) – those congregations were from opening time onwards unmarried salesmen and clerks, or men rubbing against the constraints of marriage, easy laughers, congenital anecdotalists, purveyors of endless jokes, connoisseurs of a certain type of smut. So Walter gradually ceased to receive invitations to take part in the oratorios, distorted his voice so as to produce that kind of deboshed *bel canto* much liked in pubs, and the songs which went with it, such as 'No Rose in All the World' and 'Like a Golden Dream'; at his worst he was being paid in pints.

When at weekends he came in very late, after the pubs had put him and his mates on to the pavement where they gossiped sloshily until he went for the tram and a groggy ride home, he would find not only a miserably worried mother and a dried-up plate of supper but an Aunt Ethel primed and tinder-dry, like a projectile of great power pointing straight at him, ready for firing at the slightest touch on the trip-wire. There was no escape. He would slip on the door-step or slur his half-hearted apology to his mother and the rocket would go off. Ethel's tongue was violent and, for insult, her invention appallingly powerful and hurtful. In my early teens, still doing homework at the living-room table, I would instantly become sick to the pit of the stomach and look across at Grandma miserably crossing and uncrossing her hands.

Aunt Ethel had a remarkable range of tones too, small in the subjects they covered since they concentrated on the criticism of aberrant personality but, within that area, complex and surprisingly varied. Did she get them from the plays, usually domestic dramas, which she and her woman friend from Huddersfield saw from time to time at the Theatre Royal? Had they been handed down orally from generation to generation? Was she an original genius? Her style was extremely theatrical and abounded in stagey ejaculations, studied pauses, rhetorical questions, upliftings of the eyes and deafening conclusions. But it tore you apart and I hope never to see or hear its like again. There was an agonised spirit in there but it would not give an inch in pity or qualification or benefit of any doubt, not whilst it was actually possessed. 'Ah yes! Ah yes! My fine fellow! After all that's been lavished on him what do we see, Mother?' – pause – 'this drunken wreck, your favourite, who couldn't hold down a decent job for long and couldn't hold on to one of the best and most long-suffering girls in the world!'

The reference was to Jean, whom Walter had courted and

become engaged to when he was still on the chapel circuit; a very nice and proper, very much respectable working-class, chapel-going girl from a slightly better district, Beeston, about a mile and a half away, where the houses though terraced were not back-to-back and had little front gardens with railings and outside steps leading to the front doors. We all loved Jean and looked up to her. For myself, I had never before been close to a young woman like her, so neatly turned out, so soft-spoken and gentle, smelling so beautifully. She stayed loyal, though with increasing distress, but in the end her brothers pulled her away. They were right, though there was an only half-believed myth in the family that if she had hung on even longer things might have come right. The love of a good woman. I never saw her again but seem to remember that she married. She would attract men not by overt sexuality but by the suggestion of kindness and gentleness.

The rows went on, especially on those awful Saturday nights. Walter was the epicentre for the abuse but Grandma got some too for being soft with him and failing to straighten his jacket earlier. She shrank miserably into her high-backed chair and continued to rub one pale, bony, blue-veined hand against the other. Ethel's rage was torrential and seemingly inexhaustible in drive and thrust; you felt yourself being broken apart by it. I did not know then the word 'reduced', in the sense used in 'reduced to tears'. But one certainly felt reduced to pure misery by these occasions. There was no love left anywhere, not 'in the whole abandoned world'; all was a waste of volcanic rancour. It's not right, you whispered within yourself, without realising then what an all-embracing moral judgment you were reaching after. Years later, it was discovered that Ethel had gallstones; it was a sort of relief to think they may have been partly responsible. On the other hand she was not all that much better tempered after the huge things had been removed and put in a jar on the mantelpiece.

Aunt Annie received her share for being soft, for not joining in the attack, for being like her mother in spoiling Walter. She sat there looking thoroughly fed up rather than miserable, but said nothing, knowing that if she once answered back, the assault would intensify and lengthen. On other occasions she knew how to provoke Ethel slyly, as a way of getting her own back. No one had as much stamina, as much stomach, as Aunt Ethel. But Annie would look over at her brother with an expression which said: 'Underneath all this, Walter, you know where you've gone wrong'; or she glanced at the stairs up which he might by then have staggered out of the typhoon. For such times Aunt Ethel had perfected a kind of ventriloquism which enabled her to carry on the attack on those who remained in the living-room whilst at the same time, at well-crafted intervals, casting her voice upstairs to where the beer-and-fags-full snoring form now lay on the bed next to mine.

Winnie came in for a scalpel flick or two for not taking any interest in, or responsibility for, the way things were going at No. 33. 'Go on; use us like a boarding-house, young madam; we know that's all this place is to you.' Winnie said not a word and if her face showed anything it was merely a slight and disconnected distaste for what was going on. Fairly soon after arriving in Leeds – and I have no idea how they met, given her almost resident-hermit-like existence – she began to be courted by Albert, a men's hairdresser. She was a plump, dark, prim young woman who always came in in good time from her evenings with Albert, a careful girl who drank hardly at all and I guess kept her virginity until they married. She had a basic, undemanding, good nature, as is common in people whose blood seems to run slow and cool and who are not disturbed by intellectual or emotional switch-backing. She and Albert used to have a longish Saturday evening cuddling session in the angle of our backyard and the wall of St Joseph's Roman Catholic School – ('What's Winnie doing, out at this time?' 'She's saying goodnight to Albert') – and after that she would come in and go straight upstairs, whatever the bullets flying loose or aimed at her. Quite silent, no return of any sort, inviolate, a little bit of Sheffield in the night.

I was safe from severe attack until my teens and then attracted plenty. Until then, I was chiefly the recipient of intercalated warnings as the battles progressed – Aunt Ethel's sense of shape, pace and chiaroscuro was very highly developed – about where I would end if I went on the beer; all fuelled by the sense that here was one who might really break out to a better going-on and must at all costs be prevented from letting those prospects slip. There was a half-hidden insinuation, like kettle-drum taps in the background, that some aspects of my behaviour already suggested that I might easily go down that route. For many years after that I felt, if I entered a pub, both guilty and raffish.

Occasionally and usually in the morning, especially Monday morning with the dull routine week ahead, the rows passed beyond the verbal into the physical and fully three-dimensionally theatrical. Sunday was the second most common day for rows, again for obvious reasons: there were bad memories of Saturday night. On Sundays the table was actually laid for breakfast and the sugar was put on the table in a small, fluted silver bowl. It was the only object of quality I remember in the house. Not that it was a gimcrack home but, at their best, its furniture and fittings were such as respectable working-class people would buy, objects produced in quantity but meant to last, to give good service; democratic American-style objects. Such is a clock I now have on the mantelpiece of my working-room, which was on the mantelpiece at Newport Street during my time there. It has a slightly Palladian solid wood frame, a silvered face and gilded bordering. There is no indication of origin but it is evidently a relatively early machine-made object for an exact market.

The sugar bowl was different, a lovely simple example of some silversmith's art, and we sensed it belonged to a quite different level of household objects. Even if they had had the money, none of our people would have dreamt of buying it. Perhaps it had been a wedding present to Grandmother from the landed family with whom she had been in service before she married. That was in Boston Spa, a posh little village a few miles out of Leeds on the northern side and not all that far from regal Harewood. (South out of Leeds were some of the big works, the canals, the rhubarb fields and soon the collieries, a flattish non-feudal land.) Boston Spa now houses that great functional block which is the British Library's Lending Division, a strange implantation which has no doubt inspired executive developments to match. My grandma must have walked up to the big house to start work there in the late 1860s, aged about ten or eleven. Her sugar bowl was a restrained and delicate object and sat rather out-of-place in the house, like something which had strayed in from a more rarefied world, as odd as a crinoline would have been in those streets.

On Sundays, that day alone, we had bacon for breakfast. Not an egg and not the lean back bacon, but cheap streaky from the Sunshine Grocers where they let everyone have tick. Still, the streaky has more flavour. So do many cheap foods – and, now, some junk foods when they are not bland – a strong, if coarse, flavour as though to make up for the lack of the more expensive delicacies of taste. The taste leaders are tinned salmon, of course, and the very cheap mutton, which makes a better stew than more expensive cuts.

One Sunday a row blew up across the table, Ethel being in a flaming temper about Walter's 'vile drunkenness' of the night before. That brother, on whom so much hope had been pinned, was manifestly throwing all away and coarsening before their eyes. In the mêlée, the sugar bowl was either knocked violently or waved about in emphatic rhetorical anger and a swathe of sugar flew over the table straight on to my bacon. Not knowing American habits by then, I believed it against nature to mix savoury with sweet and was greatly dashed.

The biggest of all the early morning rows came on a Monday. They were sitting or moving round the table, briefly, before walking to the Holbeck factories or dropping to the main road to take the tram to work. Weekday breakfasts were usually bread-and-dripping and tea; very tasty, with salt on the dripping. On this occasion some thick-seam tripe was on the table, left over from Sunday supper. A row blew up suddenly in that hung-over or dully unexpectant air. Just as suddenly I realised that Aunt Ethel was in an incandescent rage. A piece of thick-seam hurtled across the table, hit no one and landed slap on the wall. I walked to school half cast down, half laughing, and already storing it. Aunt Annie and I could ask each other years later: 'Do you remember the tripe battle?' and start laughing. It comes back, too, when I read *Tristram Shandy* and reach Uncle Toby's recreated battles. Like much comedy, it feeds on the contrast between the domestic setting and the titanic energies being deployed. Still, regular rows were disturbing, exemplified a life of no calm, of little control over the immediate emotions and of unnecessary and unjustified extremities of harsh feeling. I drew more and more towards books and school.

Towards me Aunt Ethel's attitudes were most complex, far more complex than she or I knew. By nature, she could not forbear to put me to rights and there is always room for that in any of us; especially if the agent of judgment can operate a metronomic morality for every occasion. When she was in the mood, Aunt Ethel would have straightened Plato's jacket for thinking too much, or Shakespeare's for writing too much, or Michelangelo's for spending too much time painting. If a saintly celibate had walked in when she was roused she would have rounded on him for being less than a man. A family with one child would be selfish, a large family would prove that the parents were disgustingly unable 'to control themselves'. She would never have used such a phrase as 'fornicating like rabbits' but her tonal ability made the crudities of most such metaphors unnecessary. Some everyday phrases are so deeply associated with powerful moments in our lives that they are etched into memory like pokerwork mottoes. Aunt Ethel gave a force to the phrase 'picking a quarrel' which has never faded. She was as driven as a kleptomaniac in Woolworth's; at certain times she simply had to pick a quarrel.

She really was deeply afraid that I would take after Uncle Walter, suspecting that Hoggart men often had more of an easy, thin charm than spunk, than backbone. Such 'manly' words formed part of her most used vocabulary. If she had anything to do with it, she would make sure that I didn't go down that road. So if, when an eighteen-year-old student, I had a half pint of beer (that was rare, on not much more than a shilling a week in the first year, for all personal expenses, and must have been in honour of some special occasion), she would at once accuse me of coming home 'stinking of drink' and tell me again where I was heading. She had from the start been convinced that Annie would spoil me and Grandma not be able to put me right so that it fell to her, against the indulgences of those two and the miserable example of Walter, to keep me on the right track.

Since I was soon doing well at school she realised that I was bright and that that brightness could get me at least out of the dreary, without-perspective, working-class life against which she always inwardly and sometimes outwardly raged. My grandmother too was glad I was clever, but saw the possible implications in both vaguer and larger terms, as having something to do with 'being an educated man'; being able to speak to 'Them' as an equal, taking my place in that larger, more confident world beyond the streets of Hunslet which she knew existed but had no knowledge of. It was not the world of that large country house in which she had worked as a girl; it was a bustling, city world where men, men above all, talked well and got on and were assured; and thoughtful. They 'had respect' and that was more important than wealth.

Aunt Ethel's interest – and it was a passionate interest and, as the years passed, a passionate pride – was more like trying to make an assertion on her part as much as on mine, an assertion which would vindicate her and at the same time help assuage the memory of

Walter's wasted talents. She had no idea where I would go, end up; but she gradually became sure that I would 'show them'. I was the one who could break out on all their behalfs, who could help erase the memory of those years of swollen feet and tired backs, doing routine jobs; of the endless risk of being 'dragged down' by the district and the people around, including some of her own people, of the snubs not from real gentlemen or ladies but from jumped-up people who hadn't got two ha'pennies to rub together but gave themselves airs – those immediately above, the genteel-upper-respectable-working class; and the memory of that uncle who passed the greater part of his life subserviently behind the counter of the drapery shop in Harrogate, only to be ruthlessly sacked after all those years.

I could go on and on, for even as I write the memories, and the language to match, the metaphors available for every occasion, flood in to recall that endless clinging to respectability for fear of sinking without trace. The old joke about going out with clean or at least well-darned knickers in case you fell down and showed all you'd got or were run over, taken to hospital and undressed, was no joke at all; it was a proper precaution. The traps and the treadmill were there all the time and only by being nervously aware of them could you not so much rise as at least stay in place, keep your head above water. 'Watchful' is the word above all others.

'One may hear the most private affairs of other people but only in a spirit of respect for the struggling, battered thing which any human soul is, and in a spirit of fine, discriminative sympathy. For even satire is a form of sympathy. . . .' Lawrence was making a case for the novel but his warning applies to more than fiction. Aunt Ethel is by far the hardest of all my relatives to write about. I do not want to criticise her at all and certainly not a shade more than is necessary in the effort to draw a true picture. I do not want to set anything down in malice or self-justification; even less do I want to make her a figure of grotesque fun; or to sentimentalise her; or to excuse her out of family piety or the easy indulgence we can all extend to the dead. I would like very much indeed to be able to say with complete conviction: 'But after all she loved us,' and sometimes I feel that to be true. Perhaps by the time I have finished this book I will be able to break out and say it in the clear. Just as much I would like to be able to say: 'And after all and in spite of all I loved her.' In a way I believe I did, beneath all the emotional stresses which went on to the day of her death and can still come to life at an echo.

One of the difficulties is that there was always a hard, extrapolated, personal edge and thrust to acts which, simply related, looked like acts of pure love or simple kindness. As there is in many relationships we rather easily call relationships of love. Hate is much easier to identify and describe. It focusses like a burning glass. Resentment is easily identified too; it smoulders underneath for ever, except by an act of great will. Love has a thousand forms, almost all of them adulterated. The metaphor for it might be pure gold which has to be adulterated so as to be usable, to be mixed with other things so that it is, I suppose, technically impure. With Aunt Ethel the sadness is compounded by the fact that she was not, in spite of all her transparent and throbbing thin-skinnedness, very sensitive to nuances outside her central range. The sheer fierceness of her resenting drive itself seemed to preclude the more tolerant nuances, so acutely did she sense anything which bore on her own role and the way in which she was regarded. She soon knew, and bitterly resented, without apparently being able to take any usable message from the knowledge, that I preferred Annie. For her part, Annie, like her mother, knew in her bones that children need love; the assurance of an uncalculating love not tied to good behaviour, tolerant of mistakes, not keeping a record of rewards and punishments, able to make allowances. Without being intellectually aware that that was what they were doing, Grandma and Annie trusted the patient processes of growth.

Ethel had no capacity for letting up; she was a constant disciplinarian. A phrase such as 'Oh, that's all water under the bridge now' was totally alien to her nature and if she had heard it much in her environment she would have distrusted and rejected it. Add her fiercely wounding tongue, her capacity to make you feel flayed alive, and the common nervousness towards her is understandable. 'I wonder what mood she'll be in tonight', was one of our refrains at just after five p.m. By contrast, Annie, nervy, indecisive, made few demands and was kind; she simply had more natural vision, unknown to herself, than Ethel had been born with or learned.

I later came to realise that Aunt Ethel was not, in spite of her great energy and articulateness, really intelligent. It was she who first made me see the degree to which intelligence seems able to develop well only where there is also a strong imagination. The imagination is the fluid which can transform intellect, bare mind and drive, into intelligence – which is a more sinewy and muscular quality altogether.

Even now, it is plain, I can make little coherent sense of Aunt Ethel and wish I could; that would be a kind of breakthrough. Two memories are on balance far more to her credit than much I have found myself saying. As Uncle Walter went downhill, the almost inevitable happened. The furniture-shop proprietor found he had been pocketing some of the takings to finance his boozing. The proprietor was a kindly Jew and not anxious to prosecute. I expect he knew that he would get nothing out of a prosecution, in money repaid. But from what I heard he was also humanely concerned. Yet he wanted his money or as much of it as possible.

My grandmother was beside herself. Her pride and joy, Walter, come down to this. The threat of gaol over one of her own! True to form, I was told nothing of this; it leaked through the cracks of whispered, obliquely phrased conversations. What on earth could be done? The terrible problem was solved when Aunt Ethel surrendered one of the insurance policies she had been keeping up against her old age, and the money was paid back; or enough of it to satisfy the owner. It was a remarkable act. Why was she willing to do it? Perhaps she remembered that gifted (as they always believed) and greatly loved younger brother behind the very frightened shabby man who now haunted the house, and spent his evenings indoors, not at the pubs. Certainly she conjectured the likely shock to her mother: 'It'd have killed her if he'd gone to gaol.' There would be, too, her own pride. What a time she would have had among the 'passers' once that shame had got out; as it would. She provided the money and raged.

In her final years Aunt Ethel had, like Aunt Annie, a protected maisonette. When it was cleared out after she died they found a pile of yellowing newspaper clippings charting my career through the decades. There was reflected glory there; she referred to me among post-Hunslet friends as 'the nephew I brought up'. I hope there was, I think there was, behind all the knots a baffled, perhaps maternal, instinct and so a kind of love. But it became soured the very moment it tried to express itself.

There is little in the last few pages about cheerfulness or the normal enjoyable moments which any healthy lad is likely to have. They did exist, though not in the life of the immediate streets: in books, rather; in outings with my best friend, Musgrave; in a few school trips and in little treats such as going to Holbeck Feast with Aunt Annie. All in all, I turned inwards or, after I was eleven, put grammar school at the centre of my preoccupations; and found much help and kindness there.

I was beginning the movement out and away, step by step, slowly but irrevocably leaving that house, that home, that culture, those unhappy people to whom I would for ever after be emotionally linked. I carried their peculiar pride with me, in different, diffident or aggressive ways. After all and in spite of all, I had been luckier in my placing than either my brother or my sister. Above all, I had had the love of our grandmother.

Grandmother died just before Christmas in my first year at Leeds University, on her bed in the living-room, handy for the doctor's visits (and they were made as a matter of course) and for being looked after. I went out for a walk in the streets one evening and came back to be met by Aunt Ethel on the step with the news that she had just gone. As if under compulsion, I turned around and walked the streets again and for a long time. I was not thinking about anything; I was simply miserable and bereft and aware underneath that the terms of my life had changed yet again. Aunt Annie had by now left the house and had a step-family to look after; the relationship with Aunt Ethel was a different matter. For the second time (our mother being the first), the person who had above all given unmeasuring love had gone.

They were comforting when I got back and after all I was eighteen, not a kid. But in such experiences age matters hardly at all. When the one person who loves and is loved above others goes, all perspectives change, the sense of a landscape forward and backward and all around, the very feel and texture of the day-by-day. No number of good acquaintances, no succession of good friends, can make the whole as full of meaning and as bracing. For that one needs someone else to love and be loved by. Unless, I suppose, you are able to say: 'Now and forever we are not alone'; but for that you have to have religious belief.

I began this chapter with Aunt Annie in hospital. I finished the first draft as she died. By then I knew the nurses and kept in touch with them by telephone from work in London. There came the afternoon when they told me she had not long to go, so I took the next train.

When I arrived in the early evening she was sleeping or unconscious. I held her thin shiny-paper hand and pressed it whilst saying softly and again and again 'Aunt Annie, love, it's Richard.' I thought I felt a slight pressure in response and the doctor said later it could well have been that somewhere in the recesses of her mind that message of love was getting through. It was then I felt an overwhelming sensation which I had not known before and have not since known. It was an intense feeling of quiet happiness and assurance, of being caught up by unknown but wholly benign powers that were seeing Aunt Annie out on a tide which embraced all the universe and was wholly good; and which recognised me too. There was no gainsaying or denying it. I had not hoped for it or expected it, being agnostic. Nor do I know what it was. As it moved away, I looked at Aunt Annie and the parchment-white, drawn face seemed not only lovely, but radiant. I realised she was entering the very last stage of her last journey. She died in the small hours.

CHAPTER 2

POTTERNEWTON

Up to the age of twenty-two home was Leeds, various parts of Leeds. First, Potternewton, a small enclave within Chapeltown, as we always called it; the map suggests its proper name is Chapel Allerton; or perhaps they shade into each other. Potternewton is or was, predominantly, another of those respectable working-class-and-lower-middle-class areas, about a mile north of the city centre.

At about eight years old I was taken to Hunslet, to those massed back-to-backs of South Leeds, also about a mile from the centre. When Grandma died, at the end of that first university term, there were a few months more in Newport Street with Aunt Ethel before she and Ida set up shop. It was a badly driven time, with Ethel still unsure whether the leap would succeed and me overworking in the effort to cope with what university education meant. Her fuses became shorter and shorter. If I stayed at home to work or was in early, I was about the house too much. If I was late in, I seemed to be going the way of Uncle Walter. She tried to understand that a student had to work in the university library until it closed at, I think, nine. But there was something odd, not right, about it; and anyway she couldn't leave me to see to my own supper.

I did not want a dramatic bust-up but wrote to the British Legion in London citing my father's war-service and they gave me a grant towards the cost of university accommodation. I saw the Professor of Education, who was head of the main men's Hall of Residence, Devonshire Hall, in the inner, middle-class, West Leeds area of Headingley. He was full but after Easter put me in the one room he had for any student who might become sick. That sort of personal response was assumed then and for about another thirty years to be part of an academic's work, his pastoral duty. The following session I had a normal room. Yet throughout that time, until I was called up in 1940, through the war and until my wife and I set up our own home, in mid-1946, Aunt Ethel's address in Armley was still regarded by her and partly by me as in a certain sense 'home', even though on leaves from the army I always headed for my wife (we had married in 1942) who would be making her way to her parents' home in Stalybridge. For her part Aunt Ethel assumed and insisted that the mantle of her mother, as the person responsible for me, had fallen to her.

So there were four main Leeds's, from birth to going to the war when I left Leeds for good: Potternewton, the near-North; Hunslet, the near-South; Armley, the inner South West; and Headingley, the inner West by a bit North. The East was an unknown area which we cycled through on the way to the Wolds, themselves not as attractive to us as the Dales. All the time the tracks crossed and recrossed, our sister there, a cousin here, an aunt there, a schoolfriend over that side; again with the bicycle providing access to the look and feel and smell of each street in a way no public transport could. The landscapes of early life are indelibly engraved on the mind; for me with the bicycle as the main graver.

Even Potternewton is clear. Not sharp; it is Hunslet which is sharp. From this distance in time and space Potternewton has the misty air of a mid-nineteenth-century daguerreotype. When you look closely much of the detail can still be made out. Even in the first half of the Twenties it was a world in which few motor-cars appeared, partly because they were not very numerous in Leeds even by then, partly because our little, virtually self-contained area was off the through routes, partly because almost no one in that area could have afforded even an old banger. In such districts it was almost forty years, into the Sixties, before cars, most between five and a dozen years old, began to spot the kerbs.

That slow pace largely remained until the war, though there was some picking-up in prosperity as contracts began to be placed for armaments, especially with the heavy engineering firms. The first warplanes I ever saw passed quite low over Hunslet in the middle Thirties, about half a dozen twin-engined bombers droning slow and grim; an amazing sight from a world we only vaguely comprehended and surely – as we were meant to conclude – a sign of massive and effective preparedness. That was the point of going over the big industrial cities, a morale-boosting exercise, as the local left-winger told those of us prepared to listen. Crude stuff but typical of the time and of official attitudes towards 'the mass of the people'. I carried my new-found and second-hand scepticism home and was reminded by Aunt Ethel of the dangers of listening to the wrong sorts of people; even the mildest kind of public questioning had no place in her world, or in that of most around her.

For what seems by now a remarkably long time horses and carts were more common than aeroplanes or cars or vans. The coalman, the milkman, the rag-and-bone man, the knife-and-scissors grinder (his cart was a model of simple technology with the one big wheel serving as power unit for both grinding and trundling along) – most of those had their own horse or pony. So that small, neat, ecologically complete cycle was carried out day after day: the clatter of the horse and cart meant horse-manure within a few hundred yards; every bit was collected on hand-shovels within minutes; and the wallflowers in the window-boxes thrived.

From Potternewton a trip to the city centre seemed to us as great as their first journey from Hull to Lancashire seemed to our children; in our early childhood we hardly ever made the trip except to pass through the city on the tram en route for Hunslet and Grandma's house. Adults, whether from Potternewton or Hunslet, often went into town regularly, for work and entertainment or both. They each had their own Leeds, their own watering-holes, co-existing with other people's Leeds's. It was as though there was a basic grid for the city taking in inescapable landmarks, meeting and circulation points: Briggate, Boar Lane, City Square, Vicar Lane and the Markets, the Headrow, the main department stores, Dyson's clock under which you met people, the Arcades, the Town Hall. Superimposed on that basic grid, making different uses of the same elements and so acting like different-coloured removable tracings, were different people's different Leeds's: young people heading for the Locarno or Mecca or their equivalents at any particular time, middle-aged middle-class housewives heading for Schofield's or Marshall and Snelgrove's for morning coffee, Jacomelli's for lunch, perhaps the Queen's Hotel for tea. Uncle Walter's kind made for the off-Briggate bars, the cultured to the Grand Theatre, concerts in the Town Hall and exhibitions at the Art Gallery; working-class families took in Woolworth's, the Markets, a favourite pork-butcher's and Lewis's; each made their own city from the one city, according to taste and the lengths of their purses. My own pre-war Central Leeds was Salem Chapel, the City Library,

Woolworth's and the big covered Market, very occasionally the Majestic cinema in City Square, a couple of favoured but just as occasional fish-and-chip shops and public meetings at the Town Hall about the threat of Fascism and war.

The working-class housing areas ran in an arc from east through south to west, as determined by the lines of communication to and from Sheffield with its steel, the Midlands and London; and by the manufacturing centres to the south-east and west, especially Manchester with its cotton, and the ports on each coast. I suppose it was just chance that North Leeds was hillier, and had views as well as the cleaner air which comes from a lack of heavy industry. North-west and quite near were the great Dales which were felt by all social groups to belong to them, and west and south on the road to Manchester and Lancashire were the spines of the West Riding and the woollen townships which fed Leeds so that it became the greatest centre of ready-made clothing in the world at that time, or so we were told.

The unmistakably massive working-class areas of Leeds were Hunslet and Holbeck and there was jealousy between them, as though two mongrels were always ready to square up to each other. The Dewsbury Road area and Burmantofts did not have such clearly defined characters. Our own Potternewton, whose spine was Potternewton Lane on which we lived with our mother, was an odd, washed-up, working-class pocket within a very slightly better-off district, surviving there like a widowed pensioner among cheap semis. You came out of town on the tram and went first through Sheepscar, a Jewish area largely home for many garment workers whose grandparents had come in waves in the mid and late nineteenth century to escape the pogroms of Eastern Europe and lived then in fetid courts and alleyways. Many were at first used as sweated labour but later unionised themselves and fought back. Things were a lot better in the Twenties for them and for the small wholesalers and retail shopkeepers, but not salubrious. Sheepscar was a first staging-post for Jews who became successful. Their loaded pantechnicons then went north on the main tramway route, past our lane end up to the cleaner air and semi-detached houses of Roundhay and then, if they became very successful indeed, to the detached houses of Alwoodley and even Adel. That built-in sense of the need for movement, movement upwards, was alien to most of the Anglo-Saxons and Celts around them.

From Sheepscar to Potternewton Lane you passed, amid the acres of lower-middle-class housing, a small patch of what had once been just-middle-class housing and was still respectable. I had a remote relative there, a sort of quarter-aunt; her house had a high, bay-windowed sitting-room and narrower areas at the back to lodge the long-gone skivvy. I only began to know her properly when I was in my teens and even then she seemed inhibitingly genteel. She was certainly genteel, as a kind of nervous defence against the roughness of life outside her prim and devotedly Nonconformist world. She was 'kindness itself' underneath and so was her husband, a large, shy, Joe Gargery kind of man who performed some sort of specialist blacksmithery – wrought ironwork perhaps. She once told me, with shining eyes, that in all their married life they had never exchanged a cross word. I felt that was odd at the time but put it down to the quarter-uncle's wholly mild, ruminative nature. Clearly they would not discuss issues which divide and he would do more or less what his wife wished, admiring her activity of mind as he surmised it. She ran an elocution studio in the front room.

Long after I had left Potternewton I went back near there, to her house, seeking elocutionary help. Not to learn to speak posh or to recite verse in public but because since I had first begun to speak I had had a speech defect, an impediment which prevented the proper formation of 'r's' and 'l's' so that both emerged as 'w's'. No need to stress what opportunities for bullying that gave, all the way up to and through grammar school. For a dozen years the schools' services did nothing about it; indeed, I was not referred to them; that some kids spoke imperfectly was to be expected. There were plenty of more obvious ills to be concerned about such as nits or rotting teeth or bad eyesight or plain undernourishment. Still, my defect was for years a source of some misery, many disguising manoeuvres and much compensatory activity in fast and extravagant talking. At grammar school, sixth formers took it in turns to read the lesson for morning assembly and naturally to me the thought was dreadful. The English teacher and the headmaster, both interested and watchful, did their best to find a passage with few 'r's' and 'l's' and the ordeal was gone through. At that point the matter came into full view since I must have mentioned the assembly hurdle to Grandmother.

Then someone, and it could well have been Aunt Ethel, decided that 'Aunt' Alice, the elocution teacher, should be approached and I cycled up there. After two visits she realised it was beyond her competence and I was referred (all without fee) to a more specialist speech lady towards whom 'Aunt' Alice was slightly deferential as to a senior consultant. This lady had an even bigger front room as her professional base and a life-size pottery head on a stand there, in the way that dressmakers have dummies. Literally within minutes she spotted what was wrong: a 'lazy tongue' which had never learned to lift back and up for the 'r's' and 'l's'. Eighteen years to find that out. I spent the spare minutes of a month saying over and over, chiefly in bed at night, selected passages full of 'r's' and 'l's', a special diet of exercises for the upper palate front and back. After those few weeks I came away cured except that even now in moments of tension I can slip back; not in a prepared lecture but in a rapid question-and-answer session. For me ever since, and no matter what else I find in *Macbeth*, that play recalls first of all (the highly professional lady had asked me to find my own passage):

> Stŕike Heaven on the face, that it ŕesounds
> As if it feĺt with Scotĺand, and yeĺ'd out
> Ĺike syĺlabĺe of doĺour.

At the start, saying that last line was like climbing Otley Chevin within my own mouth; whilst Uncle Walter snored in the next bed of the attic.

That was in the middle Thirties, about ten years after I had gone to live in Hunslet and forty-odd years before Chapeltown declined and became a kerb-crawlers' magnet, many of its houses in multiple occupancy. In our day it was dull with the dullness of a pursed-up, tight, cliff-edge gentility. The tram stopped at Potternewton Lane where we got off and walked down to our tiny courtyard with the stone cottage at its back. Others crossed the road to the Ministry of Pensions' fitting centre for limbless ex-servicemen. Another permanent memory is of men with wooden legs or steel arm-fittings, the Pinocchio-like mechanics of early artificial limbs, standing at the gates waiting for the tram to town. I expect they had some sort of travel pass. So I simply assumed from the time I began to take notice that a sizeable proportion of the male population was in that condition. The image faded but swam into focus again on my first visit to France many years later. The seats reserved for those crippled in the First World War, still so marked and first seen on the Metro from St Lazare, brought back those bundles of lost-looking men.

A little way up on our side of the main road was the tram depot with a turntable on which trams not going on to the terminus at Roundhay could be swung round and set off for the city again. For me at the age of seven that depot gave one of the earliest intimations of the fact that there were public issues which concerned us, that people didn't just live within their own cocoons. We were intensely solitary. We had hardly any visitors. Occasionally, neighbours would drop in for a minute, usually to bring our mother a bit of something they thought she might be glad to have. Or now and again Hoggart relatives would call. I do not remember visits from any of our mother's relatives, from Liverpool. We did not take a newspaper and nor did our immediate neighbours since they were most of them living on what they still referred to as 'the Lloyd George pension'.

In early May of 1926 I saw a cluster of men standing at the entrance to the tram depot and was told by a boy whose father had a job that they were on strike, that there was a General Strike. The phrase was entirely new and with it came a first crack of light on to such concepts as workers against employers, industrial disputes, action by workers' groups in defence of their rights, into all that elaborate and swirling pattern and drama which forms a permanent part of the mental landscape of almost any adult and most children today. That was all, a cluster of men, presumably a picket but not an aggressive picket; they looked rather as though they were uncertain: no placards; no chants; no university students manning trucks; no marches or police presence. So back to our enclave where the all-embracing, careful widow's wing covered us again, behind the closed door.

There was a tiny area, a few steps down to a stone-flagged yard with bits of rough grass growing between the flagstones, a shared night-soil lavatory for the couple or three houses which occupied the yard and at the back-end our tiny place. Gone now, of course, long gone. The living-room was straight off the yard, with a black-leaded range round the fireplace and a clip-rug in front of it. A small scullery at the back of that. A staircase rising out of the living-room and upstairs one very small, one slightly larger bedroom. The physical enclosure mirrored our psychological enclosure. It was like sharing with a few other denizens a small hole in the lower part of the bole of a big and busy tree. Leaving the bole, going out of that yard, you entered a different world and could just hear the hum of Leeds.

Across the road as you looked south was a modest, lost-looking field, like a scruffy countryman who'd been left behind. It was probably let to a farmer further out. I once saw a cow calve there. At the far side of it was one of those almost equally out-of-place clusters of privately owned cheap housing. That too was a foreign world and we never expected to set foot in one of its dwellings. If we had, we would have been frozen at the sight of the trappings of splendour, chrome biscuit barrels, lamps with bobbled fringes, colourful three-piece suites, full-length curtains on a rail, hot water systems and inside lavatories. We belonged mentally not only to a different world but to a different era. We and our neighbours were the very poor and the very old, a tiny forgotten group tucked into a forgotten corner of one of the bigger cities in one of the richest continents on earth.

There was a meagre, dark, bakery shop whose back door entered our yard and front door opened on to the next, slightly bigger, yard. It was run by an old woman with a hairy mole on her chin, who seemed to live alone behind the shop. Over her front door was a jangly bell on a piece of flexible brass which she needed since she was usually in the back, baking. On Fridays she baked yeasty currant teacakes; those she had not sold she let go cheap at the end of the day or passed to someone like our mother, someone very poor indeed. I remember her not only for her teacakes but also for her kindness. We may have been Mrs Hoggart's fatherless three but she did not – some people did – make you feel put aside, something not to be involved with.

That indicates yet again the main pattern of our lives. We were so closely cared for within the enclosed family that when even now I see, or see film of, a driven bird flying to its nest and earnestly, anxiously feeding the open mouths there the image of our mother comes to mind. We had virtually no lines out to lives, interests, concerns, beyond ourselves. This was not innate selfishness or self-absorption; these were the terms, the ground-plan of our lives forced on us by the stringency with which our mother had to operate. School friendships stopped at the playground gates, since there could be no exchange of visits; we were the only kids in our yard so no one else played there. Our only visits were to our paternal grandmother in Hunslet. We belonged to no sporting or recreational or community or school groups; we were wholly outsiders because we had to be so much insiders and, since we knew no other way, we did not seek to belong. At least in the beginning. Perhaps as we grew older and heard of school mates going to this or that club or group activity we learned to say, to ourselves at least, that we did not want to belong, knowing that we could not anyway. Perhaps this is in part the origin of my continuing and by now inextinguishable initial suspicion of almost any group (demotic cycling clubs excepted). Many such groups gain their allure not only from their declared interests and pleasures but from the knowledge also that there are others outside who do not belong. Since we were always the non-belongers, those who would not be invited, we built our own defences.

Similarly, children in our position quickly learn to interpret adult tones of voice, not simply hostile tones but, much more importantly, uncaring tones, the tones of voice of people who speak of you as of an outsider and a lower form of outsider, voices talking about you as a problem, one which has to be solved no doubt but which is still an outside matter, an irruption, voices which address their own children in the low tones of love across the tea-table but which switch key, if only to the carefully polite, when they turn to you; and the worst voices will even discuss you with others in the third person, in your presence: 'They might be better off in a home, you know.' By contrast I remember, one night not long after I had gone to live with Grandmother, hearing her talking about me downstairs to a neighbour, with no knowledge that I was overhearing. Perhaps about my health or something I had told her about school. I heard the voice of unquestioning attachment and felt I had entered port again.

In Potternewton our pleasures were entirely home-made. Outside, one went for a walk up small, known, stone-walled lanes and snickets, across bits of open ground or up to the largest local air-hole, the cemetery, where there was a flat gravestone of potted-meat marble which in the warm sun was lovely to lie on. The first regular unaccompanied venture into the world outside home came on starting school and it too had a homely, cottagey air; or so it seemed in comparison with the later savageries of Hunslet. Again, the contrast was between a village feel and an urban feel. In Potternewton we were as if enclosed and the great city breathed and droned outside and away from us.

Yet that is to make the gap too extreme. In an obscure way we felt part of the entity Leeds and proud of belonging to it. We sat very low at the table, our part in its communal life was minute and inconsiderable. We could not share in the greater part of its civic pleasures since they almost all cost money: the theatre, music, the Roundhay tattoo, shopping in Briggate and Boar Lane. Our public pleasures had to be free: to the parks via a tram ride, say, and that only on a special weekend. From the various possible Leeds's, ours was the bread-and-dripping version.

Yet I do not think we felt 'deprived'. We knew even if we did not articulate, and knew from an early age, that we were 'out of most things'. We took that for granted without resentment or sense of deprivation; we did not consciously make those sorts of comparisons. I think our mother would have resented and rejected the word 'deprived' in its common modern usages; it would have suggested that she was being seen from outside as a social problem, by people who felt they had a right to make such judgments, a right she would have resisted. It is said that members of the Royal Family, living not in the world of day-by-day getting and spending, carry no money. In our moneyless isolation we were nearer the feel of the Royal Family than that of the tradesman's or skilled workman's family down the road. We inhabited our own world, a largely self-sufficient world, within the narrow scope set by the weekly Public Assistance payment. Our mother made the home seem not only self-sufficient but a law unto itself, its habits and styles God- – that is, Mother- – ordained. Where others did differently – going on holidays, getting fish-and-chips from the local corner shop in the evening or, most exotic of all, at Friday teatime, going to a Saturday matinée at the pictures in town – these were in our early years less activities to be envied than outlandish deviations to be ignored. Thus our inner defences were yet more firmly built. Our mother had a smoulderingly powerful pride and self-respect; she knew that she was doing her best, doing right by her kids and she took care, though I do not know how far this was conscious, to imbue us too with the conviction that our way of life was quite simply the right and only possible way.

Many years later I recognised much of her in Mrs Morel. She had come from what the Hunslet Hoggarts called a 'better class' Liverpool family and her husband's people were always slightly in awe of her, of her rather reserved propriety, refusal to be patronised and fierce care for her children. She had been christened Adeline Emma but was known as Addie; 'Addie fights like a tiger for her kids,' the

Hoggarts used to say. They were surprised that their Tom had won such a woman as his bride. A photograph of him which turned up only a few years ago, a moustached soldier in coarse First World War khaki and peaked cap, may give a clue. Even now a solid masculinity comes out from the faded sepia. You could have cast those two very easily in *Sons and Lovers*.

They said, as they would, that she had lent her favourite brother some of her inheritance so that he could set up in his own draper's shop, and had never been repaid. If everyone had their rights . . . That phrase was part of the mythology of working-class families, a lost pie-in-the-sky comfort. They said similarly that our Hoggart grandfather had been a clever man, far too clever to be no more than a boiler-maker in an engineering works; that he had invented a form of clamp for lifting large sheets of steel which gripped all the harder as the weight increased, that he had not patented it, that the firm had used it from then on and he never got a penny for his invention. If everyone had their rights . . .

For what reasons I do not know, our mother had left her family and found work in York where Tom Longfellow Hoggart met her at Strensall Camp, serving in the canteen. That is the story; I know of no evidence. A bold and unusual act by a young unmarried woman in those days, though no doubt the war was already shaking some assumptions about what women could and could not do. She was widowed not long after the birth of the third child, Molly, in April 1920. Tom was then three and I was one and a half. I have no memories of our father; he has a few. One is of a tall man – 'in dark clothes, I think. The whole scene is rather dark' – giving him a book of wallpaper patterns to play with, and of sitting with it on the floor in that little living-room, under the window and behind a high-backed chair. For us all, then, our mother was the sole pivot of our early lives and of our understanding of life.

Her loneliness must have been considerable and continuous, in that minute, tucked-away cottage in that lost little area; a far cry from her solid, shopkeeper's-style home in a respectable part of Liverpool. I do not even know how they landed up there, found the place. There was her husband's family in Hunslet but that was about two to two and a half miles off, a long way, and the return fares on the tram (sixpence or ninepence for the lot of us) could not have been afforded without good reason. Nor would she be likely to have found the sort of balm she needed there, no matter how great the goodwill. Her own family appear to have written her off; on the two occasions I remember meeting them after her death they seemed rather grand and somewhat removed. Whatever may have been her spirits before she married, it was not surprising that she was not a gay woman when her children knew her. We simply accepted her total commitment to doing all she possibly could for us. With it went the air of one constantly driven almost past bearing, and sometimes a kind of hardness and asperity, a poverty of patience with the tantrums and self-dramatisings of children.

I have no idea what sort of marriage it had been. Had they been led above all by physical passion? Had our father a nice wit, or that kind of engaging manner which Uncle Walter certainly had? She was slim, with dark hair given to soft waves, and finely drawn features; Molly inherited them. Photographs of her, in which she is invariably in black with dresses reaching her shoes, still show clearly the delicate, thin-boned face, very large eyes, a mouth closed in a thoughtful line and some elegance of bearing. A respectable, slim young married woman, in no way coarse or heavy. The Hoggarts do not, generally, look coarse or heavy either, but they do tend to squareness and fairly early fleshiness. That young woman looks like one who will find it natural to keep herself to herself; she did so, in a sense even from us. She could hardly have confided in young children but neither did she, even when hard-pressed, let us see much of what she was feeling. She had to hold on and hold in, or be swamped by emotional stress.

In the late Seventies, on the death of Aunt Ethel, those who cleared up her effects sent me a *Book of Common Prayer and Hymns Ancient and Modern*. On the blank page before the title-page there is the inscription, in a scrawly but not unused hand: 'To Tom Hoggart from his loving Wife Addie 17/9/15'. They had presumably married sometime in 1915. She was two months pregnant with Tom when she wrote that dedication. Underneath she had written: 'May God watch over you and keep you safe'. Then, as if on a further impulse, she had squeezed in at the top of the small page: 'God Bless You'. When I first read this I was – I still am – greatly moved. It was like meeting our father and mother, together, for the first time, like both a confirmation and a blessing.

It might be said that the inscriptions are merely formal, formally pious as of their day. I find myself resisting that interpretation. 'May God watch over you and keep you safe' draws on a direct Christian background and, however close or loose that connection may have been by then with our mother, seems at the moment of writing to have been fervently said. There is love in those three lines, uttered in the style of the day and of that war, styles no longer unselfconsciously available. I am, it is clear, working hard to explain and justify the powerful feelings that page woke in me. That prayer-book, a gunmetal watch without hands, a 1914–15 service medal in a brassy metal, some sort of General Service medal inscribed: 'The Great War for Civilisation 1914–1919', his identity tag marked 'C.E.' (surprisingly enough, since the family were Primitive Methodists – though even in my day old army hands advised you to register as 'C.E.' to avoid any discrimination and be submerged in the great majority), plus two or three photographs of one or the other of them, are all the physical baggage from or about our parents that has been carried from their generation to this.

So there, in Potternewton, she had been left on his death. Even if work had been available and the idea acceptable to her or to others she could not have left the three small children, not without an extended family to rely on. Working-class traditions in Hunslet as elsewhere would normally have brought that extended family into play in such a situation. But it worked because, usually, only a street or two separated the parts; there was also that separation of our mother from the assumptions of working-class families. So she carried on. Her health was not good; she was congenitally 'chesty' and that in those days was extremely common and meant at the least bronchitis and perhaps incipient consumption.

We were on the Parish, the Board of Guardians, Public Assistance. She had about a pound a week in all, though I imagine they also paid the rent which would be only three or four shillings a week. They took great care that you did not blue the public funds on beer, betting, trips to the pictures. No doubt they had had problems, so they gave the weekly allowance largely in the form of grocery coupons exchangeable at specified grocers only. Ours was a branch of Maypole, over towards Meanwood. Such an allowance provided, was meant to provide, no more than a bare living, one just above the level of undernourishment – so long as the mother knew how to buy cannily and well, with great good sense. Only recently an elderly working-class woman remembered the need for that skill: 'Say that such women had little education. They were clever.

They were clever in many ways'; because 'nothing is cheap if you haven't got the money to buy it'. Even today when I see young mothers in the supermarkets filling their trolleys with prepared packeted foods which are always much dearer than their raw materials, I feel a mild moral outrage. Our mother had, quite literally, to count every penny. When you have seen a woman standing in frozen, clutching misery whilst tears start slowly down her cheeks because a sixpence has been lost and difficult readjustments have to be made, you do not easily forget. There was also a clothing allowance for us, again not large, and usable only at certain shops. I feel fairly sure, especially from later experiences at shops which specialised in what was known as check-trading (whereby people who could not lay hands on ready money bought a 'check' for, say, £10 plus a premium, and could then buy clothing immediately but paid all back over twenty or so weeks), I feel fairly sure that the value in those shops was not good, that prices were often higher than straight competition would have permitted and quality not as high as it should have been. I remember even in my early teens being directed only to certain rails of suits. But we children had to be 'turned out well' even if that meant trying to supplement the cost of clothing from the unspecified part of the weekly allowance. Especially at Whitsuntide, for working-class people in the North the traditional time for giving children new clothes. On Whit Sunday you then went round the family and near-neighbours, showing off the outfit.

It must have seemed unthinkable to our mother, even though she was not straight working-class herself, that we should not have been newly kitted out then as other children were. Not to have done that would have been a final admission that she was on the ground. One such Whit Sunday stands out, when we were about four, six and eight. She had managed to put Molly into a pretty little flowered frock and Tom and me in identical blue-and-white 'sailor suits', no doubt suggesting a school performance of *H.M.S. Pinafore* but very popular at that time and vaguely patriotic. There was a whistle on a cord in the top left-hand pocket and we shone with our splendour. These are unusually exact details because Aunt Annie gave them to me only about thirty or so years ago. She had been deeply moved by the sight of 'Addie bringing her three bairns with such pride' to Hunslet for the paternal grandmother, the aunts and uncle to see.

In addition to the calculations which must have gone on to make those outfits possible, our mother must have had to fadge during the week before so as to be sure of having the tram fares. We come back to that particular, largely unrecognised, enduring hardship in the lives of poor people, especially if they have self-respect: that they have no room for manoeuvre, and must endlessly calculate. Everything is so much easier if there is a little to play with. It seems an ironic and perverse extra burden on the poor that they must, if they are to survive and not sink, manage their money like accountants. Nothing can be allowed to spill over, hang loose, be casual at the edges. There is no scope for odd movement, no play in the fabric of daily life. That lost sixpence, a small false move into a minor extravagance, and the sum simply does not work out, the jigsaw come together.

Among my early reasons for respecting that unmistakably upper-middle-class Kingsman, E. M. Forster, was his insight into and compassion for such things. He had the percipience and generosity to have Margaret Schlegel say, of the prickliness and worrisomeness of people on the edge, that it is much easier to be relaxed and nice if you have a bit extra to play with: 'Money pads the edges of things. God help those who have none.' Later in the same conversation, which came like an illumination to me at sixteen, he has his character say: 'The poor cannot always reach those whom they want to love, and they can hardly ever escape from those whom they love no longer.' But that last half-sentence points to a whole other area of possible unhappiness.

Recalling all this, I still wonder how our mother managed. Did some of her family after all send her money from time to time, the little which might have made all the difference to her difficult going on? Did that brother of whom she was said to be particularly fond help her, especially if his business prospered reasonably? Or was it all calculation within the Board of Guardians limits, with that intense pride as a spur?

It was, I feel sure, a pride which forbade whining or self-pity or begging letters or letting yourself be dragged down; a determination that though nothing was likely to recover her own situation or give her blooming health, her children would not only not suffer but would do better, would do some of the things she might have done; if only . . . No wonder that the immediate refrain in Newport Street, if I announced that I had passed Matriculation or Higher School

Certificate well or got a place at the University, was: 'Ah, if only your mother could see you now.' When my pronunciation became 'educated' and my adult intonations developed they would say I sounded like my mother.

Her determination that we should not sound and be Leeds working-class might have seemed, to some rapid-judging outsiders, a striving above all to hold on to the level of family respectability she had herself been brought up in; no doubt it partly was. To some modern social observers it might seem yet another variant of aspirant or deferential working-class or lower-middle-class attitudes. Perhaps so to some extent; but, unqualified, those would be over-simple categorisations. She was right to see much in the lives of some others in similar positions – when she had to go to public offices about an aspect of the children's health or about clothing coupons or any other benefit which had to be asked for and signed for – to see much which, though explainable and understandable, was not acceptable if self-respect was to be preserved; not refuge in the beer jug or in a shiftless, gossipy letting yourself go. We could not have been aware of all this fadging at the time; not so as to be able to articulate it. But the sense of it came over, and was later confirmed by remarks in the Hunslet house about her attitudes in those years.

The impression given is that, since she would not have accepted such a letting-go in herself or justified it because of her circumstances, she would not patronise those in similar circumstances who had let go, would not explain away their weakness by blaming pressures she had herself resisted; hence the occasional asperity. I do not assume she overtly judged these others in that way and perhaps she did not even half-consciously make such a judgment. But she had made it for herself. She seems unlikely to have accepted any explanation of her condition which took away her own responsibility for being where she was, and her duty to do all she could to make sure she was not dragged down to a point where she lost self-respect.

She took the Public Assistance money; she had to. But she was neither subservient towards the donors nor regarded those payments as a 'right'. Others might do that in her name, not she. I cannot imagine such a phrase as: '*They* ought to do this or give us that . . .' passing her lips. She did not seem to think that the world owed her or us a living; her outlook was unillusioned and rather chill. If she had ever been invited to consider socialism and its aspirations her immediate reaction would have been, I suspect, quite unbelieving. Which is not to say that, in different circumstances, she would have gone on rejecting such aspirations; they would have been likely to touch her more gentle side. But such larger communitarian assertions would have seemed unreal to the world she had to battle in; and her encounters with authority, though she would sometimes meet kindness as well as a colder officialdom, would not be likely to give her a warm glow, a feeling that we belong to each other and are to some degree responsible to and for each other – that attitude which, it is said, led George Orwell and his first wife deliberately to go short on their own rations during the last war so that unnamed others might benefit. That sense of 'others' one may not know but to whom one is committed, that single word used in that way, creates a community, a fraternity. But it starts in neighbourliness and about that our mother knew something, at least.

Some observers almost insist that a large proportion of urban working-class people have long been politically radical, and that to suggest otherwise is a sort of treachery, especially in one who comes from the working class. But the great majority of working-class people have been unexpectant, politically as much as socially and financially. That has been the story of their lives and so of their assumptions. To recognise this neither diminishes them, the majority, nor undervalues the importance and the courage of those who have over a century and a half been active radicals. Of the three great European democratic principles, most working-class people have not spoken much about Liberty: they have always fought for it when the need came. They have a deep-seated belief in Equality in so far as that means that each of us is at bottom, in basic humanness, as good as every other; and that is different from a populist levelling. As for Fraternity: they have lived that out day by day for centuries. It is the strongest single working-class principle and its expression runs from simple habitual acts of neighbourliness to the mottoes on Trade Union banners, by way of a host of institutions for mutual help, friendly cooperation and support – especially in times of crisis.

Little is said about fraternity as an important social principle in this latter part of the century. Tawney noted the lack some decades ago and it has widened. Strange, especially since latter-day Conservatism so markedly undervalues the principle, that this range of attitudes which have for so long been centrally important to working-class people and so to the emergence of the best sort of British democratic socialism, and which still survive, has been so little recognised and drawn upon by late-twentieth-century socialists.

Our mother had to survive in the not very accommodating Twenties and to ensure that her children survived as well as she could possibly ensure. Her lack of deference to public authorities was founded not on ideology or theory, nor I would think on religion. It began in self-respect but, in so far as she felt she had a public claim, rested in the fact that her husband had served as a regular soldier in both the Boer War and the First World War. On my birth certificate his occupation is shown as 'housepainter', but he seems to have been in and out of the army as much as in Civvy Street.

I have always assumed that she, not he, was the organiser. Certainly, our pattern of eating recalls yet again the need for skilful management, usually by the wife and whether or not the husband was alive. I do not remember ever seeing a joint of meat on the table; but that would have been true of most of our near neighbours. Even families with a regular breadwinner would usually have a joint only at Sunday dinnertime and that would have been likely to be the cheap Argentinian beef. I decided after I had seen the Hunslet Engine Company at work and learnt that it exported its engines to South America and indeed almost everywhere, that the beef was made available, along with the tinned corned beef, through the proceeds of the engine sales – which in a complicated way they were. Chicken was still expensive, still something talked about as special, a café meal for those who ever managed that, or the laid-on lunch for a workers' outing. The only solid meat I recall was a bit of rabbit occasionally.

Other than that, stews, minces, porridge, bread and margarine, dripping; and the first biscuits tasted, through someone's kindness, at five or six years old. But cocoa, cheap jam (blackberry-and-apple was the staple, much as apricot jam is today in hotel breakfasts right across East and West Europe). Cheap tinned condensed milk spread on bread was a very special treat, its cloying, gooey sweetness a certain hit with children. The cheapest condensed milk was very sweet indeed, very grittily sugary; another staple in many households. In Hunslet later, I met a peculiarly rich and yellow ice-cream which children loved. One day I found by accident the place where it was made; a broken-down backshed which the Public Health inspector should have closed long before. In it we saw the Italian proprietor, before he shooed us away, ladling can after can of cheap condensed milk into his machine.

The combination of penury and our mother's good sense meant that our diet was probably healthier than those of many kids nearby. Such junk foods as there were were not for us; and on a shared penny a week one couldn't buy much in the way of sweets even at that time; the ha'penny sweets were of peculiar and dubious provenance. So we were in good health and were, all in all, happy children as young animals in good health are. Certainly my own memories of those days are predominantly cheerful. What I have said about the rigours of poverty is true but naturally based on later reflection and the comments of others about what it must have been like for our mother; it was not a day-by-day presence for us. Similarly, though many of the memories are striking and sad, that is because those are just the moments which do stick.

Again, happiness is much harder to pinpoint than unhappiness; but the moment of happiness or, perhaps easier, of contentment can sometimes be captured. I can recall one such moment which was in its nature also one of the earliest moments of self-awareness and self-consciousness. I was coming from school and was probably just over five years old. As I rounded the yard corner I saw the old lady at her bakery shop door and said hello. She smiled back and said: 'Hello, Sunny Jim. Always cheerful.' Perhaps she said that to all the children around there. But it was the first time I had heard it, or registered it, and I took it as a personal description and compliment, a judgment from an adult not of our family. That was the first time I saw my own personality from outside, as something which was noted by and affected other people, which they could and would like or dislike or simply ignore. I suppose I also began to register then that the impression we make on others can be adjusted by us, that we do not move through the world cocooned in our own completed selfhood, causing no reverberations other than those we have instinctively put out and which are our affair and no concern of others; if we ever think that far at that time of life. So the elaborate antennae for approach, response, withdrawal, adjustment, honouring the emotional or merely friendly cheques we put out, all build up. Most of all from that tiny incident I took the idea, momentarily, that I was a 'cheerful' lad; generally happy. As no doubt my siblings were, most of the time; that must have been some consolation to our mother.

There were no special problems at school; it was friendly and interesting. There was no bullying in harsh streets. There was sufficient food and tasty, in a living-room so small that it could be kept warm even by a near-penniless widow. Discomforts rather than unhappiness were what we experienced from time to time: red, chapped legs above the knees brought on by the rubbing of short trouser legs in damp and chilly weather, or chilblains in winter.

These memories of up to about eight years old are, after all, few and it is hard to know why some stick and others do not, except for that rough rule that the sad remain more often and can be brought to the surface more easily than the happy; perhaps partly because they are likely to be sharply etched by a particular event, whereas happiness is a continuing condition of which you are not strongly aware until one of the sad events breaks it. Like the condition of good health remembered from a hospital bed.

Another rule of thumb these efforts at capturing and making sense of memory have made explicit is that embarrassing moments, instances of some shameful act beyond the comfort of self-righteousness or righteous indignation, stick stubbornly towards the surface of the memory so that you remember them freshly every few weeks even after decades; especially, 'the awareness / Of things ill done and done to others' harm / Which once you took for exercise of virtue'. Some, perhaps the worst, are so utterly blotted out that if someone reminds you of them years later you can insist with complete conviction that they did not happen. Then gradually over the next few months, like a piece of detritus dislodged from the floor of a deep pond by a stirrer with a stick, they rise into the full light of memory and assert their truth so that you literally blush with shame; from then on they join the others in the front company. But these are likely to be memories from periods later in life than those I am now describing.

The more dramatically telling moments of childhood remain fixed, like old snapshots still only slightly faded. Do they, as the surrounding and qualifying detail fades so that they are sharper than seems credible after so long a time, become by that process distorted, adjusted to our wish to make a picture and a story which fit our needs both as the storyteller and as a person driven, underneath, to put together a personality we can live with?

Here is one, rooted like ground elder. I first gave a description of it in print thirty years ago; it is as fresh now. One day, coming back from an excursion to the Maypole grocers, our mother set the tea. The usual simple meal, except that on this occasion there was a slice or two of boiled ham or a few shrimps on a small plate. What had led her to buy that? The memory of earlier teas in better times? The echo of a particular tea with her husband? The stuff would not have cost more than two or three coppers but, as we have seen again and again, was an indulgence. We besieged her for some of it like quarrelsome and insistent young starlings. She was beset; she really wanted the tiny treat for herself and she showed it; she begrudged giving any away. She must have been fed to the back teeth by always having to share everything, every meagre thing, of never being able to have a personal indulgence. But she knew she had to give us some, a taste, which was all it would then be for the four of us. I do not remember feeling resentful of her wish to keep it all to herself; in a crude way children understand that well. Deep down we may have realised that we ought to let her keep it. But children's tastebuds have no conscience; we got our bit.

On another day she came in from a small expedition whose purpose we had not known. We sat at the old, square, scrubbed deal table for tea. She took out a pair of cheap wire-framed spectacles, every element of whose materials and style said 'Public Assistance Issue', and put them on Molly. Molly would be about five at the time. Tom and I looked blank and no doubt said something like: 'Ooh, our Molly!' Perhaps we even giggled nervously. We looked across at our mother and saw that her eyes had filled with tears, somehow held back as usual. It was as though her pretty little girl had been maimed. The scene came back to me when the first of our children was found to have a similar need. Grief would be too strong a word, but it was a wave of sorrow which echoed that of our own mother thirty years before. Sure enough, at the first meal at which the spectacles were worn, our eyes filled with tears.

It cannot have been very long after the incident of the spectacles that I came back from school at dinnertime (where the others were I do not recall, perhaps following on – or perhaps I have blotted them out) and found her lying on the clip-rug in front of the fire-range, lying not gracefully but all bundled and hunched as though she had fallen, been at last discarded by life and the times. She had been racked by a coughing attack until she fell exhausted. Her face was grey, with the lines of a long illness finely etched, as though many washes in cold water with coarse yellow soap had left fine grains of dirt there. I think we then called a neighbour and that she arranged for her to be taken to hospital; I am not sure that we saw her there before she died. The Hoggarts took over and we went by tram to our grandma's, temporarily; Molly may have been lodged in the house of a half-aunt in the next street. All this until the funeral and the making of decisions about our futures.

I have one last clear memory of our mother and that the only memory of her speaking. At some point, whether before she was taken away or in the hospital, if we did visit her there, she said to Tom and me: 'Look after your sister,' and we nodded solemnly. The funeral is a blurred memory of relatives, most of them women bundled in black, crowded in the little house before we moved off, a handful of neighbours at the corner 'paying their respects' and the statutory funeral tea at Grandma Hoggart's.

The statutory tea was potted-meat sandwiches and bread. The statutory provider was Dawes down on the main tram route, the local good baker and confectioner; he was called on for funerals and weddings even by people who could not normally afford to patronise him. Much later I discovered that the Dawes family was tenuously connected to the Hoggarts, by marriage. Years later still, a Dawes granddaughter or great-granddaughter came to read English at Birmingham University where I had a Chair. I did not know she had applied and been accepted until the Leeds connection told me, and she followed that up by calling in at my office. They were still making good bread and potted meat; memory had not deceived there; she brought some for me after her first Christmas vacation.

I do not know exactly what either our mother or our father died of. I think they called hers 'consumption', which was regarded as usually following on a bad chest and was expected to take the patient off quite soon. They said our father had died of 'Maltese fever' as a result of being stationed for a time on that island. They added darkly and predictably that if everyone had their rights we would have been awarded a whacking good pension by the War Office. Maltese fever is brucellosis and might have been contracted almost anywhere, including in Britain. But the idea that he had caught it in an exotic outpost of Empire gripped them. I know hardly anything more about him. From our older relatives there seemed to be a hint now and again that something in his past didn't quite bear looking into, but if there was such an incident I have no idea what it was. Some misdemeanour during his first spell as a regular soldier? An earlier, civilian falling from grace which had led him to take the Queen's or the King's shilling the first time? I doubt if anyone can tell us now, or deny it.

Immediately after the funeral there was a conclave in Newport Street. So far as I know no one in the small group of my mother's relatives who came from Liverpool – no doubt summoned by a telegram; in those days of few telephones, telegrams were almost always the bearers of bad not good news – made an offer to take care of any one of us. We would have been quite a burden. I heard one of them remark that children's homes, orphanages, were 'very good nowadays'; I have been told that Ethel at least partly agreed. There was a split second of fear before Grandma said she would not like to think of that. The working-class sense of family solidarity had asserted itself and they locked firmly around us. The Liverpuddlians withdrew and I recall seeing them only once subsequently, when Tom and I spent a few days over there. Perhaps they thought three even for a short visit would be too much, for Molly was not with us.

There remained, for the Hoggarts, the problem of what to do with us. No part of the family could be expected to take more than one. So Tom went to Aunt Madge in Sheffield and stayed there until he was finally called up in the last war. I expect they sent him farthest because he was the oldest. Molly went to the elderly half-aunt in the next street, widowed and with one or perhaps a couple of unmarried daughters still at home. So Molly could be near at least one of her brothers. I was without doubt the luckiest, in staying at Grandma's. What prompted the division as between Molly and me I do not know and I still wish for her sake, though not for my own, that Molly and I could have reversed places.

That was the end of the Potternewton phase and it seemed for years afterwards, and to some extent still does, almost pastoral. It was enclosed, as I have stressed. Even if our mother had lived, that little group more or less cut off from the world could not have retained its privacy. The phase was temporary, like the innocence of early childhood itself. It was pastoral because of the hidden-away nature of the small group we lived among, as in a lost hamlet in Mrs Gaskell. Or so it seemed looking back from Hunslet which was wide-open, roughly bustling, harshly working-class; and Jack Lane Elementary School was the microcosm of the Hunslet style.

This account is little to dredge from that hinterland of memory where it has been lying so long. Even more difficult to assess is what habits, what attitudes, what typical forms of behaviour those years encouraged. In such an assessment it is impossible to separate the Potternewton from the Hunslet period, or at least the earlier Hunslet period. I think I can detect five qualities absorbed or strengthened in those years.

First, a sort of stubborn pride which soon becomes self-righteous, a mixture of cockiness, drivenness, obstinacy, doggedness. 'Holdfast is the only dog, my duck'; 'I'll show them'; I owe you no subscription; a thin-skinnedness and a bloody-minded digging-in if brusquely or improperly pushed (that last a useful substitute for moral courage).

Second, that suspicion of all groups to which I have already referred and which in turn soon becomes an awkward and even sour emphasis on individuality, on going it alone though the cost is plain, high and simply not worth it on a sensible assessment. And yet resentment at being left out: so a quickness to take offence, a wishing to be liked but a determination not to care if that does not happen; and hence a tendency to hang from the chandeliers of the world's parties, in but not of them. This attitude extends to not feeling fully at home in England. Ironic, since I am sometimes thought of as one who writes chiefly about aspects of provincial Englishness. In some respects I do not at all like the English. There are characteristic English manners and styles I intensely dislike, and they include both the airs of those who feel themselves superior and the ingrained seediness that many working-class people accept as normal. There are also long-standing English traditions I love deeply and which I have met in no other cultures. But England hardly knows herself and knows least of all her own better parts. She sticks with her self-indulgent stereotypes.

Third, the fear of being out of a job, running out of money. I could not easily have become a freelance. Not because of timidity or time-serving or selfishness or meanness, though I expect I have the average share of all those. Rather, an ineradicable feeling that one must be sure of being able to keep the home going, of keeping a roof over their heads. 'Look after your sister' was straight out of that book of cultural commandments as was Aunt Ethel's 'Take good care of Mary' on the day we married. When our first child was four months old, I had a nightmare in which he was lost, and the undefined but overwhelming feeling of guilt indicated that the fault was mine. I sat up in bed and, still asleep, said out loud: 'Now I see what Bacon meant. "He that hath wife and children, hath given hostages to fortune".' All those years of no room to manoeuvre saw to that. Not years of 'Yes, love, have an ice-cream', 'Here's the money for the pictures', 'Tell the teacher you can go on the school trip/have that set of special paints/buy that educational magazine every week'. Instead, years of 'You know we can't afford it. I haven't got the money', and all the variants on that. Which is why I like cornucopia-places such as Woolworth's, or Lewis's Food Basement on a Saturday afternoon (ham on the bone, spit-roasted chickens, huge cream cakes), and never have a sad heart at the supermarket. Still, once I have indulged in one of those places a voice at the back of my head says 'You'll pay for this.'

The fourth characteristic is linked to the third: the need to gain respect and by my own efforts. Which seems to be above all by writing, not by professional positions attained or by making money. By writing, for respect; but not only for the respect of others; even more, for self-respect. And for more than that – because of the conviction that this is how you may begin to get hold of your life, make more sense of it, in some way command or at least understand it better; so no activity is more testing and in the end enjoyable.

Fifth, the conviction of the need for love, which need not be demonstrative in speech or gesture, nor only personal (though that must be the ground of it). In notes I have made over the years, I find some similar recurrent moments – such as Cordelia's brief and absolute dissolving of her father's sense of guilt towards her: 'No cause, no cause.' Even more powerful since, without a trace of generalised public goodwill, it broadens the sense of love far beyond the individual: during his trial, Dostoevsky's Mitya falls asleep on a chest and has 'a strange dream'; it calls out in him, through the sight of starving peasants and a freezing baby, 'a passion of pity' for others. He rises and makes to the court a quiet, joyful and convinced assertion which overrides and transforms his own dreadful situation: 'I've had a good dream, gentlemen.'

CHAPTER 3

NEWPORT STREET

We come back to Hunslet in the late Twenties and the Thirties, to the house in Newport Street, to Grandma, Aunt Ethel, Uncle Walter, Cousin Winnie and Aunt Annie whose death got this story under way. It is plainer to me now than it has been before that the two sisters executed a constant arabesque in my mind. It would be easy to pose them in a good sister/bad sister relationship and I have been on the edge of that. But it would be an over-simplification. Annie was unmalicious, certainly, and astonishingly tolerant. If someone had reported that a man in the next street had taken to keeping a donkey in the scullery and bedded down with it in the living-room, she would have said something like: 'Well, I never . . .', or: 'What next!', or: 'Fancy!'; and then she would have laughed. Aunt Ethel would have been likely to say it was disgusting, shouldn't be allowed and wasn't anything to laugh at. From her we had an ever-present sense of a shadowy body of moral guardians who allowed this and just as surely would not allow that.

As she aged, Annie became increasingly indecisive and worrity; Ethel remained rock-solid in her instant allocation of all new aspects of experience to the 'yes' and the 'no'. Annie had a lived-into shrewdness of judgment on character which occasionally and suddenly showed itself through the generally soft and misty lines of her attitudes, like a shaft of sun through fog. She was capable of saying something like: 'Yer know, 'e's one of those men 'oo can't ever say nay to 'is wife. She's really like a bairn to 'im. Of course, 'e's that much older. Still, 'e's made a rod for 'is own back' – which caught and summed up a great deal.

Ethel tended to keep a high-minded romantic novelette on the go but I do not remember her producing judgments like those occasional ones by Annie, judgments which seemed to have slowly emerged from daily experience and from a hardly aware mulling over it. Ethel was hot for certainty and absoluteness in judgment but the uncertainties and qualifications of reality meant that she was always disappointed and had to be disappointed. She had exceptional canalised and canalising force. In another life she might have been a very effective priestess of a particularly rigid cult.

For Annie as age crept on the edges of her character, never very well marked, became increasingly blurred and the movements of her mind like an old-fashioned corset bursting out all over; or like something which was gradually liquefying; or like one of the cupboards in her sideboard. She would ask you to open the right-hand door and take out something for the kids. Easter eggs, Smartees, coconut 'snowballs', mixed bags of chocolates, small bottles of fizzy drinks, confectionery of all kinds, lay in a jumble there.

She seemed old, they all seemed old, when I arrived from Potternewton. Annie was probably then in her middle thirties, Ethel a good few years older and Walter a few years younger. The first weeks and months were lonely but at least Molly and I could see each other. Tom must have had the hardest time of all, but he never remarked on it, nor has he to this day. He has always been unself-pitying and unself-dramatising. The Sheffield household was large and the one-legged uncle something of a sergeant-major. At eleven, Tom got the first scholarship to grammar school of anyone in our whole known family. He was allowed to take it up but homework, he once told me with amusement but giving no impression of blaming anyone, had to be done on the tram coming from school in the evening and going back there in the morning. At sixteen, after the School Certificate examination, there was no question of his going on into the sixth form; he was expected to go to work, but to a white-collar job as befitted one with his high level of education.

But to come back to Newport Street when I arrived. Such figure as Annie had ever had had gone by that time. Her teeth were already false as were those of most of her age, men and women. One was very much aware of false teeth; adults bending over you were likely to present rows of startlingly regular, cheap-looking gnashers. They put them in a glass at the side of the bed. I once, in the dark, took a drink from what I thought was simply a glass of water but soon found Uncle Walter's teeth knocking against my own. We were also much aware of corns, bad eyesight, corrected by cheap spectacles (Woolworth's usually), indigestion, flatulence and constipation ...

ailments, I suppose, which came from poor diet, insufficient exercise and ill-fitting shoes.

Most people did not get the right kind of food or enough physical exercise ('hiking' and 'rambling' were not working-class pursuits except among a few of the more self-conscious young people), so many were pasty-faced. But it was a less waxy complexion than one can see, for example, in working-class women in the USA, their hair still in curlers as they trundle round the supermarkets loading trolleys with junk food to take out to the car. Women's bodies in Hunslet were not in good shape after twenty-five or thereabouts. Eight hours a day sitting at a sewing machine did not help. Men who did heavy manual work would be very well developed muscularly in certain ways, though often had beer-bellies by thirty. Odd, though, that another characteristic male figure in those parts was thin and whippet-like.

Our puritanism made us shy about admiring the body except in certain prescribed particulars. Young lads or vulgar adults could say of a girl that she had 'a right pair of tits' or 'smashing legs'; not much more. More acceptable tributes spanned just as narrow a range. Very common were: ''E's got a right chest on 'im' and: 'She/'E 'as a lovely 'ead of 'air.' Yet all in all the body got little direct verbal attention among adults. The most developed reactions were to facial expressions, as in: 'She gave me a meaning look,' or to tone of voice, as in: 'Don't use that tone of voice with me.'

About physical matters, most girls learned from their mothers by simple imitation and then usually after marriage and, above all, after the arrival of the first child; so many habits which did not encourage good health were passed on. Up to marriage a girl could be extremely ill-equipped. When I was about fourteen the daughter of a neighbour married and the couple went to Blackpool for the honeymoon. The girl, an only child, was doted on by her father and mother and waited on hand and foot. Her mother did all her packing for that momentous trip. So unused was the girl to shopping that in the middle of the week her mother received a letter from her saying she was constipated and could she be sent some Bile Beans.

If she had not learned something about such things before, and she may well not have, she no doubt learned a good deal in that week about a man's sexual expectations, would become in that sense at least a fully-fledged woman. She'd learn, as they always said rather brutally. She could well have had a baby before the year was out; and be even more often round at her mother's.

Annie wore heavy glasses all the time I knew her and had a skin complaint which made the lobes of her ears inflamed, with broken skin. 'It's because of her neurasthenia,' they used to say; I knew that word long before knowing 'neurotic'. For ailments the longer, stranger-sounding names were preferred. The neurasthenia was felt to be the inner nervous complaint which caused the skin to break out, and that they called 'erysipelas'. It is also known as 'St Anthony's Fire' and 'the Rose', both wonderfully evocative names but country or village names, not Hunslet names. Over years nothing seemed to be done about it and one was simply used to seeing Aunt Annie stroke the inflamed place, presumably at moments when it irritated. In a stranger, I suppose it would have seemed off-putting (and to a stranger also), but I grew as used to it as to a mole on the chin. I expect Annie had visited the doctor on whose panel she was registered, that nothing effective came of the visit and so she just accepted the condition. We too simply accepted that Aunt Annie had neurasthenia (not 'was neurasthenic') and had erysipelas, much as we accepted that she was small and short-sighted; nothing to be done about any of it.

The majority of respectable working-class women in Hunslet and its neighbouring working-class areas, notably Holbeck, headed for the large clothing factories of the sort at which Ethel, Annie and Winnie worked – Montague Burton's, Sumries, Weaver to Wearer are only the first that come to mind. They produced for almost all types of market, from the near-bespoke to the cheap and nasty; so there was room for everybody, but a pecking-order between factories and jobs. Working-class children grew up assuming that all the womenfolk around them were expert and rapid at sewing.

Below the Leeds 'tailoresses' were the office cleaners, the canteen workers, the barmaids and others in a range of unskilled and ill-paid manual jobs. Above the tailoresses and out of reach were the secretaries, town-centre shop assistants, receptionists, those in jobs for which you had to be 'turned out well' and to speak reasonably properly. We had no sense of levels of work for women above those. So the tailoresses formed the thick middle seam of respectable women in work, married and unmarried. The unmarried of all ages formed a particularly strong contingent.

Most of them came back from the factory in the evening, as our three did, to something resembling a high tea, though ours would be in the lower end of the range: some tripe, a bit of boiled ham, a piece of fish; and always the unspoken assumption that bread and margarine would fill it out. They would talk about a new charge-hand who had turned out to be a tartar, or who was nice and helpful; or about the latest sallies by the comic on their line, a woman with a sharp wit. She could usually be relied on for saucy remarks and repartee to or about the men. The men were greatly outnumbered and alternately badgered or made up to, both with sexual overtones but with no promise of a cashing-in; this was internal, workplace stuff and the rules were well known on both sides. When it was discovered that some man and woman in the factory had indeed been carrying on, the rest were quite shocked.

They talked too about the whims of 'that madam', the 'passer' on their line. I felt sure that Aunt Ethel would figure in many teatime stories. The women also got fun from a state visit by some of the top men in the business who spoke lah-di-dah and lived in Alwoodley or Adel or even Harrogate or Ilkley.

Until we got a wireless set, which would be about 1930, such desultory talk went on in our house well after tea, intermittently, between the sewing and ironing or dab-washing. As Grandma grew frailer, some housework filled the space till bedtime, which came early. Neighbours rarely dropped in during the evening; that was more a morning habit – working-class life could be private and neighbourly at the same time. But Grandma would retail any news of the immediate district, a fall on the ice, a new baby, a visit from 'a man from the council' about something she could not understand; tying the others loosely into the neighbourhood.

Aunt Ethel had a strong mind and much energy to run it, as her capacity and staying power in family 'rows' showed. She was determined to break out from the tailoresses' year-after-year routines, and could be very decisive and courageous in following that aim. She and her friend Ida, from Huddersfield, threw in their dull but safe jobs late in 1937. They realised such money as they could, Aunt Ethel by surrendering what remained of her insurance policies after she had sold some to save Walter from gaol; I expect Ida cashed in her policies too. They set up their own women's outfitters. It was a corner shop with some living accommodation incorporated, at the end of a terrace of back-to-backs, itself part of a number of such terraces which climbed up the hill towards Armley Gaol. The venture succeeded, partly and perhaps chiefly because they started so close to the start of the war. When the war began, existing shops were given an allocation with which to buy stock and that allocation would always sell. The big multiples were hobbled and the little shops for the time being saved. Their allocations were enough to give them a decent living. They were also willing to work 'all hours God sends' to alter a dress or get something somewhere for a funeral or a wedding. Just along west from City Square were the wholesalers who dealt with small shopkeepers such as Aunt Ethel and Ida, and during their nine or ten years' tenure of the shop they enjoyed exceptionally good service in the meeting of their very exact demands. All of which helped to spread their names in the streets around. They were also shrewd, bold and unabashed manipulators of the mark-up according to their sense of the length of the customer's purse, and the degree of gratitude due to them from each customer for the effort put into getting them as nearly as possible what they wanted, and on time. I enjoyed those whispered conversations in the back-room devoted to how much they could squeeze out of each client: 'Of course she can afford that. They're doing very well, him and her; all that nightwork. Anyway, look at the trouble we had getting it and fitting her.' The customers, more often than not large, working-class ladies, were grateful.

So Aunt Ethel and Ida not only survived; they prospered. Soon after the war, again with excellent timing for their needs, they sold up and went, predictably, to Morecambe. Morecambe is, or was, not clashy and raucous but mildly genteel and greatly liked as a retirement home for the respectable West Riding working class and lower middle class. The air sweeping round that great bay from the Atlantic is always called bracing, though less hardy visitors find it perishing. Morecambe in winter looks like last year in a lower-middle-class Marienbad stranded on a bleak Northern shore. Still, the Lake District is just behind and you can take a coach ride there very easily. More accurately, Aunt Ethel and Ida went to Bare, just outside Morecambe proper, full of neat semi-detached houses. With their sharp eye for social gradations they had decided that Bare was where 'nice' people were going then. They quickly put down their kinds of roots, found friends among retired people around, a café in town which did a very good plaice and chips tea for special occasions; and took steady walks along the bracing front. Aunt Ethel had at last, and for what might have been her last few years had she not lived so very long, come home successfully to her dream place, to an evocation not of *luxe, calme and volupté* but of the 'nicest' kind of English life. Its props were exactly known and named too: Mason and Pearson hairbrushes, Parker Knoll chairs, the Carl Rosa Opera Company, Clara Butt, Gilbert and Sullivan, the *Daily Express*, Boots's Library, a world of 'good not trashy' objects, good as the genteel world to which she aspired defined it.

But she continued, in Morecambe and after, to lack wisdom, the imagination that can learn from experience if it is fed by patience and tolerance, the ability to trust in the long run, or to put up with other people's irritating ways because you realise that, underneath, their instincts are good. Not for her to echo Keats's charitable: 'Men should bear with one another'; or Virginia Woolf's rejection of the role of moral policeman to others: 'But after all we are not responsible' – such understandings as may come to us whether or not we have read a single book in the whole of our lives.

Lacking them, and I am not sure how well they can be learned by some people, Aunt Ethel could seem in a very exact sense of the words 'inhuman', 'remorseless'. After Ida died, she remained in Morecambe for some time but with increasing difficulty. Finally, she asked a very gentle cousin of mine, over in the West Riding, if she could have accommodation in her home. She was there for quite a long time until the husband, also very kind, realised that his wife was near the edge of a breakdown. Such force did Ethel still have as she went into her nineties. They managed to get her into comfortable 'sheltered accommodation' nearby and still tended her closely. It was a devoted, heroic effort and covered a large part of their own middle life. Now and again she would express great gratitude, though often to others who might thus be expected to feel obliquely criticised for their own comparative lack of attention to her, or as evidence to outsiders of the affection she elicited and the warm recognition she could tender. More often, she demanded, and complained to and about her niece.

Eventually, her heart giving increasing trouble, she had to be taken into hospital. Within a few days the house-doctor was describing her, at ninety-three, as a very disruptive influence he wished to be without. She had been ticking off the nurses in a manner which we in the family knew only too well. To them it must have felt as though they were having their hides skinned verbally, a quite new and frightening experience. Her last conversation with my cousin, only a few hours before her final heart attack, was a forceful plea that she be taken out of the hospital and again to the cousin's home. The thought must have been, to my cousin, almost unbearable. But it was couched in the terms we had known by then for half a century, calculated to get under your skin and stick like burrs or barbs, to make you feel almost unbearably guilty, ungrateful, insentient and worthless.

Way back, as I slowly climbed the academic ladder, Aunt Ethel increasingly boasted about me to her colleagues at work. Between being a shop assistant in Huddersfield and setting up shop with Ida, when she was working as a passer on the make-up line of a large, ready-made clothing factory, there was a widow on the same passers' line who had one child, a son, also at grammar school. We had met once or twice at the adults' instigation and had put up with one another for the duration in the amiable way which recognises that, though you feel no ill-will towards the other, you know you will never become friends. Between this boy's mother and Aunt Ethel there was keen, edgy competition. Once the woman let drop that her son was given ninepence a week pocket money. 'Bert (the name they used at the time) gets that too,' said Aunt Ethel, no doubt promptly. I did not; I had threepence. I could sympathise with Ethel's lie, but I did wish, way at the back of my mind, that she had felt the need to honour it practically.

The more torturing moments were when she bought me presents. She did so because she sensed that the racehorse had to be properly looked after, because she rather enjoyed being able to do somewhat more in the way of gifts than anyone around her, and out of generosity and affection. When I was preparing for the School Certificate examination (later 'O' levels) she said that if I gained Matric (the Merit grade), she would buy me a bicycle. It was a heady proposal, a beacon to a new sort of life. It was also carrot-dangling, frowned on today but still common and not only among aspiring working-class or lower-middle-class people. It would be wrong to hold that particular offer against Aunt Ethel. I was fifteen and a bike would be a liberation virtually equivalent to being offered a sports car or even flying training today. To move across and out of Leeds, into the country under your own power, not to be restricted to the distance you could walk, to town or back or into the next district, not to be worried about having the money for tram or bus fares;

above all to be free to decide yourself where and when to go, as well as to enjoy the clear uncomplicated pleasure of cycling itself, the steady movement, the wind over your body, the new smells, the quiet hiss, the sense of managed balance . . . all these were almost spiritual gains.

Of course I knew in the pit of my stomach, from the day the bicycle was mentioned, that I would pay for it. But I could no more have refused than Faust could have unmade his pact with the Devil. One side of me knew, even at fifteen, that I should have been able to find a form of words to refuse what was bound to be a worrying and uneasy gift. The bike was a New Hudson and cost £4.19.6. That was a great deal for a 'passer' to find, perhaps two weeks' wages. I knew that too, deep down, and recognised it as well as I was able. I knew also that I would be daily reminded of the need for gratitude; Aunt Ethel soured her own good, her own best, acts. She watched the bike as it went out and came in. If it got wet and I didn't dry it to her satisfaction she accused me of tossing her money away. For months she 'threw that bike in my face' (a favourite type of metaphor and, like many in that time, violent, as though making out life as combat). But I loved the machine and couldn't bear to think of saying: 'Take it back, then, and sell it.' Attachment apart, such an act was scarcely possible with Aunt Ethel. It would have been taken as a declaration of civil war; she would have recognised that at once and moved into an aggressive counter-attack like a dictator in response to the first attempt at a counter-coup. Aunt Annie could not have done that, nor Grandma, nor Uncle Walter. A self-willed or high-principled fifteen-year-old in a book might have; but not this one.

Eventually, things levelled out, the firing moved on to other areas and the bike became just another part of the back-kitchen furniture. Meanwhile I had joined the Salem Cycling Club. Salem Chapel was Hunslet's most famous, a huge place which needed two full-time ministers to keep it going, and the Cycling Club was in a loose but friendly relationship with the chapel; you didn't have to be an attender to join the club, and the chapel elders gave occasional help.

I have never been a member of a golf club or cricket club or squash club or sailing club, but I doubt whether any of them can better membership of a cycling club at the right time in life; at least that was true of a club like Salem in those days. The members came from the lower middle class through to the rock-bottom working class, and that is a fair spread; but the club was, in its style, classless and companionable. We were doing a simple and good thing together, propelling ourselves round the countryside in the full free air. A good club has a collective memory which is passed on as members fall out and new ones enter. Ours knew all the back lanes and hill tracks and the places where tea was good and generous (4d a person for the pot, with your own sandwiches). We were not botanists or birdwatchers or amateur archaeologists or historians, but we loved the Yorkshire Dales and, though we tended to look inside old churches, were mainly concerned to enjoy the views as we glided along with the air whipping past our cheeks. We particularly liked the drystone walls which checkered the fields and slopes; they will soon seem as quaint as the bee-hive homes of Puglia.

It was all a very simple love. We were each on our own, handling our own machines, but were also part of a group. No one was left behind, whatever the difficulties; we came home together or with the lame duck escorted by a couple of others. In that, it was like the army or the scouts but without an articulated mystique or 'philosophy'. We went rather by the unwritten rules-of-thumb of the community. The tradition was, in so far as there was a 'leader', in the care of the Secretary, and the Secretary of the Salem Club gave me an early lesson in unobtrusive and unbossy guidance and helpfulness. Coming back in the late evening, sliding quietly into Leeds with the only sound the wind, the slight hiss of the front carbide lamps and our own talk as we rode in pairs remains one of the most happy memories of my adolescence. Of groups I have known outside the home, no other has seemed more open, sustaining, honest and true to its own small but good lights.

That is slightly romanticised. I had joined the club with my friend from grammar school, Musgrave. He lived with his mother and sister. There was no father in sight though whether he was dead or just elsewhere I do not know. Mrs Musgrave had to go out to work, simply so as to have at least a minimum going-on. Musgrave himself was a very solid boy who showed for his age great *savoir faire* and *savoir vivre*, was determined to get out of Hunslet and to live with gusto. He was the initiator, always first over the wall whilst I had a think about it. One night he was riding next to one of the few girls in the club, as we neared the city. She was a quiet, neat, well-spoken girl with short bobbed hair. I hadn't noticed that we had lost them as we passed a wood on the outskirts. The next morning Musgrave called round to tell me they had gone into the wood and she had let him not only kiss her but put his hand right up her cycling shorts and 'have a good feel'. That was the limit of sexual exploration at that stage of even Musgrave's adolescence and I was astounded; but intrigued.

I owed a great deal to Aunt Ethel's typically tortured gift. Her torture continued, her unhappiness and distaste, her sour and intermittently volcanic spirit. From taking the shop, to the retirement to Morecambe, to Ida's death, the two lived together. They had worked and saved and scrimped for that for many years and did not waver in their peculiar kind of fidelity. I do not think they were lesbians, even by inclination, and certainly not in act. They were united in their embitteredness; not towards the universe since they seemed to have no metaphysical or generally philosophic leanings at all. If they ever ventured a generalisation it would be of the sort: 'She's the kind of woman who would say that – or would do that.' They had little time for most people they met, found them morally wanting or shiftless. If they had moments of a kind of happiness as a pair, I imagine that these were usually moments when they came together in criticism of someone outside. I expect that when they were alone together they also had long, sullen and resentful silences or elegantly worked-out puttings-in of the boot, at which both were expert. When others were present there was very often a half-submerged battle in play. Life was an endless, watchful calculation. If Ida got first to the washing-up after visitors had been given lunch so that Ethel – trapped – had to sit there being sociable, Ethel knew she would have to pay in subsequent sighs and complaints indicating a heroically unmentioned onset of backache (especially if the guests were from Ethel's 'side'; that is from her family). When Ida came back to the sitting-room, martyredly and after a long time, Ethel would make a pre-emptive strike, in honey-laced-with-arsenic tones: 'I'm surprised it took you so long, Ida. Did you decide to clean the cooker inside and out? Our guests were beginning to wonder whether you'd gone for a walk.' Ida would blink and put that in store; repayment later. And vice-versa if Aunt Ethel got to the sink first.

So it went on, an agonising but irrefrangible relationship, a sort of love, a sort of hate. It was hate or at least dislike which united them, that contempt for most of the world outside; fuelled by a fierce, damped-down and turned-in sexuality, by a puritanical self-righteousness, by scorn, and by a huge sense of loss, of having missed something. So they brooded and bickered wherever they lived and for as long as they were together, until Ida's death.

In Morecambe they made a succession of remarkably close friends very quickly, usually married couples of their own generation and retired there like them, with whom they went to Christmas Eve dinners in sea-front hotels or on outings; the other pair usually had a car. Just as quickly they went off each couple, found them less than satisfactory and, say, coarse. Always those who had been now rejected had to be cast into an outer darkness, stripped of worth. There were no half-measures in their world and no half-tones; all was lurid black-and-white. 'Well, it didn't quite work out – a pity, but there we are' was not the sort of sentence they would have been likely to use.

Above all, they were genteel with the painful strained gentility of assistants in the 'better' shops, distorted sub-Marshall-and-Snelgrove vowels and semi-detached locutions. Their gentility tortured not only their vowels; it tortured them. All was a sort of genteel aspiration, the search for perfect pitch. They would go to a sale of the effects of a large house and come back with a magnificent coal-scuttle of oak with elaborate brass fittings and entwinings, meant for the large and expensively furnished lounge of a mill-owner's stone dwelling. It sat by the fireplace of their semi like an out-of-place and ill-at-ease gun-dog. There was a baffled poetry in their gentility, a dream of England and of 'nice' English life. A Christmas card of a half-timbered and thatched cottage, the sort of cottage of which Anne Hathaway's is the epitome, all tangled with colourful climbing things across its front – that hit the exact spot. Even today I cannot read the word 'doilies', meaning a paper table-mat in an imitation lace pattern, without hearing again the prim way Aunt Ethel would say, if visitors were expected: 'Let's get out the doilies.'

When our first child was born Aunt Ethel asked: 'Are you feeding him yourself?' 'Yes. Why not?' 'Well, you see, some people think it's not quite nice nowadays.' But when she saw the baby being fed she said: 'I do think a baby at the breast is the most beautiful sight in the world.'

The magical power of words came into its own here too. 'Pos' or 'chamber pots' were provided under the beds. Odd, since their semi did have an upstairs lavatory. Presumably commonsense had intervened; after a certain age few of us can go the whole night without a pee; and the landing was dark and chill. 'Po' was not thought to be nice and 'jerry' was even worse, very vulgar; 'chamber pot' seemed proper. But after a time that too became unusable, too nakedly obvious. For a time 'the article' was the preferred word as in: 'You'll find an article under your bed.' A birthday present perhaps? That soon became tainted on the tongue and gave way to the menacing 'the thing': 'There's a thing under the bed.' It was a lesson in the cultural accretions of language, in how no word is in itself pure or impure, neutral, objective or biased; in how words can become tainted in time with what they indicate and so have to be moved on from.

I suppose Ethel and Ida were ashamed of or at the least very uneasy about their bodily functions; that one had to pee and shit was inescapable, but we didn't have to talk about it, make jokes about it, or, so far as this can be managed, admit it. The lavatory in each of their homes reeked of one of the more heavily perfumed 'toilet deodorants'. The blend of that with the smell of an evacuation was more unpleasant than the smell of shit itself, like a rank and fetid growth concocted in a shifty laboratory, a poisonous but ersatz jungle plant. But it too, like the words for the things, and no matter how much they stepped up the deodorants, eventually said to them: 'Someone's just had a shit here.' So they took to leaving a packet of cigarettes in the lavatory and suggesting their guests might feel like a smoke to reduce the unbecoming smell. There were then three smells: shit, heavy deodorants and cigs. Aunt Annie, who had a slightly scatological side, told me she would sit there puffing away like mad and the smell was something awful.

Back at Newport Street in my first years there, in the second half of the Twenties, Winnie seemed to be writing home much of the time. Inadvertently, she gave me my first sight of a girl's breasts. I must have been about ten or eleven and blundered into the scullery in search of something or other. Winnie was at the sink, stripped to the waist, giving herself a good wash; that was the only wash-bowl in the house but it did have hot water from the fireback boiler. Her back was solid, sturdy, well rounded. She turned to see who had come in, clearly not guessing it might be me. She was set back when she saw me, being a most circumspect girl. I saw two large, low-swinging breasts like very big King William pears and found them disturbingly beautiful. I realised much later from foreign travel that, if there is a model English working-class breast, it is shaped like Winnie's. When you walk on continental beaches or see the topless shots so favoured by producers of television travel programmes you wonder why many women over there seem to grow breasts like little apples; Cox's Orange Pippins.

In due time Winnie married Albert. He was by then a hairdresser in one of the large Leeds hospitals. It might have been St James's. He shaved patients before operations and after death, and cut hair in the intervals. It seemed to give him a reasonable going-on and Winnie continued at work. I liked Albert very much. All he wanted was a quiet life with Winnie, no climbing, no malicious gossip, no fret. He accepted the universe as it was, seemed to wish no one any harm and remained mildly sunny. They moved off a long way, say two and a half miles north-west to a new terrace development slotted on to a bit of spare land in an area of respectable working-class housing, marginally above Newport Street in the fine calculus of status round there. The two-bedroomed boxes could be immediately recognised as gimcrack constructions, meant to be what are now called 'starter homes' except that the phrase is favoured by a more expensive end of the building range than Winnie and Albert were involved with. I hardly think they were buying the house, though; that would have been pushing the boat out spectacularly; you don't throw up muscles like that unless you have more 'go' than Winnie and Albert.

They were, even for our family, narrow in their demands and outlook. Winnie could hardly wait to get Albert back to Sheffield and that would be another reason for not buying the house. In the meantime she ensured that they made regular visits, with Albert always complaisant, to the big, crowded but firmly controlled, nest. They did not have well-developed or varied senses of humour. But they were slow-burningly good-natured. In all this and in much else they were exceptionally well matched. They were, as it were, modest and moderate in all things; to have been snide was way beyond their range or dispositions; they behaved well and did not resent any one else's success. Their horizons were close and they did not mind.

It was plain after a few years that I was leaving their world. Knowing little about what it all involved, they did not ask much or often about my doings; they simply accepted them in an unaffected way. They were kind to me as to a younger brother. Soon after they had moved into the little house they invited me for the weekend. Unusual, that too; except that I think I had been helping with the removal, perhaps taking some of Winnie's bits and pieces from Newport Street. On Sunday morning Winnie offered to bring our breakfasts up to bed. She was 'playing at houses', enjoying being the hospitable housewife and stretching herself to a style she could not have known at her huddled home. I was asked to move in with Albert who was still in the double bed. Whilst Winnie was downstairs cooking the breakfast, he started to tell me, as a senior to a junior who is now at an age when he may be expected to understand (I suppose I was about fifteen), of the great pressure, particularly on the man, when a young couple decide not to have children for a time, to wait until they have 'put something aside'. The caution was true to the grain.

I was greatly affected by the story; it had an exemplary and even slightly archetypal quality since it concerned one of the important issues of choice which might come to us all. In fact, they never had children. Perhaps when something had at last been put aside they tried and found it did not work. Perhaps they gradually became used to being two and at some point explicitly decided not to have a family; or perhaps time just passed until they realised one day that it was now too late.

After her father died, Winnie became the linchpin of that large family, regularly going round them all, keeping up the contacts and giving practical help; and Albert played his part. Perhaps that was their best role. Our bedroom conversation had been in the early days. It is still strange to think of Albert unburdening himself to an ignorant but intrigued adolescent about the difficulty of 'holding back' when you are all worked up in bed with your young wife. This was about thirty years before the arrival of the Pill. But what about condoms? A barber, of all people, would be likely to know about those, though I don't suppose Albert would have lodged them on the mirror frame in his little hospital working-space, and most of his work there was peripatetic. A moral objection seems unlikely and so does an aesthetic. It's a puzzle. Perhaps Winnie's sexual urges were not very strong; she had strong family urges instead. We are told that many women in that kind of society, in the early Thirties, neither sought nor had orgasms, or always knew about them. These are not prurient observations. They are genuine and sympathetic questions, prompted by that Sunday morning conversation in bed, about a style of life, a life of many fears and inhibitions, which now seems a hundred years away.

In the end and inevitably Winnie took him back, like a homing pigeon with a mate it's found on one of its trips, back to Sheffield, away from the sinful city. I saw little of them after that and the war cut a great swathe in all such contacts. Tom kept me roughly in touch, being also fond of Winnie and Albert. I saw them thereafter at the odd funeral, Winnie a dumpy black figure with a face that increasingly showed both the heaviness of the Hoggarts and the even more jowled quality of her paternal side. But she was still quite unaffected. 'Hello, Richard,' she would always say, with the intrusive 't' very clear, 'how are you going on?' If I had reported that I had become Foreign Minister she would have been likely to say: 'Oh, I see. Very *good*,' as she would if I had told her my local plumbing business was doing well.

My last memories are of Albert's funeral and then of Winnie's, not all that long after. The images merge: a windswept cemetery above Sheffield, the heavy, squat women's figures all in black, the men also awkwardly in black, that so often ill-fitting and insistent black; then back on at least one of the occasions to the usual funeral tea and the catching up with the news; a sense of drifting on a tide. The due phrases at such times are always ritualistic. Lawrence caught it well in the funeral of the older Morel boy, William, early in *Sons and Lovers*: 'You niver seed such a length as he is!' and 'My word, he's a weight!'; the first said by the father, the second by one of the miners carrying the coffin. Both of them are verbal wreaths, tributes to the power and beauty of the young man who has gone. The more conventional formulation for the more common older deaths might be: 'Ah, she did look peaceful,' or 'She looked so young.' More down to earth, and when someone quite old has died so that people come from several decades in the past to pay their respects, you may hear little whispers between the women at the back as their eyes sweep round the gathering: 'Eh, is that so-and-so? Ah'd never 'ave believed it, 'asn't 'e *aged*!'

Winnie's story has taken me into the Sixties, more than a quarter of a century after the Newport Street household had broken up. When the tenancy finally came to an end, Grandma was dead, Annie married with a largish family of step-children, and Walter married with a son. The events that led to his marriage prompted another succession of whispered conversations, sedulously intended to keep things from Grandma: 'She mustn't know. It'd kill 'er if she did.' I doubt it; she was tougher than they knew or liked to think, especially in her attitude to sexual matters. Sometime after leaving the furniture shop, Walter had met two sisters in a pub, living together with no other family members in sight, and neither in good health. One became pregnant by Walter and they married; the decision was kept from me, and I rather think from Grandma, until the marriage had taken place. The new sister-in-law was usually referred to as 'a poor thing'; that was not a moral judgment but a reference to her health. I cannot remember her ever coming to Newport Street but Aunt Annie kept in touch and had considerable respect for her and for the way she coped, rather as she had respected our mother's coping. The boy did very well so both mother and father must have been proud of him; something recovered.

As I dive back once more into that time I am impressed almost above all their other characteristics by the inwardness and privacy of such households (I am deliberately avoiding the word 'home' but am saying '*such* households' because, in spite of all our differences from the families around us, we were in that closedness typical of many, probably of most). The physical focus was the coal fire which burnt all day and almost every day except when the weather was really hot; it was needed to supply hot water through the back boiler. And people seemed to feel that, when there was no flickering fire in the grate, the household couldn't come together; and since the streets did not get much sun the room would be chill most days of the year without a fire; more, a fireless grate looked 'cheerless', unwelcoming, as though you were getting ready to flit.

Except for the very poor, the coal fire was a pivot of working-class life, part of the basic pattern, taken for granted, one of the three or four constituent elements which helped lift the lives of all but the poorest to the level of the bearable (others included mains gas for cooking, cheap imported meat and cheap tinned fish and fruit, especially salmon and pineapple – the meat, and the imported wheat and much else, boons for the urban poor but ruin for many farmers and their labourers). How far cheap coal had been available to the rural poor before they moved in large numbers to the cities I do not know; I expect hardly at all and that they made do with wood. For the urban poor the statement, 'So long as you're warm you can put up with a lot', was a simple truth. The dark smoke from those ranks and ranks of terraced chimneys was specifically a product and symbol of the Industrial Revolution and the urbanisation of working people. Cheap coal does not seem to have been commonly a benefit to the poor throughout mainland Europe, except in pockets near the pits.

In Britain, miners' families were favoured since they were given a more than adequate allowance of coal. They still are and it is still tax-free. They were not envied for this; it was felt to be no more than their due; and if you lived near some of them, deals could be struck. The main importance of cheap coal, often from pits near the big cities but easily moved round the country on the dense railway network, was its availability to the great body of urban working class people. If you got down to your last shovelful or to the residual mere dust which was always found on the empty coal-house floor, then you were in a very bad way indeed. The far end of that line saw out-of-work men in the Thirties scrabbling for very small bits of coal on pit slag-heaps, or in the North-East scraping the shore for sea-coal – the sort of images which engraved themselves on Orwell's mind. If cheap coal had not been available to the urban working class much in the balance, pattern, shape of their lives would have been worse.

So: a general inwardness in these homes, with the coal fire as its fulcrum; and visitors or 'callers' (as distinct from neighbours who might drop in from time to time) easy to list and often functional, part of the pattern, especially of the repeated financial routines and customs, of our kind of life. For us there was, of course, Aunt Ethel's friend Ida, and for years and years. She had a slightly hearty, slightly uneasy manner as of one who is for the time being coming down a social notch, one to outsiders barely perceptible, but to her important and real. I do not imagine she was fully aware of this; if she had realised it she would have been shocked. Like most people she would have denied any trace of snobbery or class feeling, whilst practising some of its forms as if by nature. Nor did we much refer to this aspect of her attitudes among ourselves; but we knew, and knew that we could never be on easy terms; a line was there which could only be crossed by an act of *lèse-majesté*. She spoke with a dry, casual authority that carried total confidence in the unassailability of her opinions. Yet even that phrasing makes the differences between her style and ours more apparently evident than they were. To an outsider she would have been, especially in her manner of speaking, virtually indistinguishable from us, an uneducated West Riding spinster with a voice to match, except that her voice had that drapery-assistant's semi-genteel overlay which to her and to us made all the difference.

Then there were Albert's callings-in to collect Winnie. He didn't usually take his coat off, but sat on an upright chair near the door, adopting the 'thanks, but I'm not stopping' stance, in his mackintosh, quietly twirling his hat, cheerful with the unaffected demotic cheerfulness of a barber to working-class people as distinct from one who serves middle-class and professional people and ends every half-sentence with an ingratiating 'sir'.

Annie rarely brought friends into the house, especially since the very fact that their usual entertainment was a slow stout or two, in a pub in town or at the least out of our particular bit of Hunslet, would have attracted Aunt Ethel's scorn directly (it did so indirectly whenever Annie set off for an evening out); a whiff of her verbal grapeshot would have routed the visiting friends who would have been most unlikely to have faced such a formidable fighting engine before.

After the relationship with Jean ended, Uncle Walter brought no one to the house; any one of his cronies at that time would have caused a storm and the storms would have increased as the friends' social desirability declined, which inexorably and distressingly happened.

Visits from my own friends were few, especially after the move to grammar school. But they were steady; especially from Musgrave, that cheerful, resilient son of a woman who cleaned public premises. He never flinched from acknowledging that. It was known that he would knock the block off anyone who tried to sneer and he was a big lad. I admired him for his directness above all else. He determined to get to university and got there a year after I did, via a kind of early industrial scholarship. He promptly changed his name to Hardy-Musgrave, adopting his mother's maiden name for the first half; he was nothing if not pragmatic. 'Goes down better,' he said. I had already dropped 'Bert' in favour of 'Richard'.

We rarely saw the insides of each other's houses; that was not the style. You knocked as you stood on the pavement, a nose length from the door, and asked: 'Is your Joe in? Can he come out?', but did not expect to cross the threshold. That is a rather grand expression which I would hesitate to use now. At that time it was part of everyday speech: 'Don't dare to cross my threshold,' 'Never cross my threshold again,' 'I told him I wouldn't have him cross my threshold.' Like 'darkening my doorstep'. Such excommunications were common form about a neighbour or acquaintance who had proved to be 'no better than she/he should be' (a strange expression, underplaying what it is really saying); and 'we might have known all along'; or we 'blamed ourselves for not seeing it all along'. Histrionic expressions were part of the staple of life. It was as though a grindingly dull existence was given more dramatic shape and colour by the way one got it into words and above all images, metaphors.

The visits from neighbours were usually brief and for precise, practical and always understated purposes, usually borrowing – 'a *pinch* of salt/sugar', 'a *drop* of milk', 'a *bit* of marge'; or to ask us to keep an eye open for an unexpected caller and to tell him or her that they were out for a while; all the way up to the occasional crises of illness, birth and death. There was a distinction between being neighbourly and being given to dropping-in. We did not practise dropping-in ourselves and did not approve of it in others. There were some who, if they once got their feet over the threshold, would be forever dropping-in and that habit fuelled itself on gossip, which we did not like.

We had a firm sense of the necessary limits and terms of gossip. Some gossip was acceptable, especially if it touched the great issues of birth, marriage and death; or was funny but not malicious. Malicious gossip, gossip for its own unpleasant sake, gossip as a cheap daily drug, gossip which fed on reducing neighbours, was by most people disapproved of. The terms of life were so delicately poised, the retention of self-respect so crucial, that anything which undermined them had to be stigmatised. Hence the verb to 'cal' which rhymes with 'pal' and means the disposition to gossip endlessly and probably mean-mindedly; a woman given to 'cal-ing' was best avoided. Gossip roused animosities and it was hard enough to keep things steady, on an even keel, without provoking differences. There was religious support here too, especially from the tenets of Primitive Methodism. In some ways those tenets, as they were put across to us, seem to have been designed not as the opiate of the people but as a set of sensible maxims for daily living in poor and difficult circumstances, calling in aid for that purpose the name of Jesus. 'Love thy neighbour' did not literally mean what it said, we knew; that would have been going too far; indeed, embarrassing. Imbibed, digested, adapted, it meant: 'Keep on good terms with your neighbour, help where you can but also keep your due distance. Better all round that way.' We did not need telling that 'good fences make good neighbours' even if the fences were only in the mind and the physical division only a thinnish party-wall.

There were professional visitors of two kinds. First, the ones you recognised as not too far from you in the social scale, as respectable working class or perhaps just lower middle class, people most of whom had at least fairly secure jobs, the petty functionaries and humdrum rabbit-track makers who criss-crossed working-class districts week after week, weaving together their routine business and yet making it humanly interesting or at any rate making it seem human and friendly: the gas-meter emptier (not 'reader' since we were on the coin-in-the-slot system; expensive but manageable and the rebates were useful), the electricity-meter man, the insurance man.

That the last of these survived so long, and to some degree still does, is puzzling. Our mother took out when I was two years old a penny a week insurance from the Royal Liver Insurance Company (of Liverpool) to meet or go well towards the cost of burying me. Nine years later a similar policy was added by Grandma. I still have them and they are up to date. There will be about £30 towards burying me. Not a handsome return but in the early years the cost of collection must have eaten a substantial part of the premiums. Nowadays I send a very small cheque every twelve months or so to a town ten miles away. Still hardly worth the bookkeeping to them. For me, a slight symbolic act I will keep up.

Before the last war, the insurance agents came to collect the premiums each week, wandering those streets marking down pennies and twopences and threepences at successive houses, passing the 'agents' of other companies on the way, having a pleasant word at each place, looking out for new business, wearing out shoe-leather at a rate which made you wonder whether even in those days their 'commission' would cover the cost of new soles and heels. A striking example of the slow, painful and wasteful nature of so many practices in working-class districts at the time – and still, to some extent.

The insurance agent's life offered those tempting percentage commissions but neither his job nor his wage were as steady as those of the gas and electric men, and steadiness was highly prized. The gas and electric men had uniforms which saved their own suits and gave them an established air. Insurance agents' suits were cheap and shiny, the uniform of the lower white-collared.

I know a young insurance agent in today's equivalent of an area slightly higher than Hunslet's in social level, a mixture of council and private housing. He has a car and tends to win the annual prize for getting more new business than any agent in his group, a holiday in Majorca for him and his wife, for example. It is easy to imagine the hard-faced men at headquarters pushing such anxious young men to their limits; and the customers bemused by fast talk into buying yet more policies they cannot afford.

Those who sold the clothing checks I mentioned earlier were usually women from the neighbourhood, earning pin-money; half-sisters of those who knocked on the door to persuade you to buy from a mail-order catalogue on instalments. They thrive today though now joined by more sophisticated systems, the working-class equivalents of Tupperware parties for the aspirant. The most cheerful of the weekly visitors – she was after all on a happy errand – was the woman who came for about twenty weeks before Christmas, on Friday evenings, to collect the money for the Christmas Club advance payments. Friday was pay night.

Those Club payments were in advance towards toys, hampers, decorations, chosen from a glossy coloured brochure. The stuff arrived as you made your last payment just before Christmas. It must have been convenient for the mail-order firm to have inputs of capital week by week in advance without having to pay interest and with an assured and calculable market at the end of the process.

Of all such low-level visitors the most anonymous was the rent man. Not the rates man, for rates were paid by the landlord out of the rent. The rent man was the landlord's man or his agent's. He was not a bully but tended to be proper and economical in speech. Those streets represented a substantial sum of weekly income to some people and he had to keep getting it as regularly as he possibly could. That was all. He had none of the promptings to be matey of the insurance man or the club-check or mail-order seller.

So much in those systems might have been expected to wither away with greater prosperity and security of work, though no doubt they revived as unemployment rose again. Some predators may hibernate but wake up when the chill returns. But much was still going strong in the 'never had it so good' part of the Sixties and up to the mid-to-late Seventies; and later. Such arrangements had been essentially a product of the earlier week-by-week, just-about-managing, domestic economies. They provided a cushion against sudden shocks, in particular a requirement for clothing (for a funeral, most notably). The Whitsun need for children's clothing could be expected and might be provided for in this way each year. But forgetfulness and intermittent or even unauthorised raidings of a pot of savings on the mantelpiece could negate foresight. Weekly payments in arrears did provide some advantages.

They also had their costs, which most customers did not recognise. They are an expensive way of borrowing money, though if you look only at the weekly payments and do not work out the true annual rate of interest they can seem cheap. You can become desperately worried if you fall behind with payments; and at the worst a loan-shark appears who has 'bought the debt' and is not too nice about getting back what he, rather than the firm from whom you had the loan, is now owed. No wonder that if the complexities of debts became too much the gas oven, before the days of non-toxic North Sea gas, could seem an easy way out. For suicides who had lived alone, the standard joke was that at any rate the Gas Board wouldn't get any payment for the gas they'd used to do away with themselves.

I have already said a little, based on experiences before the last war, about the disadvantages of taking out clothing checks, especially the suspicion that you were directed in the appointed clothing stores to goods which were particularly poor value. Why else did the salesmen, sizing you up as you entered, ask immediately whether you had come with a check? Those salesmen recall yet again what is becoming a small, recurrent leitmotiv, the cheap shiny suit and its relation to hanging on to respectability by your fingernails. People in this trap are often the keenest to keep up the most marginal of differences, becoming the sniffer-dogs of class-distinction, since they themselves live by its existence and spend their lives on one of its knife-edges, where 'keeping up appearances' is a primary rule. One such man, clearly much concerned with keeping up appearances, served me *de haut en bas* with my first long-trousered suit at thirty shillings. I hated it from the start: a dead, greyish thing, the cheap cloth hard at birth and destined to shine within weeks, the sort which any West Riding mill worker or ready-made clothing worker, using an eye for quality which they could not often apply to their own purchases, would instantly recognise for what it was. Even at thirty bob it was not good value.

Years later, in the days when university external examiners were given first-class rail fares, I travelled from London to Brighton on the Pullman and met the most practised of all sniffer-dogs. After only a few minutes, the chocolate-and-fawn, tight-uniformed and tight-arsed attendant assigned to that car came to me and said: 'Excuse me, sir, but you do realise this is a first-class carriage?' I resisted the temptation to do a Lucky Jim, and said: 'Yes, and I've got a first-class ticket.' But what a remarkable intervention – the vicarious snobbery of the congenital servitor, the petty uniformed zealot – to have decided that I did not 'look first-class', to have had the nerve on behalf of all genuine first-class customers to decide that there might be an interloper sitting there from whom they had to be protected, to feel he was defending the Grail of first-class accommodation against irruptions from members of the mob. Yet to have been so trapped by the habit of deference or by his habitual insurance-policy manners as to call me 'sir', to start by excusing himself, and to use the rhetorical question form for what was a piece of reverse toadying. I am sure petty officiousness overreaches itself in something like that way in many other countries; but the tone and the formulation here were quintessentially true to the style of English minor Bumbledom.

Themselves working or near-working-class, the representatives of Them outside moved busily and repetitively through working-class streets spinning a web which in some ways held and sustained the pattern of life, in some ways bound and held down the inhabitants. They had a role, like that of the parasites, benign or not benign, in the animal world. That role was founded in the lack of perspective and security, and so of the elements for long-term planning, characteristic of their customers. If their functions have been weakened in the last forty or so years, that weakening has been very slow and partial. You build up relationships with the rabbit-track makers; they are sometimes neighbours; kids over-demand and you hesitate to deny them. The hawsers do not break easily.

Then there were very occasional professional visitors who, except for the doctor and the minister, lived in other parts of Leeds and took the number 25 tram from the city into the heart of Hunslet. They induced a slight nervousness but were presumably used to that; one or two might have seemed a shade superior but in general they had learned a polite though certainly distancing manner whose style and locutions were defined more by profession than by class.

The doctor would call with a readiness which seems surprising today. That would be the panel doctor, to whom we paid very little. Ours was a double practice run by an Irishman and his sister, probably both trained in Dublin. Our area had that pocket of Irish Catholic families long ago brought over by the prospect of work. Perhaps that encouraged Irish doctors to set up their plates there; as well as the fact that it was not a highly desirable area, not one in which you were likely to become wealthy, so the competition for the practice would not be keen.

During my time there neither of the two Doctors Cooke married. Their surgery was on the main tram-line artery, Hunslet Road, a couple of hundred yards below us. They had a wall-eyed Irish general maid-of-all-work, as loyal as a terrier. Nor do I remember her marrying. Apart from meeting her once or twice when I had to go to their door out of surgery hours, I saw the maid from time to time at the nearby butchers. She would be asking for chops or steak, mid-week, and that marked the gulf. I do not imagine that the Cookes lived high however, and I doubt if they drank (unlike the rotund English doctor in the sprawling old brick house opposite Jack Lane Elementary School: from the playground we saw the wine and spirits van unload there regularly). The Cookes were quiet, soft-spoken, quite without side. Their voices had that soft, classless Irish burr which British broadcasting, seeking in the last few decades to escape the tyranny of class-tainted tongues, has learned to value. Their voices did not mark them out and off as 'Them', as the voice of the local English doctor did, and we were touched by this. The English doctor was respected too. It was a fair bet that many doctors who came to those areas were not simply desperate to find a practice, but that they had had at the start or had developed a social conscience. Yet the English doctor accepted the hierarchy, hob-nobbed with others of his kind, the local solicitor on the main road, the Church of England parson, and congenial members of the golf club a mile or two out. The Cookes seemed to have none of that. There seemed a kind of beauty in the simplicity of their lives. They were not gregarious or hearty, just quiet and concerned.

When I contracted pneumonia, somewhere between eleven and twelve, the family assumed it would be touch-and-go; it often was in those days. The illness regularly took its course to what was known as 'the crisis'; if you got over that you were on the way to mending; if not, not. Dr James, the brother, calculated that my crisis would come in the small hours of a certain night. I was on a bed in the living-room. That was *de rigueur* with any serious illness even in a child, both for convenience and to mark the line between just being ill and being really poorly. On that night the doctor came in late and sat through into the small hours listening to my breathing, checking from time to time. Sometime not long before dawn he listened and checked again and said to whoever was with me that night, Ethel or Annie: 'The crisis is over. He's breathing well. He'll be all right now.' The afternoon of the day I came down with the illness someone at school had given me three or four of those highly scented sweets – were they called 'silver cachous'? – which look like tiny, chromium-plated ball-bearings. As I ate, waves of nausea rose from my chest. They are instantly recalled if I so much as smell such a sweet even today.

The sister, Dr Jessie, a very gentle woman, took a special interest in Molly. That aunt at one remove who had had the kindness to take her in was not a clever woman. They were as a family respectable but very narrow and, it was felt in Newport Street, slightly below us in that not one of them was in a white-collar or supervisory job as some of ours were. They were basic, manual working class of the chapel-going sort, turned in, unimaginative, of the very soil of Hunslet. A score of years after I left there, a boy from that branch of the Hoggarts got to Cockburn High School, their first.

Why did they take Molly in? They would receive a weekly allowance for her from the municipality, but she must have been something of a burden to them, being only six or seven. The aunt was widowed and her family all grown up, though one remained at home. Above all, I think, they took her because of that rooted family feeling: you don't let your own go into an orphanage. There can also be, in such a decision, a touch of watchfulness towards the neighbours: 'We'd never let one of ours go into a home, no matter how good they said it was.' I expect both feelings were in play when Molly was taken in. Once there, she was not shown the love Grandma showed me. Such love needs a degree of imagination, no matter how unaware its possessor may be of that gift. I do not think they were actively unkind; they were, rather, insensitive. It was simply assumed that when Molly reached fourteen she would leave school and go into a clothing factory. By then they had moved to Pudsey, a mill township just outside the Leeds boundary and now incorporated. Molly duly went into t'mill. She was bright and imaginative, with a romantic disposition towards books and the idea of writing. An irregular illness kept her out of the running for that hurdle, the eleven-plus exam for grammar school. She came under the care of Dr Jessie Cooke who became very fond of her. So much so that eventually she asked Aunt Emma if she could adopt Molly, giving her a good education and generally treating her as her own daughter. The answer was no, though made with what degree of hesitation I did not learn. It was a wonderful opportunity and I have continued to believe that Molly should have had it and would have thrived on it.

But the issue could not be forced. They would tell themselves they 'thought too much of Molly to let any outsider take her away' and to some extent that would be true. To an even greater degree they no doubt believed it to be true when they said it. Just as powerfully in play, I still believe after all these years and with every effort at charity, the habitual 'what will the neighbours think/say' self-regard and fearfulness would have operated. If they had let her go no amount of sensible explanation, at which they were certainly not adept, would have convinced ill-disposed neighbours that they had done so at least partly because they did not care enough for her, that they lacked the right degree of family feeling. It is difficult to blame people for acting in the way that Aunt did, in the face of such all too predictable attitudes. Too much in the weight of their background, combined with their own lack of insight, made their response almost inevitable. But it was a great pity; in the event, a very great pity indeed.

A less frequent visitor to Newport Street was the headmaster of the elementary school. As befitted a professional, though one whose profession was a fairly lowly one, he lived in a slightly better part of town and wore three-piece suits which our kind of men wore only on very special occasions and then uneasily, jingling loose change in their trouser pockets. If I had seen his suits some years later I would have recognised their multiple-tailor's origins (Montague Burton's, not Weaver to Wearer), but they were impressive in that place and time. He appeared unannounced at the door, when I was in bed with pneumonia, to ask how I was and to indicate to Grandma that he had high hopes for me. I had not known that nor had he made any special approaches to me to indicate that kind of expectation and interest. Rightly, for to have been picked out as the headmaster's pet would have been to reap trouble in the playground.

Mr Harrison was the first instance – there were others at Cockburn and, above all, Bonamy Dobrée at Leeds University – of someone watchful, slightly stiff but from a due distance attentive, who saw it as his duty to give special care to promising boys (and girls too, I expect) in difficult circumstances; who was willing to go out of his way both metaphorically and physically, as in visiting you at home. 'You've got to get on, lad', was one of Mr Harrison's favourite injunctions.

What effect did the visit from the headmaster have on me, once I was up and about again? I cannot recall any feeling of pride or privilege. I do remember a mild wonderment that he, so grand a man, could do such a thing. More important, I remember an inchoate respect for the fact that someone from outside the family could act not out of self-interest but out of at the very least a sense of professional duty and, probably better, out of human sympathy also. It was an early lesson which I was to be offered again and again, and still find slightly surprising and certainly admirable.

Then there was the Primitive Methodist minister who very occasionally called to see Grandmother. Like diplomats, they were moved at intervals. The one I remember best was a Southerner with a high, light, polite voice. His good nature shone from him. We knew he could never, being a Nonconformist minister not a vicar, be top-drawer: his position precluded it; but we were quite intrigued by his southern, middle-class origins, liked his evident kindness and, deep down, realised that there was a sort of missionary impulse in such a man taking on that job in that place.

The minister's house was at the side of the chapel and congenitally in need of urgent repairs. I cannot remember whether it was of the soot-blackened stone of Leeds or the equally characteristic cheap, red and very dirty brick; perhaps it was built of that mixture of brick with stone fancy parts which in such districts indicated a certain status just as surely as did the dentist's or doctor's plate.

The house seemed big, with lots of children rattling round in it; children very different from those of the neighbourhood. Here was where origins told; those children were kept more or less to themselves or, if they had friends, I never saw them being admitted. Probably they would at a certain point go off to one of the Methodists' boarding schools. In all sorts of decent ways that minister was not a snob. But I expect he and his wife felt that they could not let their children grow up entirely within the life of those streets just because the father felt he had a vocation to work there.

He was a kindly and rather ineffectual man. But he loved Shakespeare – far more, I guess, than he liked the annual chapel oratorios – and always cast himself in chapel productions of the plays, though not grandiosely. His anguished bleat in *The Merchant of Venice* – 'Me daughter, oh, me daughter' made the Sunday School's pressed-lads, who had also been pressed into dramatic service, feel their conscription worthwhile for such a treat.

So a trinity of religious caterpillars regularly circled the district: our minister, the Church of England vicar (I do not remember him in my time but much later met one of his successors, a thoughtful and vigorous man with a strong vision of what needed to be done in what we had by then learned to call a deprived inner-city area, and a will to do something about it); and a succession of Catholic priests who were said to rule the Irish with what Protestants would be sure to call a rod of iron.

The most regular professional visitor was also the most intriguing, socially and culturally. Miss Jubb: the name itself has a Dickensian aptness. From my arrival in Hunslet to my eighteenth year, she called monthly. She was a Board of Guardians visitor (that sounds Dickensian too) and one of her duties was to ensure that children in the Guardians' care but living-out were being properly looked after. Grandmother was given seven and sixpence a week to cover my board, lodging, clothing, everything. Not a spendthrift amount but just enough with care. There may have been occasional supplements in the way of coupons towards clothing; they wouldn't stretch to Chilprufe or Wolsey but, well deployed, could buy roughish, quite hard-wearing stuff; trousers and jerseys rather than suits.

Miss Jubb was a stout and stocky figure, her one-hundred-times-brushed and firmly held-back hair turning to iron-grey; she wore two-piece tweed suits, usually in a brownish mix; and sensible shoes. From her appearance, she might have been the head of a girls' grammar school or a senior lecturer to trainees for one of the 'caring' professions. She sat down with her legs crossed at the ankles and her hands folded on her handbag which rested upright on her lap. Her whole stance said: 'decent concern on behalf of the Authorities', kindly but firmly and totally confidently. She asked direct questions such as 'What is the boy having for breakfast these mornings?'; 'Has he had a cold this last month?'; 'How is he getting along at school?' 'Is he getting enough exercise?' She did not expect the answer to the question about breakfast to be 'An egg and two rashers each day.' Porridge, perhaps; bread and dripping certainly; she knew these were good practical provisions. She seemed to respect Grandma; Grandma was a little in awe of her.

When I took Matriculation at fifteen and a half and did well, the headmaster of Cockburn High School wrote at the base of my year's report: 'Should think of professional life.' Grandma asked Miss Jubb what that meant. Unerringly Miss Jubb replied: 'It means he could be a doctor or a parson.' She hit the two professions she knew would be recognised in Hunslet. Grandma got the gist of the message and I entered the sixth form that autumn. The Board of Guardians, sensitive in their turn, had eased the decision by putting up the weekly allowance to fifteen shillings. Again, not riches, but a doubling which would reduce any tendency there may have been to say, as was said of anyone over fourteen, that 'he ought to be bringing some money into the house by now'.

We all know the feeling, coming upon us without warning, that we have had a particular sensation before, perhaps many years before. More unusual and interesting is the opposite: the sense, at first even more puzzling, of having had a directly contradictory experience long ago. Miss Jubb came to mind again in the late Seventies when I called in on a one-day conference at which full-time social workers in London were advising voluntary helpers. In particular, they talked about how to guide people in need as to what they could claim under the Social Security provisions. It was a well-prepared meeting and in one sense very 'professional'. But there was something odd about the tone of the whole operation. It took a while to identify what the oddity was. Then I remembered Miss Jubb and was able to define the unease.

Miss Jubb consciously and conscientiously represented 'the powers that be', the public interest in an orphan, the 'proper' expenditure of public money, a code of morality assumed to be right and unassailable. She was fulfilling her role in ensuring that that code and those responsibilities were lived up to, by both sides. Her limitations and her strengths were both quite clear, her lights bright, if narrowly focussed.

What I was hearing from the social workers forty or so years on was a reverse image of that attitude. These speakers were identifying themselves with the clients, the customers, the cases, as *against* the public authorities, the providers of funds, 'Them'. The gamekeepers had become poachers. This was not only an attempt to inculcate a healthy scepticism towards bureaucracy and pettifogging minor officialdom. It invoked a conspiracy, assumed a state of war in which acts which other times and people might have thought dubious fiddles to get more money from public sources were promoted as essential tactics where no question of moral justification arose; and in which it was assumed that no one who belonged to the ranks of 'Them' ever acted out of a decent, charitable impulse.

The speakers at that conference seemed unwilling to recognise that they too were involved with questions of value whether they wished to be or not, and no matter in what way they themselves thought they approached their decisions and giving of advice. Clearly, even their rejection of such a moral relationship to their work and to their clients was itself a moral act. They were inescapably involved with questions about what their profession means, what it is for. What is justifiable and helpful public or social intervention within the life of the individual? At what points should that intervention start and stop? The speakers seemed to have given such issues hardly any thought but to have put in their place a complicated, but not complex, contestatory, cops-and-robbers, poachers versus gamekeepers model, two-dimensional, the emanation of an ideology which lacked the imaginative ballast needed in their work.

Those were our visitors; few but in their own ways a rich mixture, like a tiny but dense social tapestry. Most of the time we were each self-engrossed, each putting our suckers out horizontally from the house to a sympathetic friend or two, so as to resist to some extent the developing unease within the house, engendered by Ethel and her tempers, Walter and his misery-making slide. Winnie was looking towards marriage and the as-soon-as-possible dash back to Shangri-La; Aunt Annie, rather meek, battered but with some resilience, had more sense of fun than the others and some of the language to match it; and I was caught up after the age of eleven with grammar-school life, a world on its own and on the whole a welcoming and encouraging world; and each evening went back to chatter about the day to Grandma. I expect she understood the drift if not the details. Probably my gradual successes, as well as Annie's general amiability in spite of everything, made the last years of her life more bearable in the face of the at best tepid, at worst volcanic, grimness of the house. She liked to tell people that 'Addie's boy' was doing well; funny that she did not say 'Tom's boy'. It was as though our mother had been a visiting Lady.

CHAPTER 4

HUNSLET, HOLBECK AND BEYOND

Immediately outside that Yorkshire-Ibsenite living-room were the streets. They became less interesting as grammar school took over. The boys around were not very hostile, not those in the nearer streets; they knew you too well for that. They thought you were missing a lot, like a spotty ordinand; especially education in girls and sex. They were right; you stayed in each night or were occasionally called for when homework was finished by a boy from your school who lived in an alien area about half a mile away. The boys on the outer edges of your area could be hostile if the mood took them. Usually that meant snatching off that preposterous, peaked, grammar-school cap (ours had a dark brown base with a cross of yellow on it, as though two bananas had been carefully draped over a chocolate cake) and throwing it away.

The pattern of everyday life was like constant knitting in two colours, one laid down by school, the other traditional to those streets; the two naturally interconnected. Christmas was a highlight, with the Christmas dinner-table a clear indicator as to how things were going with jobs and money (laying-off could be ruthless and was often unannounced). Never turkey, often 'a nice piece of roast pork'; on the best occasions a capon; at the lowest, for us (though I remember it only once), a roast rabbit. Being a countrywoman, Grandma knew how to cook a rabbit and I remember enjoying it very much.

Easter we did not make much of and Whit Monday figured larger than Easter Monday, perhaps because chapel outings for children took place that day. Whitsuntide was, in general, much more important because, as well as being the time for children's new clothes, it was the first public holiday weekend of the year on which you could reasonably expect good weather. It was also the first recognised occasion in the year when adolescents could take a trip out to the country and pair off in the woods.

Summer holidays were for the few who had a man in good regular work, perhaps with paid leave and certainly with a wife who had the capacity to save and encourage him to save. The practice of wives going out to work from homes which were already doing quite well, so as to save for a really good family holiday or a better car, was more than a quarter of a century off. In the Thirties, women who regularly went out to work were usually under some kind of duress, respectable or otherwise: widowed or with a sick or out-of-work husband; or, and these women tended to get the lowest kind of jobs ('charring', cleaning offices or doing the hard-cleaning in better-off homes a mile or so away), some went out because the husband was a boozer and did not hand over enough of his wages; or perhaps both of them wanted more beer-money. It was widely recognised, though not by us, that a man had to have ''is beer money'; it sounded childish, as though you were talking about a boy's pocket money, a conceded indulgence. Unless a woman had a clear motivation to cause her to go out to work, one who did so would be regarded as grasping, out to collect extra money at the expense of care for her home and children. It was usually assumed that the husband concurred in her working; indeed, permitted it.

One might go to relatives for a few days, in summer, by bus. Even Sheffield or Stockport looked different and felt different from Leeds. I was sent to Sheffield from time to time to see Tom. I cannot remember Molly going over there, perhaps because she was a girl and younger but also because the family she was with, that single street away, were not in direct line with us and so contact with them on such matters was only intermittent.

The one seaside holiday I recall was an unexpected week at Bridlington when I was thirteen or fourteen. We went to a house offering the traditional Northern arrangement: you provided your own food, the landlady cooked it and probably offered in what we would now call the 'package' a pudding of her own making, usually nice and often excellent. A complicated arrangement if there were three or four families staying in the one house; and one which gave plenty of chances for peering without being seen into what others had provided for themselves, and finding out whether they were living better or worse than you. The system had its rituals: the landlady would expect to be asked to cook fish on a Friday even if she hardly ever had Roman Catholic lodgers, and she would not expect to be asked to cook both fish and meat on the same day at any time. So getting in first was quite important. Then the landlady could say to the second comers: 'Mrs Ackroyd has said she'd like fish today. Would something like that suit you?' All such things were explained to you as you arrived for the first time, your luggage trundled from the station for a few pence by a man with a wheelbarrow.

A sister of Ida's, Ethel's friend, married with two boys, suggested that Ida and Ethel join them. To the rest of us, a high-class idea, beyond our usual ken. Who suggested that I go too I do not know, but I feel fairly sure that Aunt Ethel would have helped with the cost of having me there; that would have been about thirty shillings or two pounds. That was generous of her and having me around on her one week of holiday away from work and home could not but be something of a responsibility, even though I spent all my time with the other two boys. No doubt the parents of the boys got fed up with her rhetorical questions, which were really designed as proud shafts of information directed at them: 'What place did you say you got in Latin, Bert?', and the like. That family was better off than we were, with a small, dapper father in a suit or, at Bridlington, a navy-blue double-breasted blazer and well-pressed flannels; a clerk. Aunt Ethel was concerned that I did not show up her, or our family, so the emphasis was on propriety. The two boys were amiable and fly; they knew how to behave at home and towards visitors. Outside, they demonstrated from the first day how to nick fruit from stalls, simply by distracting the stallholder's attention. I never had the nerve to copy them. They were not caught in the act, at least not at Bridlington.

The most vivid trip away from Newport Street came with an invitation to Tom and me to visit some of our mother's relatives in Liverpool. We arrived at a very impressive lower-middle-class district and a house with stained-glass panes in the door, a hall and rooms front and rear off it on the left. The only person I remember meeting in that house, though there must have been others, was an uncle who seemed to be in his fifties. Was that the brother of whom our mother was said to have been especially fond and to whom she was reputed to have lent money? He treated us throughout with a grave, gentle kindness which reinforced the feeling that there had been a special relationship between him and his sister Addie.

Further away, perhaps over the river, was the daughter of another of our mother's siblings, much older than we were and married to a man who was thought to be doing very well since he was second officer or some such on one of the banana boats to the Canaries which plied out of Liverpool. 'Banana boats' makes them sound like old tubs, but they were smart and carried a handful of passengers in good accommodation with good food. Tom and I were taken to tea in that house. The husband was between trips. There were two children who in all sorts of ways, beginning with the size and quantity of their playthings, seemed very privileged.

For the tea, a largish plate with a grilled fish, probably a sole, surrounded by chips, was brought on to the nicely laid table. There was a white tablecloth, something we saw only on Sundays and Feast days. The father was given the fish with some chips and the four children were each given some chips. Very puzzling. I had occasionally had tea at a working-class family in Hunslet when the meat or at least the largest piece of meat was given to the father, the breadwinner. His strength had to be kept up and funds would not run to meat all round every teatime. According to his hunger and his mood he might or might not give titbits to the children. This was not a resented practice, unless the father was a greedy guts. But it was regretted deep down and families were happier if they could give out food share and share alike. I do not remember if the Liverpool father gave bits of his fish to the children. Perhaps he did, usually, but might have been inhibited by our presence.

The memory came back when I was in the sixth form, on a somewhat similar occasion; except that no such occasions are ever quite the same. I was working after school some days and at weekends as an errand boy for the Sunshine Grocers, with whom most of the time our patronage took the form of our debt, being painfully paid off or kept level. Since I had not delivered newspapers, this was my introduction to a variety of people and homes. Even the Sunshine Grocers' clientele varied from the friendly ones who gave you a tip to the grumblers and bullies. The manager was an archetypal hired man for such a shop, though of the more respectable kind, a pious Nonconformist. I believe he was utterly honest in that he did not put his hand in the till or fiddle food away to his own home. He did, though, show me how to scrape maggots off bacon in the shop cellar and how a certain kind of light, shone on the bacon once it was displayed upstairs, made it look leaner. He was polite and understanding to customers who were congenitally in debt. In his own way he was exploited by the owners since he clearly was not very well paid. Deploying my teenage socialism, I told him one day that he was indeed being exploited. He did not take it amiss but looked at me with what Forster called the steadiness of the half-shut eye and, inevitably drawing on his biblical memory, replied piously: 'Ah, but you forget that the labourer is worthy of his hire.' I had thought that that phrase cut the other way, but it would have seemed churlish to pursue the point.

He was married, with two children, and was buying a semi out Seacroft way. Cheap semis were going up fast around there at that time. The mortgage payments would be a drain and he and his wife would want to be sure that the children were well or at least 'nicely' turned out. So it was an affectionate but slightly worried home. His kindness prompted him to invite me to tea one day, I think because he quite liked me and because I was rather different from most of the errand boys who had gone through his hands.

Just as many middle-class homes are predictably flowery-chintzy, so this striving-upwards working-class home was predictably pretty and cosy and cottony. In her own terms the wife knew how to make a room welcoming and warm, with a clutter of odd bits of pottery, especially vases, and prints. She also knew how to cook appetisingly. She brought on a medium-sized plate and the father announced that we were to have a mixed grill, the five of us. The plate contained two pieces of bacon, one piece of liver, one small chop, one egg, one sausage, a piece of tomato. A medium-sized mixed grill for one. He certainly had not been raiding his store.

He set about and managed to devise five plates of food from it; it was a loaves-and-fishes performance. I felt embarrassed for him but he carried off the serving with some style. My embarrassment arose from recognising that this was for them, perhaps had to be, characteristic corner-cutting; and from realising that the grandly styled mixed grill, shadow though it was, was special because they had a visitor even if only a penniless grammar-school boy. They were making a gesture towards me, and the mixed grill was the centrepiece, even though it was only a gesture towards the reality of a mixed grill. Go wild, lash out too often and the mortgage payments fall behind, the little girl's new dress will be the harder to afford. All in all, they both carried off the operation with dignity and without giving the impression of congenital meanness.

But the incident with the Liverpool relatives was different. An officer in the merchant navy was reasonably well paid; the house alone indicated that; they were certainly not hard up. What made them so sparing with food? Again, the weight of a mortgage, perhaps a larger one than they could reasonably afford? Or were they paying for the boys to go to a private day school? Whatever the cause, I thought then and think now that it was insensitive, however they acted when only family were present, to behave in that way with visitors – orphaned young relatives of the wife, who she and her husband knew to be living wholly without luxuries. I doubt if either Tom or I had tasted sole up to that time and no doubt we had to wait a while longer until we did.

But they were not particularly sensitive. I said something earlier about the chilling effect on a child – children being exceptionally sensitive to the meanings in tones of voice – of hearing adults talk about you as though you are not there and in a way which betrays no sign of warmth. Such an impression, felt for the first time markedly on the day of our mother's funeral, was repeated on the Liverpool visit. I recall those relatives talking about Tom and me not so much 'behind our backs' – that would have shown a kind of tact – but carelessly, with the result that we could overhear if not every word at least enough to know that it was us they were talking about, and in a manner which suggested we were outside some charmed circle, kids towards whom some gesture (but not too much, the tone said) had to be made 'for Addie's sake'. Poor Addie. She would have been first hurt, then furious that her kids had been treated like that, not with overt cruelty but with the cool casualness which can just as surely distress and deaden.

Those incidents were early lessons in belonging and not-belonging, in not having a valid entrance-ticket to many of life's important events; and their force does not seem to weaken with the years. Their adult counterpart, though not as disturbing as the child's experience, is that moment when you enter a room and hear the conversation switch suddenly and notice that the occupants are looking slightly silly and ashamed at the same time – because they have been talking about you, being snide. The expression of a lack of fellow-feeling, the rejection of one human being outside by others in the warmth of a group, is one of the most shaking types of insensitivity. The strength of my own feeling here is not a matter of virtue or of right-minded thinking; it is a not-yet-shaken-off gut-response to early experiences. We left for home, Tom to Sheffield, me to Grandma's to meet again the disinterested love, which was all she could give; but that was enough.

Such were the occasional interruptions of summer; but most of that season was passed at home or in streets which sometimes became so hot that the tar between the cobble-stones melted pungently and smelled like Victory-V tablets. The smell triggered off routine, repetitive remarks about it being 'a scorcher'. Now and again one had a vision of the few boys who were at the seaside and reckoned that they were swimming, going out in boats with their dads or hovering round their mothers' deckchairs asking for another ice-cream. It was a kind of envy but a mild form; you would have had to take the whole family packet to get that sort of holiday and few families nearby, though they were often better off than we were and did not quarrel so much, looked attractive as swops; quite early, their interests seemed limited.

So where to go? A cheap tram-ride north and up to Roundhay Park, which had been Leeds public property for half a century by then, the centrepiece of the city's many green spaces, was clear favourite, especially when 'penny returns' for schoolchildren were introduced at off-peak times in the holidays. Or one might be more daring and less a follower of the most popular taste and go east to Temple Newsam, a great house and park. Roundhay Park and Temple Newsam were good instances of nineteenth-century and early twentieth-century philanthropy and civic foresight acting together.

No one of my generation went to concerts in the Town Hall, obviously; nor to the Art Gallery or into the gods at the Theatre Royal or the Grand, except when we started at grammar school and were prompted – and then only if something cultivating was on, such as *St Joan*, with Sybil Thorndike still going strong. But the great parks were classless, like the Public Library; they belonged to us just as much as to any other citizens of Leeds, whether those others were from Roundhay itself or Adel or Alwoodley nearby, or Headingley or Burmantofts. Those parks and the Dales were our air-holes as much as anyone else's and we did not feel graded when we were in them. Big cities without some of the right kind of public provision on that scale or without some such hinterlands are doubly deprived.

If you were unable to get out on a particular weekend, and that happened more often than not, you could always sit on the step, the door open as far as seemed decent, so that what wind there was could waft into the living-room, a cushion to soften the stone or brick, a book, and an eye out for whatever might be happening in the street. By late afternoon a cooler breeze usually came up so that you were sorry to be called in to tea. Sometimes you asked to be allowed to take your tea on to the step. On one such day Grandma had been baking and had at the end put 'oven-cakes' in the bottom of the oven, made from the left-over bread dough and looking like large teacakes but with the consistency of ordinary not sweetened bread; they tasted better when fresh, chiefly because they had such crisp crust all round and the white inside was springy and warm; and moist, since the margarine or butter had melted into them.

On this occasion, a Monday during the school holidays, there was a little tinned salmon left over from a Sunday tea at which we had had a couple of family visitors, and Grandma gave me that on a sizeable piece of oven-cake. Not a lot of salmon, but it has a strong taste so a little, spread carefully, can go a long way; the pepper, salt and vinegar mix with the oily juice from the tin and the seasoned mixture seeps into the warm cells of the white inside.

I then had for a few moments a sensation of unpremeditated and unalloyed happiness. A difficult and dangerous phrase to use in English, but it is apt here. Among many reasons why I admire Chekhov is his willingness to try to describe such moments, as in the short story 'After the Theatre' in which he captures a young girl's unaffected sense of pure contentment. I guess it is not an accident but an emanation of the English spirit that when we try to describe such a sensation we slip into 'un' words, as I have done three times in this paragraph. We find it hard to go straight, positively to name the sensation, so we circle round it, saying not this and not that, un-this and un-that, as though our readers will have to infer the still light in the middle.

What I experienced on the step that day was more than a boy's elemental pleasure in a succulent snack, though it was that certainly. It was a brief sense of being wholly at one with the world, at peace. The weather lambent, the house at the time not too much threatened, school no doubt going well and for the time not making demands, Grandma's bright gesture of affection in offering the sandwich, the body presumably in good shape. It would be far too much to claim that 'blood, imagination, intellect' were running together, but in a small and immature way something like that was happening. One felt simply that one was an at-ease part of the created world and for the moment the endless anxious sense of unfinishedness was still. Until I met my wife I experienced only three such moments, but all are as vivid now as they were at their times. The latest I have already described, at Aunt Annie's bedside.

Autumn brought its own small peaks in the cycle. Bonfire night, of course, though that never meant much to me perhaps because it was a noisy, chilly affair with kids squabbling and a claque of gossiping housewives on the fringes. Today's professional middle-class version, in a garden with school and neighbourhood friends, controlled fireworks, safe outdoor lights, gingerbread, baked potatoes and drinks for both children and adults – that makes a sharp, neat, little contrast.

The main procession of autumn was made up by the movements of the great Fairs, or 'Feasts' as we knew them, across the north and middle of the country. When the nights drew in, damp, with slight fog hanging in the air and the smell of burning rubbish coming off the few back gardens two or three hundred yards away, we knew that the Feast would soon be reaching our particular patch. Two of the biggest, which we had heard about but not seen, were Newcastle Town Moor and Nottingham Goose Fair . . . their names so often trailed their medieval origins, like church weddings for wholly unchurchy couples of today; a hint, no more ... And there was Hull Fair, which we came to know well in the Fifties, still big and brassy. The biggest Leeds Feast was Holbeck, with Hunslet second; on Hunslet Moor, a clinkered waste near the frontier with Holbeck. Later, when I walked on the great Yorkshire Moors, I wondered whether nostalgia had caused the country people who moved into those cities in the nineteenth century to call any sizeable bit of wasteland 'Moor'. They were unlovely spots with virtually no money spent on them by the council but presumably protected by regulations from being built on. On Hunslet Moor one evening in my teens I heard Oswald Mosley harangue the workers, many of them unemployed: an aristocratic voice preaching hatred and envy to the dispossessed or the never-possessing. We got shoved around by his Blackshirts – bouncers, bully boys, rootless ex-NCOs – for barracking.

Loyalty to Hunslet did not prevent us from favouring Holbeck

Feast, the bigger, on a bigger wasteland; and Holbeck Feast was on Aunt Annie's route from work. She had the excellent idea, in my first year at Newport Street, of suggesting that I meet her at the door of her works on the opening day of the Feast and go round it with her for an hour. The time was exactly right, since five-thirty was the period before things warmed up and also rides were cheaper then than later. No self-respecting spinster, least of all one with a young boy, would throw herself into that mêlée in the heart of the evening or later.

At any time the biggest worry for a youngster was the tendency for those who collected the fares to give short change and to have cloth ears to any protests; especially when fares were collected on the roundabouts at full speed by rough young men exhibiting exceptional feats of footwork, like boxers' sparring partners or trainee bouncers. But from five-thirty to about seven there was plenty of room on the clinkered paths, time to choose carefully what to spend your one-and-six on, to get the exact change from Aunt Annie so that you could less easily be fiddled; and time to stop and savour the unmistakable fairground smell: hot engine oil, clinkers, toffee apples, brandy snap, mushy peas, cockles and winkles with vinegar. All in all, a dreadful compound but still, more than any other mixture of smells, instantly evocative of English working-class life, as powerful to us as the smell of some herbs must be to an Italian peasant.

Smells always come first and sounds second; then sight, taste and touch in that order. Of all sounds, swirl predominated and still does, with the pace set by the great machines swirling in every direction, and every year in more complicated ways. They were serviced in the morning by those same scruffy young men who had taken the fares the night before. Surprising that there were not many more accidents even than there were, given what havoc a loose nut can cause on machines as complex as those. Were there multiple fail-safe facilities? Were the inspectors super-efficient? Were the young men closely supervised by the grizzled, solid men who could be seen now and then moving between the packed-together transporter trucks at the back, and who looked as though they could fix anything, from a threshing machine to a steam roller. Or did those roughly casual, bird-hunting young men of the evening before change character when it came to servicing machines they respected?

Clearly, the thrust of all the clamorous competing noises was meant to put the customers into a rushed-away condition, where judgment on how to get best value and pleasure from your cash became more and more difficult as you were sucked into the maelstrom. So you went in with the usual cautionary phrases: 'Take care, now. All they want is to part you from your money.' The clang and bang of the beautiful, big, baroque steam organ was the fixed main indicator of stress and emphasis in that relentless process, the bull elephant of the whole herd.

It was in many ways very enjoyable indeed. It was so blatantly, so vulgarly and insistently and uncharmingly out to separate you from your money that it neither patronised you nor awarded you any false importance or status; you were just a coney. The Feast had a foot, a rather mucky foot, in an older England, not in the world of smooth consumer persuasion.

The layout of the Feast had its formalities. There were three concentric though not regular rings. The big stuff was in the middle; then, sheltering under the rim of the big stuff, the smaller stalls – hoop-la, rifle booths, dart-throwing stalls and the like. Perhaps a further ring of those too. Then on an outer ring the larger stalls offering larger prizes. These stalls needed more space so that people could stand back and throw with a full arm at coconuts, or kick footballs in the hope of winning a huge, garish, plastic furred doll owing more to debased Disney than to any earlier tradition. Plainly fire hazards, filled with unmentioned and probably unmentionable stuffing, the prizes announced their origins in very small print and in as obscure as possible a place: German, Japanese or perhaps a cheapjack, fly-by-night British workshop. Their successors today come from Taiwan, Korea, Hong Kong; even the most inaccessible prizes, big transistors or ghetto-blasters, are no longer likely to come from Japan or Germany; those are by now too good, too dear.

Especially on that outer ring, the nervous expectation of being cheated ran strong and true. It was known that a child would be given a cheap and nasty prize, well below what had been won, if the stallholder thought he, or she, could get away with it. At the limit a pair of policemen, who walked like twin proctors down the aisles, could be called in. That ring contained also the gypsy fortune-tellers, the biggest rat in the world (usually, a South American coypu), and the girl in satiny bra and pants lying on a bed so hinged that she fell into a bath of tepid water if someone hit the bull's-eye;

and best of all the Wall of Death riders. More than anything else, as distinct from everything else on the fairground, they had style, dignity, courage, coolness; it showed in every gesture in spite of the foolish trappings they were kitted out in. Whatever the tricks used to spin out the act, it was dangerous to hurtle round the vertical walls of that wooden drum held there only by the force of your speed whilst the safe spectators watched from the upper rim. One slip, and at the least you would have a broken limb or two as you fell to the floor with the machine on top of you.

There was a touch of the clean Hemingwayesque world about the Wall of Death, as compared with the rigged boxing ring next door where young labourers who fancied themselves were invited to take on the professionals. They were mostly silly cheats, those side-shows, harmless but childishly deceptive. The Wall of Death was the working-class fairground's link with the world of stunt flyers, matadors and all callings in which men and women really do take risks with their limbs and their lives because they like the thrill of the gamble and the entry to a world of style which a more conventional life would not offer them. So whilst the boxers who would take on the local young men strutted and made feints and snorted on the wooden platform next door, the Wall of Death riders sat on their machines, occasionally gunned their bikes but above all looked into a middle-distance as though wholly caught up in the experience which had gripped them beyond anything that had gone before in their lives, and brought them out of their homes, their jobs, their local towns to this succession of bare platforms, the crowded caravan at the back and that Wall, night after night.

There was a fourth rim: that formed by the living accommodation for the fairground people: caravans which ranged from the huge and dazzlingly well appointed, all cut-and-coloured glass in windows and lamps and mirrors, with much fringed curtaining, usually gold and red or other such bold colours, from those to the tiny ones which might have come from a tinker encampment. With them were the load-carrying trucks which had to be kept out of the way during operations, whereas the power-supplying trucks were right up there within rim one.

Around that background living accommodation there had taken root yet another of those stories which gave a little sexual excitement to adolescents of both sexes. It was believed that those rough young men who so acrobatically collected the fares for the rides slept in the big empty covered trucks; and that they were always on the lookout for girls willing to go on their mattresses. A folksy idea, drawing on some of the same myth-making elements as 'The Virgin and the Gypsy'. Lawrence refined his story out of folk-myth into his own kind of symbolism. Hunslet girls were likely to be different from Lawrence's. In Hunslet or Holbeck a shy girl, almost by definition proper as well as shy if still a virgin at sixteen, would not allow herself to be led into the darker by-ways of the fourth rim. Those who did go were more likely to be girls who 'knew a thing or two already' and were excited by the incandescent bustle and glare of the Feast which threw their repetitive days in the clothing factory into the drabbest of backgrounds, so that those shabby young men looked dashing. Adolescents were intrigued by such stories because they were felt to be rare examples of breaking the mould; the Leeds tailoresses did not have the reputation of the Nottingham girls who worked at Player's tobacco factory ('Player's Angels', the available Carmens of the Midlands), who descended on favoured seaside resorts like unabashed trollops.

Smell, noise and lights: they formed and must have formed over centuries the main fairground triumvirate for assailing the senses; picking up right across that time any new aid, especially those which push out noise and light. This last century has seen the fastest and greatest developments of all, from what already seems old-style Tannoy to the most sophisticated public-address systems and sound synthesisers, from strings of bare electric bulbs through plastic strip-lighting in bold colours picking out the outline of the stalls' rims, to circling multi-coloured discs for powerful lamps to shine through as in an open-air dance-hall. As you walked home the smells persisted for a few streets, the thump and rattle lasted for half a mile to a mile, depending on the wind's force and direction, and the light still glowed as you looked out of the attic window before getting into chill flannelette sheets. Aunt Annie and I would have stayed only an hour or a bit longer and by then she was tired after a full day's work. I liked to think of going back with a pal or two but never did, at least not until the sixth form.

These key events ran along the year like colourful but tatty mixed beads on a piece of string. Grey string: Walter on his downward path, Ethel's moods worsening, particularly when her gallstones made themselves felt, the other four of us taking what shelter we could under our different headlands – Grandma in memories, her lips moving soundlessly as she recited them to herself by the fire, Winnie with Albert, Annie with her handful of spinster seamstress mates, me with school.

As I moved up that slope, through Matric, Higher School Certificate ('A' levels) and a scholarship to the local university, so Annie, like Grandma and Ethel, became more and more proud of me. They all tended to watch for signs that I might be committing one of the worst of sins, 'getting above himself', though they watched with different degrees of severity and readiness to rebuke, tick-off. That range of working-class phrases which is typified by 'I can't abide a stuck-up person' does not express, I think, envy. It can recognise differences and is glad that someone is 'getting on', above all by merit and hard work. Its root is much more an insistence on equality in basic human worth, a sentiment and conviction which must be recognised by everyone, the successful as much as the unsuccessful: 'The poorest he that is in England hath a life to live as the greatest he.'

They were not entirely clear what was happening to me, and their vocabulary mirrored that difficulty. ''E's ever so bright, yer know, ever so clever and 'e seems to be able to carry all before 'im. Mind you he does work 'ard, very 'ard. And 'e 'ardly ever goes out.' That was about the measure of it, but it did very well. After the war my wife and I and the children visited Aunt Annie twice or three times each year, in a warm little back-to-back terrace house in Hunslet Carr, the southernmost bit of Hunslet. She had to be jollied at the start of each visit out of a slight touch of deference. One silly joke usually wafted that away.

There were only half a dozen houses in that terrace and they shared a couple of outside lavatories and a dustbin area, slotted in the middle. Picking the key off the hook near the door and the toilet paper roll – torn-up newspapers having by then been superseded – was as evocative as the smell of Woodbines. Aunt Annie liked to call in some of the neighbours so they could hear us talk. Like Miss Jubb, she knew how to place things for her audience: ''E talks just like a doctor, doesn't 'e?' Our three children, articulate in a way Aunt Annie was not used to, not 'nicely turned out' in the best working-class manner but whom she could recognise, from the way their hair was cut and from the unsmart informality and good quality of their clothes, as adhering to another range of habits – all responded warmly to her unmistakable affection and were unaffected with her.

For her part she remained almost always open about her own emotions, without looking over her shoulder at likely effects. She was 'not a great reader'; that is, she never read a book. When she watched a play on television and it gripped her she entered it and, as the old lady is said to have done at a performance of *Macbeth*, would literally call out to the hero that the villain was creeping up on him or would tell the young husband that his apparently gracious young wife was a bad 'un, playing around with that other fellow and not at all to be trusted. Like almost all of her generation and class, she found self-analysis and family-analysis disconcerting, not the sort of thing one did, likely to lead to 'showing yourself up'. When she saw me on television in the late Seventies, talking about what her mother had meant to me, this event was a revelation.

She had missed the first showing of the television programme and wrote:

> I know I have been a long time in answering the letter about the television programme as I didn't know how to tell you that I didn't see it. I was waiting every day all the week and when the time came it went clean out of my mind and when it came to me it was just going off. I was so upset I didn't know what to do. I couldn't write you and tell a lie. But, dear Mary and Richard, I do hope that you are not annoyed. Because the real reason is that my memory is going. And I can't remember anything for long. I am still upset about it as I don't know what it was about because I think it was something you wanted me to see. So if it was when you write again let me know what it was about. I do wish I could remember things . . .
>
> So now I send my love to everyone and I hope you have a lovely holliday and I hope you are not too upset about me missing your programme.
>
> Love to you both, Aunt Annie

Like our mother's inscription in our father's Bible, such writing shows the difference between virtue and virtuosity in expression. Aunt Annie saw a repeat a few weeks later. Autobiographical speaking by her own nephew about her own mother, seen on television screens right across the nation but, even more perturbing, in the houses around, was as difficult to comprehend as someone shouting family secrets to the crowds, naked, from the top of Leeds Town Hall. But she quickly realised that it was an expression of love for her mother. The moment we got in her front door on the first visit after she had seen the programme she had to tell us that she had found it deeply moving and almost overwhelming. What she said was exact, economical and graphic: 'I had to sit down. I was that overcome.'

Such memories kept flooding into my mind as I sat by her in hospital, her mind wandering, her knickers on awry (usually both legs in one opening until the nurses got to her), her corset wrongly hooked up and back to front, as she sat in one of the flowery chairs in the sitting space at the end of the ward, occasionally telling someone that her nephew runs St James's, the only eminent role her mind could grasp for me in those late stages.

In my early years at Newport Street Aunt Annie must have been, at bottom, lonely. There was the affection and the fellow-feeling with her mother, as of victims huddling together. There were the few friends. She 'liked a drink', a phrase which can cover a range of meanings, from the most simple – that the person referred to liked a single modest drink or perhaps a couple from time to time – to the imputation of drunkenness when it was said sarcastically: 'Oh, he likes a drink all right.' Annie was well over into the more modest part of the spectrum.

She could spin out half a pint of stout (not Guinness; Mackeson's was thought to be more milky and hence more nourishing) with all the ease and assurance of someone used to making things go a long way in terms of time bought: a cup of tea at a station cafeteria as you hung on in the warm; twice round at the pictures if the attendant didn't see you; or, no doubt for some, tea and cakes made to last a long time at the Queen's Hotel.

There were exceptional, ritualistic occasions when the atmosphere could get giddy and then Aunt Ethel had to be borne in mind if there was drink around. The visit to a local pub immediately after work on Christmas Eve was the outstanding occasion. It seems a shame that Aunt Annie could not have been allowed to come in slightly oiled, very cheerful, looking forward to Christmas and full of affection for all. But you knew she would have given herself a shiver and shake, like a dog throwing off snow, just before she got to the front door, so that she could not be immediately accused of coming home stinking. The atmosphere was inhibited, or there was a blow-up anyway; probably both. There were other occasions, sometimes with drinks in the factory itself after the machines stopped: girls leaving to get married or saying goodbye to someone moving out of the district; sweet sticky sherry or even stickier cheap port were the staples.

Thus Annie went on until she was about forty. At that time, I think prompted by an acquaintance, though perhaps there were deeper impulses in play – an apprehension that a club might offer a more lasting relationship than a pub – she began going to a Working Men's Club, not in our exact neighbourhood (that was delicacy) but within easy walking distance, say three-quarters of a mile. It belonged to the WMCIU, the Working Men's Club and Institute Union, which the Rev. Henry Solly inspired in 1862 as a sober and earnest attempt to provide working-men with a place to congregate other than the pub with all its threats to family finances.

I wrote something about these clubs thirty years ago but they have greatly changed since then. At the time I first came to know them the clubs had three main qualities, two of them not intended by their founders. They were places in which members could drink at a penny or so a glass cheaper than in the pubs and with no sense of the need to hurry in ordering the next one. Second, many of them, to judge by their names, appeared to have political affiliations. The one I knew best was called a Liberal Club, probably in deference to Lloyd George. But like every other club I knew or heard about, its political activities were non-existent. Third, most clubs were cooperatives run by committees of management, many of which ruled very firmly. They did, as their founder intended though not quite in all the ways he intended, form a community of sorts out of their members, and in some respects a very sophisticated community in its rules and mores.

Their rules for admission, expulsion and points in between were elaborate and mature, quite as mature as those said to be exercised by London clubs. They did not practise black-balling, but they had delicate yet firm unwritten rules for, let us say, finding it not possible to admit certain people and for getting rid of a member who was becoming a nuisance. They had rules about caring for members' widows; and for giving members' children an annual treat or one at Christmas and one in summer; they took some care for members down on their luck – the 'whip-round' was the immediate tool for giving first-aid. They were male-dominated and often male-chauvinist; and they exhibited the easy, self-flattering gallantry which can go with that attitude, in the buying of drinks for wives, girlfriends and elderly women relatives.

At their best, the clubs were like extended families with a coherent culture and an authority within themselves which the looser framework of ordinary everyday neighbourliness, always subordinate to the stresses within individual families, did not provide. Much of that must have changed. In the Sixties and well into the Seventies they often became very prosperous and constantly added new halls and equipment to house the bigger and bigger weekend shows they were by then providing. Weekend singers and stand-up comics were part of a long tradition but these new halls and bookings suggested small adaptations of Las Vegas rather than the traditional English working-men's club shows.

During the Sixties, the youngest child of the Sheffield aunt, Madge, who took in Tom did the club circuit with a magician's act which included sawing his strapping wife in half. One evening they took his mother, by then a huge matriarch, to the show. It included a stripper whom she found remarkable. 'She got right down to nowt but three tassels,' she said, and paused. One expected a moral denunciation on the lines, 'Eh, it were a sinful show,' matching her judgment on Leeds. But she added only: 'An' yer wouldn't believe what she did wi' those tassels.'

E. M. Forster's distinction between flat and round characters is useful: we do tend to see people as flat until they surprise us, do the totally unexpected, the out of character. We ourselves are never flat, always fluidly unfinished. It was through her visits to the working-mens' clubs that Aunt Annie startled everybody. There she met Jack Birtle, a widowed miner, with seven children ranging in age by then from somewhere in the late twenties to about ten. The oldest of the four boys was in that imperial offshoot, the police service in India, and married to a Eurasian. Two others, one also married, were miners, and the rest – another boy and three girls – still at school. They lived in New Holme, a featureless miners' village a few miles east of Leeds, just off the Selby Road.

That Annie was courting became known in our house at first indirectly and caused a slight tremor and some rather pitying smiles. When it was known that the suitor was a miner the smile disappeared and concern set in. We had been slightly deferential towards Uncle Walter's Jean and that house with a bay window and a bit of railing. A miner, with a council house in a miners' village, was near the bottom of the scale we recognised.

Jack was obviously 'a rough sort of chap', though one who might with time be elevated to the accepted non-commissioned status of 'a rough diamond'. That did not happen, though he never disgraced himself. Aunt Ethel did not like the affair and let that be known. But like Charlotte Lucas, Aunt Annie showed that dogged resistance which otherwise habitually timid people can muster when they sense that something important to their future is in play and in danger of being taken from them. She kept going, Jack hardly ever appeared in the house, but eventually they announced that they were to marry. That was put up with after much heart-searching and it was assumed that the wedding would be a quiet affair; as it was. I imagine that if her family had tried to stop her they would have failed. So Annie went off to become an instant mother of seven. We missed her very much, especially Grandma and I, and worried about how she would fare in those raw, miners' conditions.

She took on her ready-made family with a combination of nervousness and phlegm which worked very well. The tendency to worry we knew well; the phlegmatic, taking things as they come, long breath, had not so far been seen much, not been much called upon; she drew on unsuspected biological or cultural stores.

After Grandma died round about the Christmas of 1936 I went to New Holme fairly regularly; particularly in the first months to get away from the assize-court atmosphere in that women's outfitters on the Armley corner. The council house, though stuffy, was an occasional relief. There were no books and no conversation above the local level. But there was an undemanding going-on. There were quarrels and squabbles and explosions but not the sort of sheer unhappiness and sometimes misery we knew so often. That was what drew Annie to place her future there.

Jack had run the family in a rough-and-ready way; inevitably, since he was putting in a full set of shifts at the coalface and getting home dog-tired. In some important ways he had also run it well, had had the good sense to develop a set of routines and patterns which ensured some sound basic elements. Sunday dinner was always the same, always very savoury and always at the same time. Having 'got it going' he would slip out for a pint at the club but always be back not long after one o'clock to put it on the table. Others of his mates, still with wives, would hang on longer, knowing all would be ready when they did finally show up at home. The really late ones, unless they had submissive wives, would get it in the neck when they finally wambled home.

The centrepiece of Jack's Sunday dinner was always a solid brick of that ubiquitous Argentinian beef with hardly a hint of fat; it may have been topside. It would cost no more than a bob or two on Castleford Market, especially towards the end of Saturday afternoon when he did his weekend shopping, knowing that prices fell then. That, with mashed potatoes, carrots and peas and a thick, Bisto-brown gravy over all, was not only full of flavour but nourishing; and there was always plenty of it. He kept good order throughout and even the boy who was already at work and feeling spunky knew better than to muck about at the table.

On Saturday and Sunday evenings Jack changed into his one decent suit, perhaps his one suit, put on a bowler at a slightly jaunty angle and rolled away to the club on his extremely flat feet. That outfit, together with his unnaturally perfect set of false teeth, fitted him, also perfectly, to his environment; but he was not a joke: he was more Lowry than Andy Capp. That pattern of hard work, care for his family, and insistence that he had earned and would take his time for play, was very well held in balance and one of the best lessons he had to offer.

Aunt Annie gave up work and slipped into all that, running the economy of the house much as he had. It was a simple working machine and only an unwise person would have disrupted it in the search for, say, more gentility and smartness. She had the good sense to see that it wasn't a bad way to run things in a household of that size and with that income – only two wages coming in at the start, and I do not suppose the boy at work was asked for much towards household expenses. The realisation by Aunt Annie that she would not make much headway if she strove towards even the sub-chintzy, a suspiciousness of gentility anyway, a touch of lethargy which was always with her, combined with the intuition that Jack had got things about right, all these made her adapt more successfully to her new environment than anyone would have predicted.

She also had the sound instinct to give special care to the three girls, who must have been about thirteen, nine and seven when she took over. In the early years she was never without one just going into puberty and she worried about that, but with a clumsy effectiveness, realising that Jack could not provide the special attention they needed then, from coping with menstruation to coping with sexual urges; the atmosphere, if she had not gone there, would not have been more than minimally sensitive to girls in that phase.

She slid, also easily, into the weekend clubbing and into her role as a wife who sat in a mixed group of Jack's pit and club mates and their wives and took part in long but desultory conversations which usually became, sooner rather than later, each confined to a single sex, like two more sets of complicated weaving going on and around all the time. She slipped into the routines which governed the drinks chosen by each sex (a favourite awestruck expression about a certain kind of woman – a bolder, or harder drinker – was 'She's real mannish') and the intervals at which those drinks might be expected to come up; she slid into all the rhythms the sub-culture laid down.

She and Jack were back at the house about half an hour after closing time, since there was always conversation on the pavement outside the club. This part of the evening's talk was more urgent and insistent than that in the club itself, as though they felt they had so far forgotten something important or failed to get the right stress or, since they were not likely to be able to talk again till the next weekend, that by then a good story would have gone off the boil.

I do not remember seeing either of them drunk, though Jack would usually be slightly oiled. Seeing me working at his living-room table when he got in he would become Polonius, say how glad he was to see me pressing on, urge me to 'teach 'em a thing or two', to get away from all this. If, as happened occasionally, he had had one too many for Aunt Annie's barometer and went on too long, she would say mildly: 'Oh give up, Jack. 'E knows, 'e doesn't need you to tell 'im. Come on up.' There was tact there too; she would not compare Jack's owlish confidence in giving me advice towards a great future with what he had himself achieved. She did not damage self-respect. 'She never made him lose his manhood,' they are likely to say in working-class judgments on one kind of admirable wife. It is a more colourful form of Ibsen's 'Take the saving lie from the average man and you take his happiness too'.

Whether Annie slipped just as easily into the practice of the marriage bed I do not know. She gave no sign of shock or distaste. Perhaps she would not have spoken about it to me, but I think I would have come to know if there were problems. If I had ever thought about sex-and-Aunt-Annie before she married, I would have assumed she had had no sexual experience at all. Which will seem to a modern outlook ingenuous on my part and unlikely on hers; but I would have been right. Jack's rules of morality in sexual matters were ungenteel, direct and strong. Not long after they married he said to me, with exclamation marks all over his bumpy face: 'Eh, Bert, do yer know' (underlining pause) 'yer Aunt Annie were a virgin when we got wed.' I felt slightly piqued at first, as though he had hinted that the family might have sold him a second-hand car pretending it was new. Of course Aunt Annie was a virgin; that was what you were before you got married; at least, Hoggart women were. Equally clearly, it had not occurred to him that this would be so. Our own position was not founded in lack of sexual feeling or even in an abstract code of virtue; it owed something to religion but not to the Roman Catholic kind of injunctions on chastity before marriage; it belonged rather to that aspect of Primitive Methodism which transmuted much of morality into respectability and made that the arbiter in such things as in much else.

On another occasion Jack saw my girl-friend, later my wife, reading in his strip of back garden one sunny Sunday, with her knees up. He came in the back door and announced: 'Eh, she's got a right pair of limbs on her, that lass o' yours.' It was unabashed admiration, and by its explicitness and the clear indication that he had had a good look would have shocked Newport Street to its prim core.

On still another occasion he came back from his Saturday night spell at the club with Aunt Annie to find the house empty. One of the family had been left in the house with a girl. When Jack got back the young couple were walking to the girl's home just down the estate. Jack spotted a stain, like wallpaper paste or starch, on the shiny American-cloth of his sofa. 'The mucky buggers,' he said, 'Ah'm not 'aving it.' He knew dried semen when he saw it, though neither Aunt Annie nor I did. He also knew very well what went on in the hedges and ditches and back alleys and wasn't fussy about that. But he suffered a touch of the Lady Macbeths at that moment – 'Woe, alas! What, in our house?' – and he didn't like his sofa stained and thought his lad and the girl should have had more sense than to let that happen.

The marriage with Jack lasted, though there must have been very difficult adjustments to make, especially for Aunt Annie; she was the one who had moved from one set of habits to another, a change of which her new family were hardly conscious. The five children still at home adopted her as their mother easily. To me it never seemed other than slightly odd to hear them addressing her as 'Ahr Mam'. I was not jealous for myself but was slightly proprietorial for the family, the Hoggart family. Given what the Newport Street family was like, in all its oddities and unhappinesses, the strength, the primitive strength, of my family feeling still seems surprising.

Aunt Annie took it all in her low-keyed way but I doubt if she ever seriously or for long wished things otherwise. She did not hide her new family's inadequacies from herself or condone what she thought were improper practices. But she had done something which neither Ethel nor Walter had found it in themselves to do: she had been offered a future quite outside her normal family expectations and had, without any compulsion except her own inclinations, 'opted for life'. She had chosen circumstances and a role in which, whatever the shortcomings, she counted and was relied on. The Birtles were not working-class respectable like the Hoggarts; nor were they drunken, feckless, brawling types. They had their own kind of respectability, which here means, as it should most of the time, self-respect; rather harsher in its expression than ours, but of the same general cast.

The Birtles had the hard-earned prudence and aggressiveness of people who had drawn the dirtier end of the stick; they were not going to be put upon. The girls were not likely to open their legs wide until they had a reasonable assurance of marriage; the men were not going to be mucked around with by the deputies at the pit, the dole clerks or any other petty functionaries. Words for positive values are hard to come by nowadays; rejecting or disillusioned words come more easily. But thinking of the Birtles and trying to ensure they are not written-down I find myself reaching for such a phrase as 'in the truth'. 'In their own kind of truth' might be a face-saving formulation but is unacceptably relativistic given the strength of their position.

There are some truths – self-respect above all – which should matter as much to miners as to dukes. The Birtles had had few opportunities: once a miner always a miner; it was not easy to break out of that mining belt and it was a tough place. But they had their self-respect and kept it.

They stuck together and locked into a defensive ring against any threat from outside, with old Jack facing forward like a battered but still pugnacious bull. The children felt the usual sibling jealousies but also felt, perhaps all the more because they had been without a mother for almost a decade, part of a whole; in the current fashionable word, they felt 'bonded'. That Northern working-class possessive form apropos a member of your family which I used in the first sentence of this book – 'Ahr Alf', 'Ahr Nellie', 'Ahr Mam' and 'Ahr Dad' – did convey their sense of connection, of being part of a larger possessive whole, of not being only discrete individuals.

I saw the Birtle offspring fratch more than once and some of them could be nasty if pushed. I do not remember them being sarcastic or malicious. It was difficult to work there on my weekend visits: we were all on top of each other and the three bedrooms crowded. But the general feel of the household, the lack of certain types of nervous strain, especially that encouraged by fear of the next outburst, the lack of a sense of old to middle-aged individuals almost filling the place, with few if any expectations, all this made the weekends pleasant bits of time out.

The countryside helped. The surrounding district, though only seven or eight miles from Leeds, was still country, not outer suburbia. Not exciting country though it rolled a little; nor lush: the winds straight from the Urals, it was always said, saw to that. The farms tended to be tatty, the bits of common and woodland scruffy; a few pitheads showed in the middle distance and one or two pimples of land had been taken over by people doing well in Leeds, on which to build wholly unvernacular red-brick, large, centrally heated boxes whence they drove their Rovers, Wolseleys and Rileys to work in the city. The miners' brick rows and circles stuck out like weals on the already battered countryside, neither belonging nor merged.

In spite of all that, the miner saw it as country and still to some extent practised that double life Lawrence described: they were manual workers in a big and heavy industry; they lived not in country villages but in special blocks of modern council housing plonked on the nearest piece of cheap available land; their indoor recreation, at the club, was much the same as that which went on in the hundreds of such clubs in the middle of the big cities. Yet they still felt like countrymen on Sunday morning and set out for long early walks. There were rabbits about and a few pheasants and partridges; their relations with the local landowners were at the best guarded. Some had ferrets, working ferrets. On their long walks they might hope to knock off a rabbit or two or even a bird. But also they did evidently like the walking itself and had a range of favoured routes through the fields and bits of woodland. Eight hours or so a day underground for five days a week, some of the time on your knees, meant that you valued the chance to stride upright with a wind blowing; so long as you reached the club or pub door just about opening time.

Wilf, the miner son, must have been in his late teens or early twenties in that second half of the 1930s. He had a good eye and ear for a story and soon realised that he had a ready listener in me; so he saved them up. Sometimes they were about outwitting the police (you needed big policemen, in pairs, in those parts, to take on drunken or recalcitrant miners) or the colliery management; but most of them were about his and others' sexual exploits in the neighbourhood. Sometimes they were merely stories of conquests; more often they were better than that, and had a dramatic or quixotic quality which he could recognise and knew I would appreciate without knowing what it was we were responding to.

A story of the first type would be about playing rummy one weekend evening in the home of an unmarried mate. He found that the mate's sister was rubbing the length of her leg against his, under the table. Eventually she announced that she had to go outside to the coal shed at the back for a new bucketful, looked at Wilf, and he duly offered to help (which should have aroused the suspicions of anyone who knew Wilf's supineness at home). Once at the coal shed they had a quick one-two or blow-through and were back at their seats before the others – especially the father and mother – noticed any delay. Wilf's dramatic world was full of available girls, though I suspected they were a stage army with a few going round and round doing duty for a pretended great many.

If he was to be believed, Wilf's weekends were dotted with such exploits. One of the more bizarre was about helping a mate (it was a life of 'mates' who stuck by you even in the silliest of escapades and especially against the police, to whom they would lie as a matter of routine and from whom they expected a thumping if they caused annoyance). This mate asked Wilf to go with him to some nearby woods one evening; he suspected his girl-friend or fiancée was playing fast and loose with him, and needed Wilf's support in case a fight developed. They found the couple on the very point of copulating. The man ran off after getting no more than a thick ear; they had little anger against him, since he had merely taken his opportunities. The girl begged for forgiveness from her boy-friend and promised never to let him down again. 'Tha'd better not,' he replied, 'But first yer can let me mate Wilf 'ave a crack. 'E's done me a good turn tonight and better 'im than that daft bugger 'oo's just run off.' The girl agreed.

Not long after Jack's death we found ourselves talking with one of the women from the Birtle family, during a visit to Aunt Annie's, about the great changes in sexual manners of the last two decades. I suppose we had mentioned a girl we all knew who was living with a man, or a man we knew living with a girl, without either of them seeming disposed to marry eventually (the phrase 'trial marriage' now has an out-of-date and even otiose ring). 'Ooh!' said Aunt Annie, rather shocked but not out to rush into a quick moral judgment. The younger woman then made one of those remarks which transform flat into round characters. If we had been inclined to underestimate her clarity we would have been forced to think again. 'Good luck to 'em,' she said, 'Ah think they're right. If Ah had me time again Ah'd do that. If Ah'd lived wi' my chap for a year or two Ah'd niver 'ave gone on to marry 'im. But in ahr day that were the only road open.'

Even whilst enjoying those occasional weekends at New Holme I also knew they could be only a phase; but it was a helpful phase within a difficult period. Pulling up out of Leeds on the New Hudson bicycle, I felt glad each time to see the irregular line of pitheads with their great wheels suspended high over the shafts and the slag heaps to the side, still then as bare as a baboon's bottom.

With some intermission that line stretched right down to South Yorkshire and the coal fields around Doncaster and so down again to the Nottinghamshire and then the Leicestershire coal fields. The end of those outcrops rather than an imaginary line at Watford marks the real end of the North and Midlands and the entry to the softer South, the property-owning South, the executive South, the clean South, the suburban South, the mock-Tudor and half-timbered South which, on the rare occasions one passed through a swathe of it on the way into London, had all the tugging attraction of an Ealing film, and made a Northerner feel more than ever outside, cut off from an altogether softer, more wrap-around, less harsh-edged England.

When Jack Birtle became too old for work down the mine he decided not to take a job at the pit surface; he wanted a change and more money than that would have brought in. So he sought the stewardship of a working-men's club. At first, rather like a doctor starting out in the Thirties, he could only find a succession of *locum* jobs, standing in for stewards who were ill or taking annual holidays. From that, now rather like a parliamentary candidate, he graduated to being a name on a list of possible stewards for the area he favoured. Each club being autonomous they made their own choices, but they shared information about candidates and, even more important, about 'bad 'uns'.

Jack finally got his niche, a small and at the time shabby club at the far end of Hunslet; but you've got to start somewhere, as he inevitably said. He took to the job as though all his life had been a preparation for it, for keeping order, keeping on the right side of his management committee, exercising the virtually regulatory fiddling. Sometime later one member of a club management committee told me they expected, assumed, about ten per cent of fiddling from any steward. Given the turnover at some clubs and the fact that, unless the taxman found a way in, those proceeds were tax free, a steward could salt a lot of money away. If, my informant said, the reported weekly takings made them suspect their man was getting greedy they called in the auditors and perhaps the police; but the police were a last resort. Much better settle it yourself, make what arrangements you could for some repayment, sack the culprit and see he went on the blacklist.

The clubs I knew were not criminal haunts; they were in many ways extremely respectable. But their attitude to small-scale portable property was relaxed and flexible. They firmly believed that the bosses saw themselves all right by perks from the works and so they too simply assumed that you fiddled what you could, that barter was an honourable form of trading – I can get you a bag of coal or a bolt of cloth if you can get me an electric fire or a dozen tins of stewed steak. In my experience only Birmingham surpasses Leeds in the bartering of knocked-off goods. The war gave the trade a great impetus. They were quick to point out, as they tried to slip you a tin of something which the London North Eastern Railway Catering Division didn't know it had lost, that the bosses could eat out every night if they wished and still have their coupons. It was a complex trade and involved a fine sense of judgment as to how many tins of this or that was equivalent to a repair job on your radio or to the plumbing.

By the time Jack went into that first club I was almost through my studies on the other side of town and had for some time been well settled in the university hostel, thanks to the grant from the British Legion. On occasion they also gave me a clothing grant. I remember an avuncular, pipe-smoking major who doled out what he could, willingly. Fish and chips may have been threepence, five Woodbines twopence and beer a few pence a half-pint; but still a bob or so a week did not go far. So, once they came to live in the club in South Leeds, I took my washing, at her suggestion, across town each week to Aunt Annie. We kept that from Aunt Ethel. She would have done it if asked, but the emotional price would have been high; and she would have been angry that Annie had offered and I accepted. On Monday or Tuesday I would cycle down to the bridge over the Aire, the main class-dividing line in Leeds, and then a mile and a half south to Hunslet Carr, hand in that week's and collect last week's shirts, towels, underwear; and have a cup of tea and a sandwich of 'something from the cupboard' – bartered ham or red salmon maybe – before setting off back.

On one visit Jack was not to be seen and I asked where he was. 'In t'cellar,' said Aunt Annie, 'but Ah shouldn't go down there if Ah were you. 'E creates like mad if Ah so much as put me 'ead round the stairs. 'E spends ages down there after t'beer's been delivered each week an' it's more than me life's worth to ask 'im what 'e's been doing.' Jack emerged from below after about a quarter of an hour, holding a small medicine-type bottle with the remains of some dark brown liquid in it, like gravy browning. 'The buggers,' he kept saying, 'the cheating buggers.' He asked whether we had any chemists at Leeds University. Would they be able and willing to tell him what were the contents of such a bottle? What is it for anyway, I asked. He told me unabashedly that he mixed the contents of the bottle – a quarter of a pint at the most – with several gallons of water and added it to the brewery's beer, thus making a handsome profit for his own pocket. He was swearing because the 'buggers' who sold him the stuff were charging one and sixpence and he was sure it was worth only a very few coppers. One and sixpence to produce several gallons more of what seemed like beer was not a bad bargain, even in those days, and even if those who sold the anonymous liquid were making a hefty profit on the one and six they charged. Jack seemed quite unable to connect the two kinds of cheating or to realise that the other parties would think themselves entitled to some of his large rake-off, by way of a particularly generous mark-up on the raw material value of the dark liquid. I asked him whether the customers had spotted that their beer had been adulterated. 'Adulterated!' He reared back as though I had accused him of poisoning his mates. Then he played his trump-card. Actually, he was doing the members a favour: 'They like it. They like it better. They grumble at me if I miss a week because them buggers 'aven't brought me a bottle.'

In one of his favourite bits of intellectual jackdawing, Auden liked to recall that the upper classes on their raffish side and the working classes on their more spendthrift side have long had much in common, especially their by-passing and conning of the hard-working, respectable middle and professional classes of which Auden was proud to be a member. Belloc made a similar point:

> The Rich arrived in pairs
> And also in Rolls-Royces;
> They talked of their affairs
> In loud and strident voices.
>
> The Poor arrived in Fords,
> Whose features they resembled;
> They laughed to see so many Lords
> And Ladies all assembled.
>
> The People in Between
> Looked underdone and harassed
> And out of place and mean,
> And horribly embarrassed.

Jack had a walk-on part in that old scene. He had not been free or able to go to the races when he was down the pit; but the relative prosperity of club stewardship released him and he began very occasionally to go to local racecourses, not to football or rugby matches. Just after the war, when we were living on the north-east coast, he announced that he would like to spend a few days' holiday with us. We had not realised until then that Redcar races were due. So he came and patronised them each day with the assurance of a landed gent or a big bookie. In the evenings after his meal he went to the local working-men's club at which he had reciprocal rights much as Harvard and Yale and suchlike clubs' members have rights at the Savile or establishments like that. He was no trouble as a guest, therefore; he enjoyed his meals but was out at his two main interests most of the time. He had a well-practised capacity for picking up acquaintance and was never lonely.

We used to know when he was approaching home because we could hear from several yards, through our front-room window, his by then well-lubricated, flat-footed roll. He moved like someone walking across Christmas tree decorations in stockinged feet. There was also, most nights, the sound of another voice since he would have a new-found mate who had decided to walk him as far as our door. He had too much tact to invite the other in, nor would it have been expected. They would be talking all the way, fifty to the dozen. Working-class women can be tireless gossipers. After a couple of beers, many men can equal or beat them. They would stop for minutes outside our window to finish a skein of repetitive talk, much of it in ritualistic phrasing. When Jack finally came in on one of these nights he was full of a particular item. The new friend had boasted about how much he earned. Jack was curious and dubious so in the end the friend had offered to reveal exactly how much he had made the year before. At this point a strange delicacy overcame Jack. 'Nay,' he said, as though the other man had offered to exhibit his wife in her nightgown. 'Ah nivver ask a friend what 'e earns.' But it was too much to brush aside and finally delicacy was smothered by sophisticated self-deception. 'Ah tell yer what,' said Jack. 'Tell me 'ow much income tax yer paid last year. That'll do.'

Meanwhile the little club thrived and grew. Among much else it had by the early Seventies a huge new concert hall elaborately wired for sound, and multiple lighting. By then Jack had died and we had had another of those funerals which have by now become such a habit that I could draw a map of Leeds and South Yorkshire made up of crematoria and graveyards, most of them windswept and all of them as sad in appearance as the events they provide for. True all the time to his own considerable shrewdness, Jack had been salting his profits away and just as predictably putting them into houses, since there is 'nothing as safe as 'ouses'. Actually these were not all that safe: they were two or it may have been three old-style back-to-back terrace houses facing the club over a cobbled dead-end street and producing only about a pound a week each in rent. Still, they were property and Aunt Annie inherited them, and it was in one of those that she lived before the protected maisonette became available. That was when the council finally, having condemned them some time before, said the houses must come down for redevelopment. She would not get much for them, perhaps a few hundred pounds; but the maisonette was warm and comfortable and the nearby Birtles helped her to move in. It was from there that she was taken to St James's for what proved to be the last few months of her life.

In the new place she was able to keep up most of her more cherished routines, especially the regular visits to the club; a Birtle or a son-in-law drove her and a neighbour the half-mile there. She was not a maker of casual club mates as Jack had been; but wherever she lived she soon made one or two good friends whom you might well find sitting with her when you arrived. She was obviously good-natured, even though a great worriter; but she made no demands and would listen to the longest of hard luck stories, making little sympathetic keening noises, and that must have been a kind of comfort. So the neighbours tended to depend on her rather than the other way round, for the healing power of confidences. That unmalicious readiness to lend a sympathetic ear was accompanied by an eye for a funny situation and the ability to describe it; that too must have endeared her to the rather lame ducks who so often were her later friends.

Her family would solve most of her own problems – fuses blown, doors which stuck, blocked lavatories; and she tended to have a tricky form or letter or two on the sideboard waiting for me to decipher next time round. By now she was in appearance a typical, mid-to-late-seventies, working-class woman, even more shapeless than she had been in her thirties, but yet not large, still in touch with her step-children and their families, living opposite the only surviving son and his wife. They treated her as if she were their natural mother, which included both reassuring and scolding, especially when she dilated too long on her aches and pains.

She loved language and especially metaphor; I doubt if she forgot any colourful image she had heard. Grandma and I enjoyed them, the others seemed not much to respond to them. I drew on her more than anyone else in recording working-class metaphors in *The Uses of Literacy*. The image I always remember first, and it sets the tone for most of the others, was her description of a self-righteous, easily outraged woman: 'An' yer know,' Annie said, describing a typical reaction by that person, ''er eyes stuck out like chapel 'at-pegs.' It is a superb image and invokes more than an individual's self-righteousness; it also suggests how that attitude fed on the narrow puritanism which chapel culture could encourage. There were many others: 'Ah reckon she'd like to 'ang 'er 'at up with 'im' (marry him: Aunt Annie liked hat-pegs); ''E thinks a lot of 'imself. *'E goes with 'imself*, yer know' (of a man who is his own claque and cheerleader as he strides through life). I do not imagine Aunt Annie invented any of those images; she knew how to use them, though – as well as the more obvious, always dramatic but over-used locutions of the area, such as: 'It's as true as Ah sit 'ere, if Ah nivver get up again.'

At one point in the second half of the Seventies an old widower began to pay court to her. We met him once, sitting on the other side of the fire, best suit, silent, shy. Aunt Annie kept glancing at us, slightly nervous of what we thought, anxious for him not to be in any way cast down by such a bunch of people from another world, wanting to share later the slight comedy but not at his expense. Her comments after he'd left brought together, in one, her sense of the humour of the situation and her own still strong commitment to the way she had been brought up.

He had startled her by asking her to go for a week's holiday with him to Bridlington. That too rings true. Scarborough or Blackpool would each have been wrong, off key, the one slightly too lower middle-class, the other slightly too vulgar. She did not turn the idea down out of hand; she realised he was a lonely old man, quite lost now his wife had gone: 'He keeps back death the way he keeps back phlegm/in company, curled on his tongue'. 'There'd be nothing funny, you know,' she said, meaning there would be no suggestion of sexual hanky-panky; she was very anxious not to be misunderstood. Then she gave a quick smile and said she had felt she had to tell Aunt Ethel who was by then well into her eighties. Aunt Ethel had not greatly liked the idea but did not go off the handle. She said solemnly that since 'our mother' (Ethel's preferred usage) was dead she, Ethel, had to advise her younger sister. It was this which touched Annie's funny-bone. How long would the unmarried Ethel go on feeling *in loco parentis* to a sibling who had had several decades of marriage, had seen her husband buried and some of her step-children too?

She did not go to Bridlington, and I think made up her mind for herself. She was tired and feeling old and by then probably could not dig up the boldness of will which all those years ago had set her off on her life with Jack and his family. But she was chuffed to have been asked and protective of the old man's self-respect. She thought around for something suitably dignified and respectful to say about him and finally came up with: ''E's a very *clean* old man,' as though we would be reassured to know that he was not one of those old men who are forever hawking and retching about the place. Sitting at the side of the fire he certainly did look like a clean and well-behaved old man; like Stan Laurel's uncle.

Aunt Annie will no doubt reappear in these pages, but that is the end of her direct story. Except for the cremation. They brought her from St James's to lie for the last day or two in her own home and from there the cars took her and us to the tattier southern side of the Leeds ring-road – like a fragment of the old Great West Road – to Cottingley crematorium. Cottingley does not go in for curtains closing electronically or coffins, now out of sight, sliding back or downwards as the canned music swells. The coffin stays where it has been placed until the service ends. Then relatives go up to it, touch it or kiss it and leave.

True exactly to form, relatives who had not seen each other for years came from as far away as Harrogate and Sheffield, and there were dimly remembered faces from New Holme. Most moving of all was the small group of old working-class women and men, club regulars most of them, who had come to pay their respects and stood in a ragged line slightly to one side, not being 'family'. 'Very nice,' Annie would have said. They were like a chorus reminding us of some eternal verities: friendship, memory and above all death. Our own children, unprompted, came up too and that would have pleased her very much indeed; I doubt if she ever knew they so loved her. None of us, all now living in the South, could stay for the funeral tea.

CHAPTER 5

INTERLUDE: LEEDS AT LARGE

For me, a known and homely landscape is first of all the sky above the houses. After that, a few vivid visual images, a mélange of sounds, some touch and taste, and underlying all a great many smells. That is the mental baggage. Taken together it means, and always will mean before all other places, Leeds.

Even now, coming into the place on the way to see Molly, in the warmth of a railway carriage, knowing how wet and dreary and unkempt and grey and shapeless, all of a heap, it must seem to the stranger in the seat opposite, this November day, that combination of light and sound and smell pulls like a large maternal breast. We lived for ten years, through the Fifties, in the East Riding of Yorkshire, in Hull. The great arching skies look as though they stretch from the middle of the Atlantic to the far east of European Russia. There are no hills but you do not miss them because the sky and its changing moods are dominant. The trees are huge and thick, not lean, scraggy and windbent; within their shelter are wool-churches as big as small cathedrals. The potatoes are so large that most of them used to go for crisps. I have some nostalgia for that landscape too; and for Hull, especially as the lights came on between four and five on a winter's evening. It was all in all a happy time, with the children each in their first decade, dependent and clustery. Say 'Saturday high tea at Jackson's' and it all floods back. These memories are more contented than those from Leeds, satisfyingly familial. But they are not Leeds. Leeds memories are more basic, as hard to shake off as a scruffy dog which shadows you down the road. So are the typical properties of that landscape. To go round a Woolworth's in any town or city you land in, no matter how far away it may be from home, is like having a quick fix from a drug you became addicted to very early. At their peak they were the paradigms of working-class stores: in the prodigal layout, the open bazaar, slightly Arabian Nights effect; in their exact sense of what their kind of customers wanted to buy, especially for the home; in the indisputably working-class girls on the counters; in their recognition that our kind of people cannot resist 'a bargain'; in their whole garish but accessible feel.

Recently, in an as yet unreconstructed Woolies, I passed the Pick and Mix counter which is usually sited near the exit so that they catch you, slaphappy, just before leaving. An old man was there, addressing himself with care to picking from the vivid variety of toffee and chocolate and liquorice and coconut and other nuts and nougat and marshmallow and Turkish delight and sherbet.

I looked down and sure enough there was a little mongrel on a lead, a typical tyke but adoring and biddable; like the tiny, attentive dog Carpaccio gave Saint Jerome in the picture of the holy man in his study. In Venice, that; but seeing it there I was instantly back in Leeds in the Thirties, in those streets where the movements of old men at the times when able-bodied men were at work and most housewives indoors doing the housework were the most common street-traceries. Even though most wives lasted longer than their husbands, there were plenty of old widowers. Dogs were often important to them in two apparently but not necessarily contrasting ways: as something to be 'master' of when there was nothing else to 'master'; and as something to love when there was no longer a near human being to love. All old men, we knew as one of the thousands of small facts of life, have 'a sweet tooth'. Woolworth's exotic mixtures on the Pick and Mix stall have been effortlessly adopted by the customers, especially the old men, because those sweets are the linear descendants of the old-fashioned humbugs which were the old men's staple in my own early days.

An old bachelor was a sadder figure than a widower because he had not even the memories of a married life to fall back upon. Why had he not married? No doubt for a number of reasons. In a touch of sentimental delicacy towards such a man people tended to say, as though to invest him with, set him against, a romantic back-light you would never have suspected, that he had been going strong with a lovely girl but she had been taken away with consumption. Similarly the more gentle and prettier spinsters who might have been expected to marry, were awarded fiancés who had been killed in the war and whom they had loved so much they couldn't bear to take up with another man. A touching Tennysonian romanticism on each side.

The bachelors might live alone but more often took refuge with a brother and sister-in-law or a sister and brother-in-law. They were free of commitments on the whole and usually liked to go on errands: to the council offices with the weekly rent, to the butcher or grocer with a list or the chemist with a prescription; that kind of activity pleased both sides. I once saw a little old man walking down a terraced street hand in hand with a boy. He had a lad's grin himself and occasionally gave a little hop and skip; he sniffed as though his nose was running a bit. They knocked at a door together, both by now smiling broadly. The daughter's house perhaps. At any rate, they knew they would be welcome. A cameo of ease in three generations.

Old widows often used to be in the bosom of one of their children's families, helping with the grandchildren; or they stayed in their own homes long after their husbands had died, until they could carry on no longer. In black, and often with black shawls over their heads, I saw them as late as the mid-Sixties, in Belfast. Those dark bundles, the faces peering out with the fragile bone-articulation showing through where the flesh was thinning off, were like an arrested sepia print from Leeds in the Thirties. It is clearer to me now why the people I most respond to include grandmothers and grandfathers, lonely old bachelors and spinsters, slightly charming broken-down boozers and sweet-natured girls. We learn some of our sympathies early and for good, like ducks being imprinted.

Further out than those streets and beyond the city's public parks, but before the 'real country' began, was a band a mile or so wide of inner fields; it too was so much part of our composite vision of Leeds that in any sorting out of boundaries it would have had to be included. It was broken up by clusters of speculative and usually cheap housing, with the sewage works somewhere there, a few smallholdings and some cattle providing the nearest fresh milk to the city. The most immediately noticeable difference between this band and real country was that the grass here was stunted and dirty as though factory smoke had been blown over it for so long that it actually grew dirty and wasn't merely made dirty each summer. The few cows looked dirty too, several shades grimier than the farm Friesians a few miles away.

In all ways the dominant and most characteristic inhabitant of this betwixt-and-between area was the rhubarb. Leeds has a ram on its coat of arms indicating its historic reliance on wool for its clothing industries. It might just as well have put a stick or two of rhubarb. Field after field marched round the outer limits of the town on the south, like a rank, deep, defensive fence; and that had a certain rightness. Like urchins, it seemed to thrive on dirt and smoke. This rhubarb was not that thin, small, pale pink forced stuff sold in supermarkets nowadays. It had as much relation to that neat pie-filler as a great miner to an effete courtier. It was huge with leaves which would have served both Adam and Eve at the same time and better than two fig-leaves. It was a Heathcliff sort of plant compared with the delicate clingfilm packets of today, the Earnshaws of the rhubarb family. It was sturdy, vivid with deep green changing to bold red sticks, thick as a labourer's forearm. We used to go to the edges of the fields, find the younger and tenderer sticks, make a quick getaway and walk home chewing.

Back home, in the streets again, the big physical markers (the corner shops were smaller markers but important in their own way, like subsidiary junction-boxes in a circuit) were the pubs, the chapels and the public library. The Rose and Crown nearby was as familiar a name as the Co-op. Membership of the Co-op suggested a more settled going-on than we had; we felt it and its customer-members slightly superior. For a different reason we did not visit the pubs, did not put our feet over their front steps.

The biggest group of brooding presences, the standing judgment on the pubs and bigger even than them were the chapels, in our case the Primitive Methodist Chapel on Jack Lane. Like the other Leeds chapels, ours did try and in some ways succeeded in being a social and recreational centre for the district. Until I was well into my teens, I went first to Sunday School and later to the early evening service. There were plays during the winter evenings such as the productions of Shakespeare our minister so treasured and, even more glittering, the pantomimes at Christmas; bowdlerised pantomimes, since no real rudeness or showing much bare flesh could be permitted. There had to be a chorus line but the girls' tops and tights looked more like armour-plating, or at least heavy-duty canvas, than erotic fancy-wear. Once, during the pantomime of another chapel down the road, a girl in heavy top and tights, singing on the line, had the misfortune to break a shoulder-strap so that a breast popped out. She was given a hard time for a longish while after. In some obscure way it must have been her own fault; things like that don't just happen; she'd probably tied it too tight in the first place, to show off. All this so as to find someone to blame for the awful embarrassment she had caused them all, the more regular and puritanical chapel-goers. Embarrassment came easy in a world surrounded by so many inhibitions about sex (and money, and drink). In less regular households and among the boys round about there was raucous laughter, not so much prurient, peepshow laughter as slightly liberated laughter at the shock to the regulating inhibitions.

Winter saw also the great oratorios, those to which Uncle Walter before his decline was invited to contribute as a visiting soloist. For *Messiah*'s success, much depended on how good a trumpeter you could get, from a well known pecking order, to fill the huge cube or dome. Backing all was the chapel choir whose front rows seemed to a small boy packed with large ladies with disproportionate bosoms; motherly. Bosom is the right word. You could hardly think of them each having two separate breasts in the face of these great mantelpieces or arching shelves. By comparison the men seemed small. Many were old, had been singing in the chapel choir all their adult lives and knew the scores of the great oratorios by heart.

The third main, shared, public institution within Hunslet itself was the public library. A new one was opened in February 1931, and became at once a focal point and attraction for at least two groups. I do not mean the women who in more literate areas expect shelves well stocked with romantic novels or the men who want detective stories and travel books. I expect some like those patronised Hunslet Library too, but they seemed not to do so in the numbers you find in middle-class areas. The two most regular sets of patrons were old men and grammar-school boys and girls.

The old men haunted the reading room; chiefly because it was warm and you could spend a lot of time turning over the pages of the daily newspapers in a desultory way. You were not allowed to go to sleep over the newspaper; if you did, a uniformed official came and woke you and left you in no doubt, even if he did not actually say it, that you ought to get on your way. There were one or two eccentrics pursuing their private obsessions but most were simply those lonely and lost old men we have met before. They lodged in my memory so firmly that one of the first two pieces I had published – this would be about 1947 – was a description of the old men in the reading room.

The life of those streets was, then, a matter of multiple fine-gradings. Any child above the age of four or five knew its own area and that area was usually no more than five or six streets. How were the boundaries decided? By types of people and by street furniture. This cluster of streets belonged to the Irish, this thought itself slightly better than the others around it, and this was thought to be slightly less respectable. Or the division came at the main road or on each side of a medium-sized road which took off at right-angles to the main road; or the walls of a small factory marked the boundaries. Superimposed on those were the divisions indicated by the regular worshippers and customers at the chapels and pubs scattered throughout, to some extent cross-cutting other divisions. That was 'our' chapel or 'our' pub, those others 'theirs'. That fine shading by possessive identification extended to all the local shops: he was 'our' butcher, grocer, confectioner; and we were quite sure our shops were better than 'theirs'.

Any attempt at an anatomy of a group of people should begin with their ways of talking, the pattern of recurrent images, the frequency with which they are used, the stresses and the tones of voice. Why, for example, was the hatred of meanness so strong in the people I am describing, as shown in their range of words to express that antipathy? 'Mean' was used, backed up by 'near', 'keen', 'close', 'tight', 'stingy', 'cheese-paring', 'skinflint' and 'close-fisted'. These words are used by people in other groups. The difference is that here they are used very frequently and with great force; and used by people who are poor and might have been expected to feel sympathetic to the need for cheese-paring. The reverse seems to operate. If you are so poor, since you are so poor, then you must not allow yourself because of that condition to decline into a mean-minded, joyless attitude; you must remain able to be generous. And that too is caught in epigrams, as in the bouncy: 'Oh, we're all right. We're short of nowt we've got', a cock-snooking at their own congenital hard-up'edness. The great generosity towards children belongs to the same emotional area: let them enjoy a sense of plenty while they can; it will soon enough have to end.

The language of neighbourliness shows similar contrasts in play.

I have referred more than once to the language of the tight kind of neighbourliness, that which is all the time aware of neighbourliness's due limits, of the need to 'keep yourself to yourself', to define unequivocally who shall and shall not cross your threshold, step through that front door which is the final and also the only physical line between you and the streets. In sharp contrast was the elegant phrasing offered to people who were welcome visitors. In a light account of the language of middle-class or professional sexual habits, I came upon the phrase: 'I think I'll slip into something more comfortable' used by a girl to a young man she has invited to her flat, to indicate that she is willing to get herself ready for sexual play. The word 'slip' also appears in a typical sequence of working-class language for hospitality, which begins: 'Why don't you slip your coat off?' – not a question but a polite invitation ('Why don't you take the weight off your feet?' is jokier, less formally courteous). The response is: 'No thank you. Very nice of you indeed. But I can't stay' ('is dinner's on); or 'I'm expecting our Elsie.' The counter-response is: 'Go on, do. You'll feel the benefit' (meaning you'll feel the benefit of it when you leave). And so it can go on, a minuet.

Two other major attitudes still recur, both forms of suspicion, the one obvious, the other slightly surprising. There is, first, the dislike of petty officials, that seam or band of employees with whom working-class people have to deal about a whole range of matters in their efforts to be in touch with, get justice from, understand the shadowy powers who really run society; and, second, an almost upper-class disdain for 'trade'. Petty officials, often uniformed which makes them even more off-putting, are likely to seem at the worst traitors to their class, at the best uniformed boobies, more royalist than the king; nay-sayers, congenitally suspicious of the lowly people with whom they have to deal; now well described as 'jobsworths' (as in 'Oh no, I can't let you do that. It'd be more than my job's worth', when 'that' is a simple and easily granted request); rigid bureaucrats ('Ah, but if I give you one they'll all want one', one of the great illiberal, closing-off British phrasings); 'How do I know you're telling the truth about what our Mr "X" told your son on the telephone?'; 'No: that's not my department/business/pigeon/affair'; 'You're at the wrong door. We only let people with that piece of paper in at Door B' (even if the corridor from B can be easily reached from the door you are standing at and it's raining and Door B' a long way round).

It might be thought that the police would have been seen as the worst petty functionaries of all and in some ways they were. But they were also different, a group on their own, as much and as unevadable a fact of life as rain. They had made a more distinct and dramatic choice than the great cluster of petty officials and behind them stood the real panoply of law. Nor were they, with some exceptions, thought to be particularly nice men, being likely to give you a hard time, a beating up, if you caused them trouble or resisted them, and many of them right-wing and racist. Not that racism as to colour was much of a problem during my boyhood in Leeds; the city now has sizeable Asian and West African groups.

In the way that certain television sequences, often come upon by accident, etch themselves into the memory, I remember seeing a programme from Leeds in the Seventies in which a policeman, brought in to discuss racist attitudes among the Leeds police, in a panel with a thoughtful and soft-voiced West Indian spokesman, revealed such contemptuous and vicious racism that one wondered whether he would be allowed to stay in the force – though his nastiness was expressed chiefly through tone of voice, snide phrasing and a clever use of ambiguity; hard to exhibit such malice in a transcript. The presenter, as is the emollient way of television, smoothed out the edges and the full beastliness of the exposure may have passed a lot of people by. I, for one, was shaken by the evidence it gave of attitudes apparently acceptable in that police force, for the man gave no hint that he was doing other than speaking for his kind. But I was not really surprised. The standard working-class phrase before all evidence of discreditable behaviour in the police was the dour: 'Policemen don't shit roses.'

I am still extremely, probably excessively, sensitive to the misuse or abuse of power in even small things and at those levels where most people cannot easily hit back. It is a personal rage founded as much on memories of petty unjust usage heard about continually as on principle.

Our family respected and sought after white-collar jobs and those could include being assistants in shops or even shopkeeping on one's own behalf – so long as the shops were of the right kind (Walter's furniture shop was on the outer edges of that kind of propriety). But in general we shared the general distaste for people 'in trade'; not just the cheating grocer but anyone committed to 'money-grubbing' through buying-and-selling. We thought there was something soiling about such activities – self-defining, low-level entrepreneurialism; independent, certainly, and self-reliant; but sharp. Where did the attitude originate? In the fact that many of the older women, much like Grandmother, had started working-life in upper-class homes and so learned at least a mild contempt for tradespeople? More likely, it carried over a countryside and community feeling which made us immediately suspicious of those people who ran shops in the city, most of whom we scarcely knew as persons and who, we thought, might be on the make, not above fiddling or adulterating. There was something aristocratic in the attitude, connected at a distance with Jack Birtle's taking his days off at the races. When I wondered what I would do after leaving school it never occurred to me to think of going into trade or commerce (nor into one of the major professions; they were socially and financially out of reach). The Nonconformist ministry, perhaps; politics, no – though that attitude may have been due chiefly to our family's suspicion that all politicians except aristocrats were only out for their own ends.

Probably most families in our kind of district at that time tended just to go on going on, to be unpolitical or slightly suspicious of politics, perhaps to be deferential Conservative voters but certainly not active socialists even if they voted Labour, to accept the division into officers and other ranks as though it were part of the natural order – of which a prominent instance for Yorkshire, so proud of its cricket, was the division into Gentlemen and Players there, a distinction which now seems to belong at the latest to the eighteenth century. Many who would not dream of voting Conservative did not by that token become active members of the Labour Party. Some were likely to become bloody-minded immobilists, not out to change things, and at the worst minor Orlicks. Yet on all sides was the assumption that we were very superior as a nation, superior to any other; and an acceptance, a virtually unquestioning acceptance, of the monarchy. Most people in our area were nationalists, monarchists, unprogrammatic and unpolitical.

By the age of fifteen or so people like me had learned to laugh at the monarchy and were moving towards socialism. By the sixth form, half of the class were socialists; of the others, most were politically unaware and the remaining few were incipient Tories who had concluded already that in selfish terms that was likely to be the best side on which to have their bread buttered.

Friends talk about the one teacher who fired their political interests. I had no such mentor. My socialism emerged from looking round and deciding that that sort of life, those sorts of divisions, were simply not good enough, least of all in a society with the pretensions of Britain. It was a Tawneyesque democratic socialism which stressed fraternity as the ground for equality and of the urge towards liberty; it was not theoretic and to have called it ideological would have been a misuse of language.

It took me years and the acquaintance of some intelligent, imaginative and humane Conservatives – whose Conservatism was based not on self-interest but on a feeling for the importance of history, tradition and duty – to learn to be hospitable to the idea of the good Conservative. Even now, I tend to assume that any new acquaintance who seems intelligent, imaginative and humane must be – or should be – from somewhere on the left.

As to working-class attitudes towards the intellect and the imagination, most writers and most politicians assume they are both positively anti-intellectual and contemptuous of the arts. This is alien to my experience. Most working-class people were and are un-intellectual and not anti-intellectual; the first arose from their condition, the second was not part of their culture. You have to be slightly up the social ladder to be both aware of intellectualism and cut off from it, to feel threatened and judged by it; so that you attack it. Working-class people would habitually react against anyone who assumed airs of any kind, in dress, deportment, speech, assumptions of superiority in mind or taste. They would not react against a serious intellectual interest in itself; hence a man in the area who is 'well-read' could be given a form of respect; so could a child whose intellect might in time get him or her out of the area.

Somewhat similarly, working-class people have not tended to be anti-art; the arts in the usually defined senses are not among their active concerns; how could they easily or generally be? The thrust of popular persuasion over the last forty or so years has undervalued art and intellect; and it is often assumed that this reflects changing taste in a majority of people. But if you talk to working people even today you are unlikely to find an active philistinism. Those kinds of philistinism may be part of the sensitivities of life at some other social levels but are still relatively unassimilated among working-class people; nor do they seem relevant to them.

The overwhelming immobility of British working-class lives still exists, the lack of expectancy (once again), the damp putting up with things – buttressed by a class-based and class-biased educational system at all levels and an apparatus of mass communications which appears to be open and sometimes even radical but which hardly ever takes on directly the major engines and processes which keep things as they so unacceptably appear to anyone who tries to stand apart and take stock.

Here is a true story of two Lancashire brothers. Both were trained just before the war as craftsman-electricians and both saw war service. One is still an electrician, a maintenance electrician to a smallish government enterprise. He is reasonably but not prosperously paid; one child has managed to get to university and so to teaching. A gain of sorts but not a major breakthrough. His style of life and, more, his sense of horizons and of the likelihood of major change would be recognised by his mother and father as much like their own, though with late-Eighties physical knobs on; no great changes, no qualitative difference, no exponential shift.

The other brother had a period of service in Australia during the war and started courting an Australian girl. After the war he came home for a while, she joined him, they married and set off back to Australia. They had three children. Now, almost forty years on, the father has retired from his post as works manager at an electrics firm in Sydney; a post he would have been most unlikely to gain in Lancashire. The older boy is a barrister and has served on a senator's staff, the daughter is a solicitor and the other boy is engaged in advanced athletics and sports.

All three children assumed access to whatever higher education they needed for entry to the professions they sought; and entry to those professions was assumed to be available to them as to almost anyone else, whatever their origins. They were not stupid children but neither were they, I expect, brighter than their cousins back in Lancashire. Their social climate was more open and encouraging so they reached upwards and grew towards the fulfilment of their aspirations like plants in a nutritious soil.

By contrast the climate offered to most working-class people in Britain is still too closed, not beneficent, turned in on itself. The unexpectancy it encourages is in part admirable, being dogged, stoical and not lightly progressivist; but such attitudes can also be resistant to change, and resentful of change in others, turning down the corners of the mouth against the prospect of betterment. Among many bad results there is, and once again one comes back to a particular word because it is inescapable, a *waste* of much talent, talent which could help all if it were given its proper opportunities.

It is typical of much in British society that the two ways of escape which are recognised and applauded at all levels are: success in show business and success in large-scale commerce, the pop star and the tycoon-entrepreneur. A society which is both commercially thrusting and class-bound in the opportunities it provides for most of its people has, by the only half-conscious adaptation of its organs of persuasion to the service of that combination of energetic opportunity for some but stagnation for most others, hit on the two opiates most likely to keep most things and most people much as they have long been. So the sense of 'fraternity', which is the wider, public extension of 'neighbourliness', has been steadily weakened.

Almost paradoxically, though, the most common quality in the tone and temper of the working-class Leeds I knew was local rather than national melodrama. Melodrama had to be found in the day-to-day or, more accurately, had to be attached to and then floated off from the day-to-day, because it gave savour to our lives and made the streets, the neighbourhood, the city and its near-countryside larger than the lives we actually led, more vivid and well-I-never'ish. We had to find exotic and at times threatening *dramatis personae* to inhabit those spaces out there.

In this the Irish had a permanent walk-on role. They had come over in dribs and drabs and occasional waves from the late eighteenth century onwards to build the canals and railways and later to take up any, usually heavy manual, labour to hand . . . right through to the building of motorways in the second half of this century. In Hunslet they congregated in one or two contiguous streets and had their own pubs. They seemed threatening to us, being Roman Catholic, with over-large families, and under the thumbs of their priests, themselves often newly brought over from Ireland. We believed the Irish drank too much and congenitally brawled at weekends. Our own puritanism gave us a sneaking feeling that in spite of our prim disapproval they knew something about enjoying life which we did not. Still, we would not have wanted to live like that, and the thought of one of ours marrying into such a family was fearful; they were like a caste.

They had their own elementary school, which backed on to our yard and a tough place it was. Still, at least two well-known men, and no doubt there are others, came from those streets and that school. One is a professor, with the build of his 'navvy' ancestors; the other, an actor, has an easy lope and a crooked grin which recall generations of Irish charmers. They both enjoy telling inflated stories about the wild life on their side of the tracks as compared with the sedateness on ours. The further away they get in time and style of life the more picaresque their stories become.

The Irish were too few and too locked in basic manual occupations to be able to engross our thoughts as richly and melodramatically as the Jews. We were told that at that time, in the Twenties and Thirties, Leeds had the highest proportion of Jews of any British city. Certainly we were very much aware of them and in complex and contradictory manners.

When they found their way to Leeds from Eastern Europe, Leeds was beginning to build up its ready-made clothing industry. Montague Burton ('The Tailor of Taste') became the best known name and had the biggest of the factory complexes. There were other big ones and medium-sized ones and a host of small enterprises producing men's and women's and children's clothing, from the finest to the cheapest, nastiest and shoddiest. Not all the firms were owned or managed by Jews, but Jews did play a big part in them at all levels. They did in retail trade too, and in the professions as their sons, and occasionally daughters, rose to enter medicine, the law, academic life.

We tended to resent Jewish prosperity, to claim that it came about chiefly through nearness, 'taking care to look after your own', clannishness or tribalism, and through all sorts of short-changing. 'They don't like a hard day's work' people used to say, perhaps remembering some smart 'Ikey Mo' who had diddled them at his market-stall and not at all remembering or even being aware of the great numbers of poor Jews who worked very hard for low wages and never got out of Sheepscar and on the road to a more prosperous life.

The suspicion was deeply ingrained and you absorbed it from the first years of playing in the street. Like the Irish, only more so, the Jews were a race apart. There may have been one or two Jewish families in our area but I do not recall them. We knew where the great body of them lived and thought it only right that that was how it should be.

Above all there was the resentment, the fear, the suspicion of their capacity for getting on, their restlessness, their refusal to do what was central to our own outlook – to take things as they are – their strange, alien, outsiders' drive. This was one main element in what I suppose has to be called anti-semitism. That was weakly but unpleasantly pervasive, like an insistent bad smell which creeps in everywhere. Once, very early in my time at the elementary school in Hunslet, a bigger boy hit me hard in the playground without cause but said it was because I was a 'sheeny', a 'Jew-boy'. That was the most convenient label to justify in his eyes taking a swipe. Boys who were Jews, in schools where they were a minority, must have had a miserable time from young brutes like that. It was also assumed that Jews were cowards and would not fight to defend themselves.

But the phrase 'anti-semitic' describes only one aspect of our complex attitudes towards Jews. With another part of our minds we had a grudging respect for their willingness to work hard, their devotion to their families and their group loyalty – much as is said today about some groups among the Asian immigrants. An admission such as this usually began with the clause: 'You can say what you like about' (meaning 'against') 'the Jews, but they . . .' (there followed the enunciation of a virtue). We knew and at the very base of our minds admired their assumption that they had a duty to give practical help to their own kind, members of the same synagogue or practitioners of the same trade who fell on hard times. We knew, again at the very backs of our minds, that though our own old people had, many of them, come from village communities to the hard and inhospitable streets of Leeds, our own sense of communal solidarity was not as strong or as effective as that of the Jews. We did have a sense of neighbourliness and practised many of its forms; but unless we were blindly xenophobic we had to recognise that the Jews could show us a thing or two.

We also, and this will not be a surprise, found the Jews sexually intriguing. That interest started with the fact of circumcision. Gentile circumcision was practised, usually on medical grounds, but it was rare. Jewish boys, we were told – most of us had never seen a Jewish penis – had a great, bare, foreskinless, purple mushroom. It made the girls feel different, much more excited, when they got a circumcised prick inside them, the older boys pronounced (others made a counter-attack by insisting that the way the foreskin rolled back on entry gave an even greater thrill). So here was another cause for resentment and envy. Jewish girls, we were also told, as we were told about almost any alien group, had an intriguing benignity to fornication and were even physically different 'down there' from English girls; and the difference enhanced the act. Of course, we wouldn't think of marrying one of them. Still . . .

A joke I do not forget, though I forget most jokes instantly, encapsulates many of these conflicting attitudes, especially our belief in the restless and sharp observation of Jews and their sexual knowingness. A Jew, a little anxious about his young wife's fidelity and also feeling amorous, breaks his habit and comes home at lunchtime. He puts his fingers up his wife's vagina and finds it wet. 'Why is it wet?' he asks. 'Because I have just had a pee,' she replies. He extracts his hand, holds it up and spreads two fingers. 'Pee don't make vindows,' he says. It is superbly witty, knowing, a million miles from a Hunslet joke; none of us could have thought of a joke like that. It was probably invented by a Jew.

On all such grounds the Jews were a very powerful element in the folklore of the city, and working-class Gentiles created and purveyed the details of that interest with endlessly renewed zest. The local representatives of royalty were a similarly powerful element. We were fascinated by the doings at Harewood House, where the Princess Royal and the Earl of Harewood lived with their two sons; a vast place loaded with treasures and surrounded by large grounds. This was not minor royalty; it was big stuff, rather like having a Covent Garden production of *Tosca* permanently playing at your local theatre.

Working-class Leeds (and in its own way I expect middle-class Leeds) lapped up old and created new folklore about the Harewood establishment, especially about the old Earl's reputed drunkenness and brutal ways towards the poor Princess Royal. Who had, naturally, to be gentle and long-suffering, being so much put upon; so everyone, or at least the great majority of housewives, felt sorry for her. The very presence of direct royal stock so near the city – certain shops in the middle of town were said to serve the great house – gave a glow to our Leeds which its counterpart Sheffield could not match; the sinful city had at least a better grade of aristocrat.

These two main elements in the city's folklore – the Jews and the local royalty – came together vibratingly, either just before the last war or latish in the Forties. The amazing tale went the rounds at the usual great speed, and was generally believed, that the elder son of the old Earl had been having an affair with a Jewish girl from the city. From the expensive upper north of the city, naturally, not from Sheepscar. Once the alleged liaison was out, firm efforts were made to stop it from the Earl's side. But it did not prove easy to dissuade either the young man or the girl. So a meeting had been arranged between emissaries of the Earl and the girl's parents. It took place in the lounge of the Queen's Hotel, that high block which looks on City Square and hangs over the main railway station.

Hardly the sort of place the Earl himself would have chosen if he had business in the city. But for the purposes of myth the meeting had to take place in the lounge of the Queen's, in the public consciousness a theatrical place and so most suitable for so melodramatic a meeting.

The hotel lounge in those years was busy at most times of the day serving tea or coffee with biscuits, cakes and sandwiches to middle-aged, middle-class ladies. For the Earl's envoys to agree to meet there would have been like doing a deal in the concourse of the station itself, under arc-lights and with a clapper-board, since the regulars would have been taking note of every gesture and doing their best to listen in.

The insistence on that particular locale underscores a basic rule of story-telling and especially working-class story-telling; *si non è vero, è molto ben trovato*; truth to the imagination is more important than a pedantic attention to likelihood in detail. Folklore must be kept up and dramatic inventions, once some unsung genius has created them, find their own way and grow to a baroque maturity because they fit so well into what the urge for local myths wants, feeds upon. So we believed it all happened, that a deal was struck and that the girl then faded from the life of the young Royal. Much later I met the older Harewood boy, by then the Earl; he might well have wondered what I was smiling at, over the table at a meeting, not knowing what a powerful figure he had been in the fabulous fictions of our lives.

That early, strong and complicated set of attitudes towards Jewishness which we were offered in the Leeds working class before the war comes to mind fairly often because, as I realised fully only a few years ago, some of my most impressive friends have been Jews, at university, in the army and later. The most powerful in his impact was Andrew Shonfield and I will write about him at a later period. What drew me to such men was first, I think, their possession of a muscular and restless intelligence, much freer than mine was from the baggage of class and of local, Anglo-Saxon place-roots. They had almost all ceased in adolescence to be Orthodox and so tended to be impatient of other non-intellectual pieties. Second, and in contrast, was their unashamed accessibility to their emotions.

I once stood in the arrival area at Heathrow with a middle-aged Jewish professor with whom I had been on a foreign lecture tour. He found a letter slotted into one of the message boards; it told him that his sister had died. His grief was immediate and overt. He leant against a pillar and wept unreservedly; his grief overrode the presence of the incurious crowd which swirled around him; it was naked, biblical, of the Old Testament. No stiff upper lip, just unconstrained grief as he said over and over again: 'My dear little sister. My dear little sister.' It was quite un-English and I was at first abashed and then rapt in a kind of respect and admiration.

The third of these powerful and novel qualities, and this I encountered later than the others, showed itself in a glad unpuritanical expression of the joy of married love which gives a new element to the definition of uxoriousness. That had had little place in the dark furtiveness of the attitudes to sex, in or out of marriage, passed on to us. Sex in the street was raw and rough and male-dominated; in the home it was simply not talked about; for 'decent' adults to discuss the practices of sex in marriage was even more strictly proscribed. We could scarcely have imagined an Israeli wife, over supper after Orthodox observances and in the presence of her husband, describing gently and joyously the role of physical love in marriage to those of her faith. A million miles from 'close your eyes and think of England' but not in any way lewd. This was a world in which faith and fidelity and an openness before sexuality came together in a manner I had not met before and found attractive and liberating.

CHAPTER 6

JACK LANE

Jack Lane Elementary School, Hunslet, was a product of the 1870 Education Act and the School Boards, a cheapish-brick building which looked L-shaped from Jack Lane itself but hid parts at the back. There was a hard playground within the arms of the L and a free-standing metal and carpentry shop in the far left corner; you passed the edge of that as you went to the outside lavatories with their tall, slate urinals. There was only a handful of classrooms; a set of sliding doors converted two of the larger into a sort of Great Hall for morning assembly. The walls were tiled, the windows high. Heating was by fires, so front seats were prized; but the less bright or the problem children were put to the front and the rest suffered at the back swearing that our chilblains all started there. Since there were several other chilblain-inducing locations scattered throughout our days, beginning with our bedrooms, the charge against the school did not hold much water. The less thoughtful teachers warmed their backsides at the fire throughout the lessons, so even less heat got through to the pupils.

I was last back at Jack Lane in late 1986 and was once again reminded how fallible memory is. That description of the buildings above, for instance, which seemed quite firm and clear as I wrote it, may be an amalgam, partly a memory of Jack Lane, partly memories of other similar schools mixed with descriptions from other people's books and shots from old films. When I came back much in Jack Lane was as I had remembered it; some of it – and I do not mean obviously later building additions – I had not remembered at all and would have argued out of existence if I had not been there to see it.

The place is now the Leeds Athletics Centre and has a rolling population of weight-lifters (apparently a speciality), people with crippling diseases which may be helped by some forms of exercise, and a number of other groups. The rooms are warm, warmer than I ever remember them; and so is the atmosphere. There was a friendly ex-policeman exercising as vigorously as his damaged limbs and a small degree of brain damage allowed him. He had been on motorcycle duty when a motorist came through a red light and hit him, just outside Yorkshire Television's studios two or three miles away; and half a mile from the site of Aunt Ethel's shop. He had had sizeable compensation from the motorist's insurance company and liked, among other things, to take himself to Majorca at intervals. A late 1980s story in a building which goes back to the 1880s, told to one whose memory kept flipping him back for half of that span of years, trying to make sense other than the anecdotal of that century, that landscape, those details, those figures.

Not far off, the M1 motorway, which ends only a few hundred yards from the very centre of Leeds, has cut a great swathe through Hunslet and traffic swishes by near the Jack Lane buildings. The history of the area all around, which included our Newport Street, is a microcosm of typical errors and re-tries in public housing over the last thirty years. The streets were cleared in 1971 to make way for the 'Hunslet Grange' development, some of the worst, most crass and inhumane public housing I have seen in any developed country: industrial-unit building in concrete blocks of several storeys, much less human than the old back-to-back streets, suggesting an attitude to or vision of those who were expected to live in them like that of a farmer using the cheapest mechanised methods for cattle rearing in uniform units.

The blocks were square or rectangular, and the one major concession to the fact that human beings had to live there was in the provision of a grassy space, a sort of court, in the hollow middle of each block. But who would relax there, in that almost sunless square frowned on by flats on four sides? Or let their children play there, since very soon the grass was rubbed bare and the areas were the handiest places for dogs and cats to shit and pee? They became dreary waste land, of which Hunslet has always had its share so it didn't need architects to purpose-build extra lots. The stairs in the blocks were dirty and smelly, and residents complained that the workmanship in general was poor and the units damp.

We can all be wise now, and angry, about the errors of municipal housing in the Fifties and Sixties, but these things have to be said again and again in case architects and town planners forget and repeat such errors. No one would want the back-to-backs to return: but the pattern of life almost by accident, or by a refusal to be made anonymous, encouraged by those old streets – or, perhaps better, grafted on to them in a way one could not graft any decent style of life on to the concrete blocks – that pattern of life if it had been understood by the planners would have said to them: not a general heartless appearance such as this, not several storeys like this, not stairways like these and above all not enclosed bare-arsed courts like these. It did not, and the inevitable happened: the units became haunts of petty crime, where girls had to be careful in the dark; and those who were trying to live respectable lives found it a more and more uphill battle.

It appears that eventually people became so fed up that a tenants' association began to press hard for rehousing, for the abandonment of the concrete blocks. They came down in 1985, so by the time of my late 1986 visit much of the area was once again half-brick-strewn waste land; but the new housing was beginning to appear in clusters: semis and the like in irregular groups, looking liveable and likely to encourage a neighbourly feeling. We do learn but at what a cost; and not only in money.

From Jack Lane School we almost all went home to midday dinner. I do not recall any school meal provision. Most mothers were at home all day and could provide for less than even the cost of the cheapest school meal. I expect some, those few whose mothers went out to work, brought sandwiches of a sort (the sandwich proper was not common around there, except at Sunday tea when there were visitors. A plain teacake, the Yorkshire equivalent of a bap, filled with corned beef, say, was the nearest we usually got to a sandwich). Some boys went down the road to the nearest fish-and-chip, or pie-and-peas, or pork butcher's shop. Some boys haunted the playground throughout the midday break. Others rushed back from home to get in a few minutes kicking a ball before the bell went.

In the beginning the playground, like the school but in a more intensified, only-half-supervised-jungle form, was a shock, since the playground at Chapeltown Infants' School had been mild and unthreatening. Infant schools usually are, but the difference here was more than that. It reflected the fact that Potternewton within

Chapeltown was itself mild and had no great concentration of unskilled manual workers. Hunslet had at its core a solid body of workers in heavy industry, and those who lived around Jack Lane and its ancillaries were more often unskilled than skilled; most skilled men moved out even if only a few streets. Whatever good qualities the Jack Lane men could show on occasion and many of them, the older men especially, behaved like gentle giants, they were bound to be in general a rough lot. Their sons expected to go into the works like their fathers – the big engine works, probably – into what they saw as a tough, masculine life which they could hardly wait to enter.

I mentioned earlier the boy who hit me without provocation, whose poverty of offensive vocabulary gave him only 'sheeny' as a term of abuse. His poverty of attitudes made him choose a racist epithet. The main point, though, was that any newcomer not born rough Hunslet working class was an outsider to be labelled and abused, verbally and physically. I do not remember hitting back on that occasion. I was very new, he was older, bigger and had his gang with him. Nor did I tell them at home; one didn't and I suppose doesn't.

Without consciously working it out I knew then that I had to establish myself in some way, so that there would be an invisible ring round me within which I could operate in the playground and the streets. This was eventually secured, partly by performance in the classroom: cleverness could be derided but after a while was furtively recognised as something many did not have, something which might after all be more valuable than the ethos of the streets suggested. So 'teacher's pet' ('swot' came in at grammar school) soon became ineffectual. More important was the demonstration of verbal ability and that, perhaps because of some vestigial folk-memory, brought more respect or at least cautiousness than did cleverness in the classroom. I do not remember consciously using my tongue as a weapon, though I expect I did, 'lazy' though it was at that stage; I expect I also used it to make them laugh. At any rate, the word got round that 'Oggy couldn't 'alf talk'; like a trick cyclist; and so I gained at least some identity.

More status, or at least a more accepted place, more credit in the anti-authority bank, was gained by an evening exploit in the early months there. By then I had made a few friends in school from the streets nearby. That evening we were in the school playground though that was forbidden. Our purpose was to collect the balls which we knew had sailed up to the high-pitched roof, rolled down and then, instead of falling back to the ground, had lodged where the two horizontal gutters of the L-shape met at right angles. The idea was for someone to shin up the vertical drainpipe at that point. Being the smallest I did it and threw a good number of balls to those below. But someone had been watching, probably behind half-length lace curtains, and the following morning the headmaster wanted to know, in assembly, who had done it. He had to, since it could have led to injury or worse. I admitted it and was duly rebuked and punished, though I do not remember how. But that consolidated my place in the playground. The drainpipes are heavily bound round with barbed wire these days so I guess I was not the last to shin up one.

I remember no regular meetings between parents and teachers at Jack Lane, and we never thought of ourselves as part of the larger provision of education made by the City of Leeds. Nor had we any sense of a possible progression; we were not, to use again a phrase which has to recur, going anywhere. The school did have a clearly defined but not complex place in the life of the streets around. The headmaster who later proved to be so kindly disposed towards me was very much aware of the English GP on the opposite side of Jack Lane in the house which provided surgery, residence and outbuildings. Doctors were certainly higher in the social hierarchy than the headmaster of an elementary school and even we sensed that. We noticed his car and the odd-job man who also drove, his maid, and his superior wife. One day the headmaster told us all at assembly of some honour which had been bestowed on the doctor. I expect it was not a distinction which would have seemed very great in the world outside Leeds: perhaps he had been made a JP. But the head told us that he had been over the road to congratulate the doctor on his own behalf and that of the school. A touch of Mrs Gaskell in darkest Hunslet.

Parents were aware of the school but largely ignorant of what today would be called its 'philosophy', if it had one other than a handful of pragmatic and largely conventional aims and points of view. Parents only penetrated its door in emergency and most had not set foot in it. I best remember, of the few occasions when parents as a group showed an interest in the school, a dreadful occasion which brought out above all a good deal of misguided and short-sighted gossip.

During the mid-morning break a master on playground duty sent a boy over the road and round the corner to buy him an apple. It was a fairly common practice and one boys welcomed. On the way back the boy was killed by a lorry. Naturally the staff and the boys were all terribly shocked, and most of all the master concerned. But many of the mothers of the district made the event the occasion for malicious gossip as though the teacher concerned had deliberately or at least heedlessly put the boy at risk. 'He should have known better than to . . .' Thereafter no master sent a boy out of school on any errand. But that boy could have been killed any day, out of school hours, playing in the streets or roads or going to the local cinema. That did not enter the gossips' heads; they carried on with their thoughtless, harpy-like group cruelty which made a bad situation worse. I remember this so clearly because not all housewives would take part in such gossip and Grandmother for one thought it wicked.

Mr Harrison, the headmaster, took us for geography. He was a rather distinguished-looking man with a well-groomed moustache, a three-piece suit and a watch-chain; until you got closer and saw that his suit was not the full fine worsted of the English G.P.'s clothing. From thirty feet he might have been a solicitor or a bank manager. Close up, the similarity and illusion faded and he was, I later learned to see, a not very commanding elementary-school headmaster.

It was an early lesson in the limits of the simulacrum; which is a fancy way of saying that you see 'lookalikes' at all levels of society, but when you come closer they are not really lookalikes.

More than any other influence, the personal strains and gains of life – illness, happiness in relationships, loss, love – make our faces whether we will or not. We also make our own faces in response to the pressures, as we conceive them, of our jobs. Similar expressions can thus emerge from vastly different levels of work and degrees of responsibility. All have imprinted on the faces of their actors a similar set of lines, jut of the jaw, tilt of the head, expression in the eyes. At each level, faces look alike – until you look more closely. Much the same can be said of voices and their often only partly conscious imitatings. This is another of those ideas which I have kept coming back to, year after year. Why? Perhaps because, like so much else to which I return, it is about identity, the sense of identity, the need for a secure identity, the fragility of identity; and, often, the phoniness of many identities we are offered or offer ourselves, make ourselves grow into.

I once saw Winston Churchill on a small railway-station platform. It was, though, the stationmaster; and I do not think he was consciously imitating Churchill, though many used to. He had a similar build and to him the stresses of running that small station must have seemed as portentous as leading the country in time of war; and perhaps for him they were. So the markings and style had become engraved but were well beyond the needs of the job. Deans of small faculties in universities can give the same impression; and civil servants who are hitting their heads at the ceiling of principal but look like ready-made not bespoke permanent secretaries. There are hundreds of petty functionaries who look like members of the Cabinet; they have taken their jobs as weightily as though they were in fact members of a Cabinet. With all of them – and this is the hard part – when you look closely you realise that the quickly observed similarity is deceptive; there are few village Hampdens. The eyes are weaker, the jaw not so secure, the sense of a brooding complex intelligence not there.

We should never take facial models or voices from real life; we may end looking like something on loan from Madame Tussaud's. Nor can a particular set of clothing, from camel overcoats to jeans or green wellies or very long necklaces, do anything important for us. Eliot knew what he was about when he said that a poet should look like a bank clerk; he did it all the time and that was a safe disguise; he was a most thoughtful and impressive-looking bank clerk and so, also impressively, looked like a grave poet. Private faces in public places are indeed wiser and nicer; but those who have grown into a public face of the wrong size and type can't easily take it off even in the most private places.

The exact opposite of the lookalikes, and they particularly flourish in France, are those petty functionaries who think and feel like petty functionaries all the time, who rejoice in being petty functionaries, who do not wish to be other, who take pleasure especially in the negative aspects of their role and so come to look irremediably like exactly that; like bad-tempered cogs, or dogs. After that, your heart lifts to see a little man or woman, fortyish, lean-faced and lined, gentle and rather worried-looking; not moving upwards but clearly a decent worker and father or mother, unaggressive, taking the kids for a walk in the park on Sunday afternoon. Not yet old enough to have settled securely within his or her identity and fate, but living honestly within a good present personality.

Standing before the class Mr Harrison awed us. Until he made his expected gesture. He appeared to have an itchy crutch and so, without being aware of it, from time to time ran the flat of his hand firmly up the length of his crutch. That was interesting enough to small boys always on the lookout for a dirty snigger; but one day he made the gesture as he pointed at Africa on the map he had unrolled from the top of the blackboard, his other hand pointing to the continent as he announced: 'Here is the Bush.' He was identified with that gesture and that remark from then until his retirement, with each generation of boys who passed through his hands. He would never know, since none of his staff would have told him.

Mr Harrison probably came from the lower middle classes; he had more style than the usual teacher from the working class and less assurance than one from the middle classes. He was at bottom a devoted and kind man; towards me he continued his kindnesses until the day I left his care.

A teacher I had for one year gave me my first full, repeated lesson in gratuitous cruelty, cruelty practised not in rage but as a form of convoluted enjoyment. He was a plump man, perhaps in his early thirties so to us seemed quite old. Clearly not very clever, he liked best to boast to nine- or ten-year-olds about his friendships with members of the Hunslet Rugby Club. We hated him without being able to say exactly why; but our instincts were sound. We could, if asked, have given several telling examples of his methods. Such as the day he taunted a rather slow boy, then expressed himself entirely out of patience, hung the boy partly out of an open window and threatened to drop him on to the concrete playground. He looked round, expecting us to laugh at his huge joke. Few did. I do not imagine we saw the homosexual element in the buffoonery but we recognised sadism when we saw it.

I expected him to have a go at me since he tended to pick on the smaller boys and here was one with a speech impediment; early on I saw him circling me with his eyes as though wondering where first to put the boot in. He soon saw that that boy at the back with the tendency to stare unblinkingly was cleverer than most and might, even if only inadvertently, show up his own lack of cleverness; so he avoided me. Not much positive educational help there, but then there was none to give.

His last shot was his worst. One afternoon, he began to sing 'Mother of Mine' in a most maudlin way, moving from boy to boy, transfixing each and asking each how he would feel if he lost his mother. He soon had several in tears, which was his purpose. His even larger purpose was to make me cry, since he knew I was an orphan. It didn't work; I gave him my baleful blink again.

Then one day he was no longer there. Gossip said the police had arrived at the school to enquire about some peculation to do with a club he belonged to; and that there were enquiries about his practices with small boys. He had fled to take refuge, the neighbourhood said in a flash, in South America. If it had been a woman teacher, no doubt she would have hied to North Africa or the Middle East to pursue her white-slave trafficking or procuring; as always, we liked our gossip histrionic and colourful. I do not know how much was true; the one clear fact was that he had hopped it. He could not have coped with Calais, let alone more exotic places, so probably landed up in Belfast or Dublin and assumed a new identity.

Like so many parts of working-class life at the time, the school was a closed world; the phrase 'open-ended' could never have been applied to it, its practices, purposes or aspirations. Over in other parts of Leeds children were being groomed for the eleven-plus exam, entry to grammar school and perhaps further. Mr Harrison knew enough not to put more than two or three of his boys in for that each year. It would be easy to conclude that almost all of us were being prepared as recruits for the big Hunslet works and were therefore given an education no better than was needed in that role, able to read basic instructions and that was about all. There is some truth in that explanation but it is too pat, too much a mixture of conspiracy–theory and ideology, insufficiently qualified.

The 1870 Education Act was born out of more than the realisation of society's growing technical needs, at many levels below those met by the grammar schools, if industrial development was to be maintained and international competition met; though that knowledge was part of the power behind the Act. Education for the masses was also seen, to some extent by both governments and religious bodies, as a means towards greater social control. Yet it had, too, a religious and moral impulse, one which would not let itself be used simply as a cloak to hide either a naked capitalist thrust or the political need for a more pacific working class. There had been far more elementary education before 1870 than is generally assumed, and much of it was provided by church and chapel.

It was much the same with the teachers' own impulses. Teaching and care varied from the rank bad to the reasonable and devoted. It could rarely be inspired, since almost all were under-trained and under-provided; but there were some who, we could recognise even then, were moved by more than getting through the day and then taking the tram out of Hunslet to a cheap semi and its mortgage. So we learned something. The greatest single weakness in the whole school, and it ran all the way from the lazy to the devoted teachers, was the absence of the sense of intellectual enquiry, of the assumption that ideas are interesting, exciting, challenging and to be challenged.

What we were taught, well or ill, came on a plate: this is arithmetic, this geography, this history; and all was dished out like rations, never presented as a matter for speculation or as something which had in its time created a conflict of opinions, or as part of a continuing process with which we were all, if we saw properly, still involved. That too, I suppose, was the way they also had been taught and taught to teach at their teacher training colleges.

Nor did they seem to have much idea of the complex social processes which had brought them and us to those daily encounters – if you could call them that – in those high institutional rooms in Hunslet. I hope they did not intone 'Well, the labourer is worthy of his hire' as they took their salary cheques; I hope some of them were fed up not just because their level of salary, their clothes, their inescapable style of life, were sub-professional and shabby but because they recognised the pressures of society and the interlocking processes of education, work and persuasion, which kept social divisions much as they always were. I do not remember an instance of such discontent.

The irony was that we were taught by those teachers to be unthinking little latter-day imperialists. Our history, when external to Britain, was imperial history – Wolfe dying on the Plains of Abraham, above all; the paradigm of the gallant English soldier and gentleman (an officer, of course), with Nelson at Trafalgar a close second and no mention of Emma; and little about Napoleon, except that he was a French villain. We heard much about the Crusades, much about the benefits British rule later brought to benighted natives everywhere, much about the warrior statesmen and little about the missionaries except for Livingstone and he was presented chiefly as an explorer.

Our internal history was concerned more with the Wars of the Roses than with the plight of the peasantry. We were given no sense of ourselves as part of the processes of history and did not expect or receive from our teachers any understanding of the way our ancestors had come from the villages to the cities as the Industrial Revolution got under way, or of ourselves as only the latest in the many generations of workers who had always been at the bottom of the heap and would be expected to assume they would stay there; 'the people of England that never have spoken yet'.

Somebody, perhaps Miss Jubb, must have been thinking about my holiday needs at that time because one year, not long after I had started at Jack Lane School, I was despatched on a camping holiday near Ripon. It was organised annually by, I think, the Rotarians of Leeds, for poor boys of the city. No doubt the best of intentions were in play as members pledged their support after the monthly lunches. But it was a bad camp because a loveless camp. Some of the children came from what used to be called 'problem' families. Certainly the people paid to run the camp treated us as minor delinquents or potential delinquents. They were quite without imagination or empathic understanding of the boys' needs and problems; they were part of the old, tenacious and endless parade of the petty functionaries who are not going to put up with any trouble or discomposure they can possibly avoid if they can snuff it out at the beginning. We decided right at the start that they were a shifty lot and probably ate far better than we did on the rations supplied for all.

On the day we arrived they issued boots. You could envisage the responsible Rotarian reporting at their next meeting that the camp had been its usual success and that as usual also all the boys had been issued with 'stout footwear'; and the members would have nodded with satisfaction and self-satisfaction. What the Rotarians would not know because they were not there – and would they have noticed if they had paid a visit, since the hired camp managers would then have put on a better show? – was the typically careless, heartless way in which the shoes were dished out. They took a quick glance at you, decided what your size was and handed you a pair without a word. Mine did not fit so I went back to the end of the queue to tell them so; they replied that they hadn't time to mess around chopping and changing so I had better get on with it. I was not alone so we swopped around and solved the problem. Apart from the more regimented bits, I began to enjoy the week, after the first day and a half; a slightly younger, lonely boy attached himself to me and most of the camp's régime fell into the background.

I do not want to overstress this seam of casual cruelty as it can be met by children who are in receipt of some public charity or another. There are plenty of descriptions of cruelties in prep-school and public-school life. But the contexts are different and so the impact and the effect. A poor child usually has little supporting and cushioning background: an understanding family, the refuge of books, a number of boys or girls in the same boat with whom common cause can be made. The cruelties tend to come to you individually (the Ripon camp was an exception) and from different directions so that you begin to expect them.

Nor would it be sensible to suggest that all the faults lay or lie on the one side. We may prefer to talk about 'disadvantaged' rather than about 'problem' families today but sometimes that is a linguistic cosmetic, a procedure for avoiding even a hint of a moral judgment, a way of suggesting that all fallings-away from whatever society regards as its current norms are the result of social pressures only, never due to the weaknesses or failings of individuals. There are poor homes where cruelty is regularly practised; cruelty which cannot be entirely ascribed to social conditions, any more than the cruelty of a belted earl might be.

Still, some areas of public institutional life provide easy havens and opportunities for people who combine lack of talent with moral laziness and a touch of sadism, like the teacher from Jack Lane who had to run away. Even in my day the Leeds Education Authority had a dental care service. Fine: but who would work in such a scheme? No doubt some with ideals of service much like those of the Doctors Cooke. Also a few who preferred a safe billet and a secure pension to the uncertainties of the open profession; and a few bullies. To save time the dentist who covered South Leeds would, as we all soon learned, go on grinding away to prepare for what would be a rough and unsightly filling, without benefit of an injection, no matter how much you reared back involuntarily. I minded him more than the Italo-American doctor at an American field hospital on Pantelleria, where in 1943 I lay for six weeks very badly burned. He took special pleasure in pulling off the bandages in the most painful way and, if I cried out, said: 'OK, Limey, you'd better sing

Rule Britannia.' He just hated Limeys, though whether because of his ancestry and Italy's recent collapse or because some Americans think us insufferably arrogant even before they have met us, I do not know. But it was a more bearable kind of cruelty than the Leeds dentist's because it was so obviously both impulsive and idiotic. The dentist was a more representative and sinister figure, habitually cruel through laziness and insensitivity, and one who had by choice put himself into a position from which that cruelty could be exercised. Perhaps the American doctor was tender with wounded American servicemen – or Italian prisoners-of-war.

Boots and shoes have a special role in the lives of poor children because they are peculiarly precise indicators. The boots doled out at the Rotary camp looked what they were, solid but unlovely job-lots, without style or taste, clumpish, like shoes for drayhorses. Similarly, you could identify the really poor boys at school because when almost everyone else had, by a certain age, graduated to shoes, they still clumped around in ugly black boots, clearly bought with some public coupon or other. Yet again the classes have a way of coming together, especially the lower and the upper as they bypass the middle.

Sometime in the Sixties, waiting in the hospitality room for a television discussion with a writer and a politician, both public-school products – and both of them extremely confident as a result, but in different ways, the one as the public-school success, the other as the public-school renegade – I noticed two things about the politician as he walked in: his bowler hat and his well-polished boots. When the politician was at the lavatory the writer picked up his hat and looked at the brand name. 'I thought so,' he said, 'not from Lock's. Cheapskate.' I noted the shiny black boots especially, since I had just read that servants in exclusive clubs and the most expensive hotels can recognise a real gentleman by whether the instep of his footwear has been blacked and polished; which would indicate a good body-servant (what a phrase!) at work. We managed to get one quick look at the politician's instep as he crossed his legs: no polish. 'Still,' said the writer, 'it's a form of snobbery for his generation to stick to boots in any weather. A hangover from school and an indication that they have no intention of becoming tailors' dummies.'

A remote relative of about my age was attending a minor Yorkshire public school of the sort which educate the sons of local businessmen and professionals who for whatever reasons do not aspire on behalf of their sons to first- or second-league public schools with a national reputation. They tend to produce people whose speech still has a basic Yorkshire intonation, though now overlaid with a clipped gentility, like a striped boating cap on the head of a burly Yorkshire farmer. One year, via an equally remote woman relative, a pair of that public schoolboy's shoes were sent to Grandma for me. Perhaps he had outgrown them. They were black, glossy and very pointed. Had he worn them at chaperoned dances with the nearest girls' public school? Or at tea-dances in Harrogate when he and his friends were let loose on Saturday afternoons? Grandma and aunts agreed that my existing shoes were 'getting very shabby' and that the pointed pair, though rather unusual, were of very good quality. They were hateful and if I had known the word 'poncy' by then would have instantly used it. Not only did they pinch the toes, they rightly attracted vilification in the playground.

After a while I complained to Grandmother who understood at once; and so in different degrees did the others. We had our pride and it was not worth even the best pair of shoes to have that lowered. Quite early, the shoes became badly knocked about and so, sooner than I had feared, were ditched. I have only once since bought a pair of shoes with a marked though not extreme point; and realised within the day that I had made a mistake, had put on my feet that bit of the past.

Strange how certain words at certain times in your life can have special force and, read or spoken years later and thousands of miles away, can call up a range of events and their contexts, the form and pressure of those days. Aunt Ethel's approving use of 'manly' – clean, not sexy, carrying himself well, a square-jawed Baden-Powell of the simple moral life – is quite unusable for me, though occasionally I wish it were available. Those pointed shoes which were accepted because my own were getting 'shabby' bring to mind that 'shabby' was a word with great resonance for us all in several different ways. It held, within those different meanings, many of the fears of the respectable working class. They did not usually notice, were not usually aware, that they were branded on the tongue (though they recognised educated speech when they heard it) but they did fear to begin looking shabby. So 'darning' (another word one hardly ever hears today), sewing and patching were regular activities, stays against shabbiness: socks, jackets, shirts, underwear, all got the treatment. 'Come back and let me see to that sleeve. Ah can't have you going out all shabby like that.'

The leather patches for the elbows and sleeves of middle-class Harris tweed sports jackets would have been a godsend if we could have brought ourselves to seek them and pay for them; and, more importantly, been willing to wear them, since they would have marked us out around our streets. I met them first at university; undergraduates on small grants knew all about them.

The fear of shabbiness was reinforced by that cycle – by which you were caught both ways – which keeps recurring as I write. Your pride and respectability made you afraid of sinking into shabbiness. Your budget allowed you to buy only cheap clothes which soon became shiny and then shabby. The sort of sports jacket one can still see on country gents in Salisbury and Newbury and Winchester and Chichester and Harrogate and towns like those – faded, much washed and cleaned, patched at elbows and cuffs with the patches themselves showing wear, but not a trace of shine anywhere because the cloth was too good for that – the sort of jacket which looks as though it was built like a battleship by a bespoke tailor thirty years ago, such a jacket was as unattainable to us as a rope of pearls, in both money and social terms.

'Shabby' to us was a very real, present and material word; it pointed above all to shabby *things*, overwhelmingly to clothing and secondarily to the furnishings of the home. I do not remember it being used directly as a word of moral judgment as in: 'a shabby achievement' or 'particularly shabby behaviour' or 'a shabby outlook' or 'a shabby conclusion'. For me, the moral force of the word when it is used in these ways is all the greater because our long-standing fear and dislike of shabbiness in clothing and things about the house was at bottom a moral judgment; it indicated that someone, yourself perhaps, had let go instead of fighting all the time not to succumb. Edwin Muir's lines: 'It was not meant for human eyes / That combat on the shabby patch' had exceptional force from the moment I read them. I had not until now realised that 'shabby patch' might seem a grotesque pun.

The Jack Lane Elementary School period lasted only three or four years but seemed much longer. One went along from day to day, with little sense of change, because one was told to do so. For almost all, life outside in the streets was more real than school and more connected with the life they assumed they would go on living to the end of their days. By the time the district was knocked down, I suppose that back-to-back street life had lasted about a century and that is a good long time – longer, for example, than British colonial rule in some now independent states of Africa. No wonder the Africans, and the British from their side, threw off much of colonialism so easily. It ran more shallowly than the culture of our streets.

The streets entertained play – marbles or tag games in and out of the snickets and round the dustbin-and-outside-lavatory areas; and offered early training and trading in relationships outside the home or school. That is obvious but worth saying because those boys and to a lesser extent girls who did not float easily in that street environment, and I was among them, often showed that lack for years afterwards and had to learn in a different place, at a different age and with different social currency, how to manage the different levels of relationships. For some of us, girls were not a problem until quite well into our teens. The hardier ones would play the boys' games and were said to be hurriedly, fumblingly and, as if accidentally, touched up from time to time in the dark of the snickets.

Sometimes, indulgent parents gave a penny for some chips, with a part-shovel of 'scraps' of fried batter which had floated free, and those were often slightly shared. Saturday could mean the pictures, usually the matinée at the Parkfield Picture Palace which had a clinker floor and charged a penny or twopence.

Reading, except of comics, was a strange land to which most did not penetrate. If you had gone up the whole length of our street on both sides you would not have found, I guess, more than fifty books in all, and most of those would have been giveaways from *John Bull*'s or the newspapers' promotions. But within a group of two or perhaps three streets you would be likely to find someone, almost invariably a single man of indeterminate age, who was known as a 'scholar' and had a couple of small shelves of books with a one-volume encyclopedia prominent. I have never seen a record of the role of such men, both in acting as clerks and amanuenses to people in the surrounding streets and in encouraging, usually with a deference which shamed you, the occasional 'bright' kid who popped up.

I understand that I was the first boy from Jack Lane to pass the eleven-plus exam. Not many years ago, I saw the school's honours board, by then in storage. It had hung on the wall of the room used as an assembly hall and listed mine and others' later achievements;

but it was a short list. To be accurate, I failed the eleven-plus examination but still went to grammar school. The explanation involves the intervention of the headmaster who, I now see, was one of those people who gave me a leg up at the right time far beyond their calls of duty.

To sit for the eleven-plus you had to walk out of Hunslet, over the 'Moor' to the edge of the Dewsbury Road area where stood the local 1902 Act 'grammar', Cockburn High School, the one to which you would without question be assigned if you were successful. You were to answer papers in arithmetic, or maths, and English. I remember a very cold walk and a maths paper which floored me; we had not done that kind of maths, which shows that Jack Lane did not deliberately train its pupils for the particular shape and form of those exams. In the circumstances precise training for the scholarship exam would have been misguided, though I suppose a bit of tuition on the side for the front-runners would not have come amiss. After good teaching, I gained a distinction in maths at 'O' level. But at that point, at eleven, I failed to gain a scholarship.

This upset Mr Harrison who must have been counting on me to break the barrier. He went to the offices of the City Education Authority, then and still – or until recently – over the road from the Town Hall and asked that they at least read an essay of mine, whether one written for the scholarship exam or on another occasion I do not know. He came back with a place for me at Cockburn. I do not remember where I heard this story. He may have called me in to his office and in his fatherly way, and with some pride, have explained that I was after all to go to grammar school and how it had come about; I rather think he did. Nor do I know, nor will I ever know, why the official concerned agreed to the change: had he looked at the essay and said – 'Why, here's a clever lad. Yes, he should have a place'? Or had he thought to himself that it was about time Jack Lane had a scholarship, the headmaster obviously put great store by it, and the boy he was promoting might have something about him?

Such speculations interest me less than the thought of what I might have become had Mr Harrison's plea failed. I know several people, now distinguished, who did fail the eleven-plus for Cockburn or some other grammar school; and stayed failed. It was not difficult for clever children from working-class streets to fail to show their potential in a once-for-all test. The test could be, and was, easily prepared for by lower-middle-class parents from other parts of a school's huge catchment area – for us, that large arc round the south of Leeds. Their children could be sent to junior schools dedicated to getting as many as possible over the hurdles; and given tuition at home.

Once you were at Cockburn and on the prescribed route, the successive steps, so long as you worked hard, seemed to follow one another with a near inevitability. You did not necessarily have to show initiative, to decide to do this or that at a certain moment, to make that kind of gamble, to break the ties of home and Leeds. Those who should have got through but did not were required to be tough later and constantly if their potential was to be fulfilled; they had by far the more testing time. Whether I would have been able to show that degree of tenacity I do not know.

CHAPTER 7

COCKBURN

I do not recall when I first consciously realised that I would – I did not say 'had to' to myself – get out of Hunslet and the life of Hunslet. I do not remember recognising this in a resentful or rejecting way; it was a blind sureness that that was the way I would go, would be led; as if a simple instinct pushed towards ways of life, ways of seeing life, which Hunslet did not offer but which as the weeks and months passed I saw could be offered in other places and were in some important ways preferable. Both symbolically and literally the first step on that journey, towards those new terms of life, was when I began making that morning walk to Cockburn High School, over the 'Moor'.

Other boys and a smaller number of girls, but in all no more than a trickle, thirty-odd scholarship holders a year, out of the 65,000 people who lived in South Leeds, were coming out of the crowded streets, togged out in their new silly blazers and even sillier caps, starting the journey away, getting on to the first of the little launching pads. From now on their main friendships would be of the classrooms not the streets; they would dance to different drums. No parents would go with them, that first day or any other. In the early months the boys and girls would not talk to each other en route; that came later if at all. As you pushed off, out of the gravitational pull of your own small ring of streets through others you knew less and less well as the rings widened outwards, the associations, the known places, the accretions of memory all thinned out: you were enclosed within yourself, looking nervously but doggedly ahead, one person going through what would have seemed to outsiders like featureless, dull streets to a new order of life, new words, new ways of behaving, new kinds of excitement, a novel sense of possible openings-out, 'prospects'. The first day at university, the first walk into a barrack-room where you will sleep as a recruit, are similar nervy beginnings if that is your disposition; neither has as much force as that first walk to the grammar school and entry to your first classroom and all the new faces, at eleven.

Cockburn's great cube had cupolas at each corner as though the architects, to relieve the functional blankness, had decided to add swirls which might seem at least slightly reminiscent of the domes and spires of Oxbridge. Otherwise, everything from the outside was unprepossessing as architecture. To us it was massive, formal, from a public area of life we had never before lived within; an impression heightened by the great hall, its platform and the morning procession of masters and mistresses in academic fig.

Inside, the lavatorial tiles up to several feet, the high windows, the wide corridors, the stone stairways with iron banisters, the institutional smells, all might have been expected to continue and reinforce that blank functional impression. But they did not. The designers had somehow hit on dimensions which were human. You can find it in other large public buildings from roughly the last two decades of the nineteenth century to the start of the First World War: teacher training colleges of which St Gabriel's, as it was, in Camberwell is a fine example; lunatic asylums, as they used to be called; parts of some pre-1939 provincial universities; some council buildings and even some mill-owners' homes. None of them were ancient or mock-ancient, not ivy-clad or turreted. But they had a feel, an atmosphere, which suggested that they were full of people doing their best to do well by those they were concerned with, not in a cheerleader sort of way but firmly, responsibly, decently. I do not know how the architects hit upon that mix but it worked. Set them against, for example, the tall Senate House of the University of London, frowning over Russell Square if a dead thing could frown, an inhuman disaster. That is a Fascist or totalitarian building, as Orwell recognised when he drew on it in *1984*. The inorganic scale of the rooms and especially of the cafeteria suggests an East European ministry with vast bureaucratic pretensions but little understanding of, or care for the lives of, individuals outside the decisions of the state. But Cockburn's entrance hall, with its bits of good curly wood and a few *art nouveau* twirls, suggested that you were joining a liveable congregation, accessible, available, firm but not frightening.

Just over the road, in an old and fairly large detached villa, was

Burton House, Cockburn's kindergarten, academic forcing-bed or allotment. A relic from the day when even more students at the senior school were fee-payers. A kindergarten attached to the mother foundation could at one time give your children almost automatic entry to the main school. Still in my day many of its pupils made that move, though I expect that by then most of them took the eleven plus examination to see if they could get a scholarship and so a free place. The fees must have been so slight that even quite small self-employed grocers or tailors or hardware-shop owners could afford them; in 1930 just over half of Cockburn's pupils were still fee-paying. The local doctors sent their children either to one of the Yorkshire public schools or, probably after some preparatory training, to Leeds Grammar School, an independent foundation near the middle of town which also took in the sons of solicitors, accountants, plain aspirants and the like, as Leeds Girls' High School did for the girls.

There was another band, composed of people who did not seek training preparatory to entry to Leeds Grammar School or Leeds Girls' High School, or even less impressive-seeming places such as Cockburn, for their children, though they had at least as much money as most of those who did. They were the self-employed artisans, such as plumbers, electricians and carpenters. Not unskilled manual workers, nor factory-employed skilled working class, they nevertheless belonged to the working class by tastes and habits. A boy might be expected to take over his father's business; to send the girl to a fee-paying school when the boy did not go to one would have seemed odd. They were among the luckier ones: they had a skill of which they were proud and which brought in good money; they were better off than the people around them whose tastes they in general shared. No wonder that if the plumber's wife came to the door when you called to ask for his help as soon as possible she looked confident, content, on firm ground above your shifting sands; the older and prouder ones could look like minor Mrs Bulstrodes.

Once, in a note for a television conversation with the poet Tony Harrison, I said he had gained a scholarship to Leeds Grammar School. I described it as 'the poshest grammar school in Leeds'. The producer, an Australian and extremely sensitive to what she understandably thought of as the usual excessive English class-consciousness, wanted to substitute 'best' for 'poshest'. Her antipodean ear betrayed her there. Leeds Grammar School was not indisputably the best in town, as the maintained grammar schools would have been quick to point out. There would be times when it was, times when it wasn't; such reputations, like those of university departments, go up and down, with a substantial time-lag, according to who is in charge and who on the staff. Leeds Grammar School certainly thought of itself as both the best and the most select, attributions which parents were glad to adopt. Others might also deliberately call it the 'poshest' but the epithet was more a criticism of its pretensions than an acceptance of them. 'Best' is another indicator altogether.

One remembers again the intensive process of winnowing which each year ensured that a few very bright children from round about reached Cockburn. After that, doggedness came in since so much in the environment had to be held off; there were few easy handholds. Most of those pupils disappeared after the School Certificate examination ('O' levels); to their parents it would have seemed like flying too high for them to stay after sixteen, especially when all around were leaving school at fourteen. The sixth-form arts class which I entered held about seven or eight, two or three of them girls. Most had parents with a little more money than the average around there, or strongly aspiring parents, or both. Most went into teacher training colleges. Perhaps after our time the teachers lifted their sights, since our year and the equally small classes immediately before and after us produced three professors, a diplomat and an economic attaché to a major embassy. Not a matter for great surprise or congratulation, after all that sifting.

Even within our group of scholarship holders, and on the whole we did not distinguish the few fee-payers, there were small differences of grading which made one or two stand out: such as the boy whose doting widowed mother gave her only chick sixpence a day for sweets; we envied him mildly. He could go to the pictures on Saturday evening with a boy similarly privileged; that cost more than going to a matinée, and he could buy a comic as well. He became plump and spotty for a time but was quite generous and amiable; in the end he was one of the very successful five I mentioned above. Neither he nor the one or two others as well-off for pocket money as he was, in the score or so who had moved up together towards the first big public examination at fifteen or sixteen, showed off or pushed their luck. I can recall no snobbery or bullying in that particular group.

This was because for the first time in our lives we were in an environment created not by accident but by selection, an environment whose main purpose was to train clever children to make effective use of their brains. There was competition, inevitably; but since we were all being pushed from outside we tended, with a good sense we were not aware of having, not to compete overtly among ourselves. The school thought of itself as training us in more than the use of our brains; it offered diluted versions of some public-school values: a healthy mind in a healthy body, responsibility towards the community and the like. But these values were not urged with any great conviction. Brains plus tenacity were the main things.

Here was one reason why my friend Musgrave, he whose widowed mother was a charwoman, was not embarrassed by that fact. Another reason was his own toughness, resilience and poise; at his perkiest he carried the situation off as though it were a distinction greater than having sixpence a day for sweets. Which it was, but not in the perspective of most teenagers. Musgrave was bright enough to have learned early some key rules about the presentation of self in everyday life, rules much above the level of and more subtle than offers to fight if anyone tried to patronise him; he was past that point early.

The girls in the class were thought of as in general slightly better off and on average rather cleverer than the boys. Whether this reflected the habit of working-class people, even the aspiring, of urging boys on to higher education more than girls, so that you had to look to the lower middle class before you found stronger expectations for girls and more girls going in for the scholarship examination, I do not know, though those seem elements in the situation. If so, the sieve for girls was even finer than for the boys. For the first year or so classes were single-sex; perhaps it was thought the younger ones would be too embarrassed or too rumbustious for mixed classes. By the time they reached the sixth form even the shy boys were sexually aware though only rarely sexually active and most of the girls were, though similarly inhibited, fully mature sexually. So there might have been a case for switching round the arrangement and separating the two, if separation there had to be, at puberty. Girls and boys were put on opposite sides of the classroom, separated by the centre aisle.

The differences in the age of maturing kept classroom romances few. A seventeen-year-old girl was more likely to find a nineteen-year-old boy-friend, one with money to spend, outside the class. There was one handsome, tall, dark-eyed girl who liked to tease the boys by, for instance, pushing her skirt up so that her hand could reach right up to her stocking top and the erotic suspenders for a scratch; that gave the boys over the aisle a good eyeful. We all knew she was going out with a trainee estate agent who had a coupé, of sorts. Her best friend, another girl who liked to flaunt some of her parts safely, had a tennis-club acquaintance; clearly they were both from a social notch above the usual. What they might have got up to on Saturday nights seemed as remote and flashily outré to us as the ways of the glossier American soap operas are now. I expect it was a pattern of tattily showy roadhouses out beyond the ring-road, the tennis club, the odd young bloods' bar in town and necking in the coupé.

A ginger-haired girl on a scholarship, after rehearsals for a school play, walked with me towards home one late evening and then asked me to see her the three or four streets to her own home. As we neared there she remarked that her mother was out and the house empty. When we arrived at the street-end she asked me in and, dopey though I was, I realised – half-realised would be more accurate – that she was hinting at the possibility of something sexual. I said my grandmother was expecting me and made off with my ears red, embarrassed but not excited. I would have been about fifteen or sixteen at the time. I remember no other such occasion.

Sex was talked about a great deal but focussed on events or alleged events away from school; gossip about them more than direct experience. As always, there were recurrent patterns of myth as to particular practices and the places in which they were said to take place; and specially selected words. There were stories of girls a few streets away who held Saturday night parties whilst their parents were at the pub, for the sexual initiation of girls and boys younger than themselves; there was a woman hairdresser who worked at home and was said to take boy customers to bed in the afternoon; there was a skivvy at a local shop who was said to demonstrate her skill at tossing-off the shop dog; which had to be an Alsatian. There were, of course, girls said to be willing to show 'all they'd got' for a few coppers: 'Penny a look, tuppence a feel / Threepence to twine the hairy wheel'; quite inventive, that. Such stories interested both grammar-school and elementary-school boys; they came together in that, since they were still in the same streets and at the same curious age.

There were 'spicy' magazines with line drawings, very soft porn in print and picture. We particularly liked the story of a film tycoon whose new secretary soon went behind a screen in his office, undressed and reappeared: 'And Gale stepped out to reveal gleaming thighs.' That became a class rubric.

Favourite locales for the stories included large houses on the outskirts where the maids were said to be complaisant towards visiting workmen, and the sands at Blackpool in the late evenings of high summer. Even more, railway carriages: we had story after story about what someone who worked on the railway had seen of the antics of honeymoon couples or casual pairs, by day and night. It was no surprise to find later that both Graham Greene and Ian Fleming recognised the potency of the railway carriage, stationary or, preferably, moving, as a sexual setting.

Above all, the local parks were the settings for sexual stories and experiences; and of those the greatest and best loved, not only for sexual but for many other reasons, was Roundhay Park. Two memories of that stand out, one sexual one not, each connected with a big public event and each trailing its disturbing, confusing and puzzling intimations. First, there was the Military Tattoo, in a large bowl of grass. Was it annual? I could not afford to go and anyway it was at night and right over on the other side of town. But in the summer holidays, just before my twelfth birthday, a pal and I went to see it 'set up', which meant going as nearly as possible to the day it would open.

After seeing the preparations in the great open bowl we wandered down Roundhay's maze of wooded paths and, round a corner, came upon two girls, much older than we were, sitting on a bench and giggling themselves silly. They were looking into a largish hand-mirror so trained as to reflect whatever was to be seen a few yards down the overgrown and bushy bank behind them. We asked what they were laughing at and they handed over the mirror. A few yards down the bank, under a bush and probably also under the illusion that he could not be seen, was a soldier, one who would no doubt be involved in the Tattoo that evening but had been given a few hours out of camp. He had a girl under him – plenty hung around the camp – and they were just reaching the full tide of copulation. I had never seen the act before and the memory remains sharp. It is above all a memory of the violence of the sexual act, seen from outside, when it is reaching its climax. I had often heard about 'what happens'. Nothing had prepared me for the sense that at the act's crisis, in its last blind moments, it is like a blow, an unrestrained and unrestrainable violence by the man; but with the woman all open and receptive and adjusted by nature to the blows. I was astonished and abashed. As we handed back the mirror one of the girls said: 'She'll 'ave a proper 'eadache i' nine months' time.'

The second Roundhay Park event was an air show. Those shows trundled round the country with a Tiger Moth and other old aircraft, refurbished after the war. Daredevil pilots did heart-stopping stunts, with looping the loop as the benchmark and favourite. At least you could see something of all that from outside, without paying to go into the great arena. Still, a couple of us wandered along the day before it started, to have a good look. They had already sealed off the arena by running a seven- or eight-foot canvas wall all round it. But things were quiet so we crawled under the canvas; and found ourselves in a small village of caravans running round the perimeter. We came upon a very elegant caravan, within and immediately outside which two young women were setting themselves up. They called us over and offered a shilling each if we would bring water to fill their various tanks and receptacles; we accepted immediately.

At one point we even got inside the caravan. I had never seen women or women's accoutrements like these. The girls were not wives or girl-friends of the pilots; they were themselves stunt pilots. They were slim and pretty, Southerners with accents which I think I would now recognise as public school . . . middle-class, public-school girls out for a life with some spice and not short of courage; it is a good long line. To them we were like coolies to a couple of mem-sahibs; they were not harsh or bullying; they entirely ignored us; and we looked. I remember above all their smell as they moved about the narrow caravan or came to the door to ask for yet more water, the smell of perfumes which suggested the exotic and the remarkably expensive. It was not a sexy smell; it smelled of the carefree, the dashing, the financially well-endowed. Here was a world in which slim-boned young women, brought up in parts of England we had only heard of, with names like Egham, Midhurst, Haslemere and Sevenoaks, moved freely and did what they wished, not hag-ridden day by day by worries about money or what the neighbours might think.

*

Cockburn's teachers were of three kinds: two main ones, with a smaller group in between. Some were unmistakably middle-class, usually from the South and with accents to match: accents we had hardly ever heard before except perhaps, and that was not certain since even these two professionals may have been locals locally trained, from the doctor and parson. There was a kind young French mistress who told us she came from Virginia Water. I imagined a great stretch of southern lake, fringed by low and half-timbered houses reaching to the water's edge, ladies with parasols, young men in boaters, rowing. Nowadays, going through that exurbanite or near-exurbanite area skirted by the A30, I think of her. She was a gentle and good teacher and we had not seen her kind of gentleness or even her degree of sophistication in our schools before that. The senior French master had a rather effete manner and sported a bow-tie; again, something rare to us, as rare as a parakeet on the loose. He was a scholar beyond the needs of the job and might well, if he had graduated in the Sixties instead of the Twenties or Thirties, have had a university post; he too taught well. The two put up large colourful posters – châteaux on the Loire, Provence, Notre Dame – to inspire us to a Francophilia approaching theirs.

The most thoroughly southern and recherché of the southern contingent was Mr Norden, the headmaster. He had great middle-class academic style and polish; that impression remained even after I had reached university and seen the style and airs many provincial professors awarded themselves. He had taught at Dulwich College. For him and for some others of the teachers in that group, to come north to a grammar school in a working-class area in a large and grimy industrial city was prompted not only by the difficulty in those days of getting a job at all but also by a missionary spirit. Not all the teachers at Cockburn, but a clear majority from all three of the groups I am describing, felt they had a special role in relation to their pupils. Their vision of what they could best try to do for those pupils was often limited culturally, but it *was* a sort of vision; and it ensured that they felt a strong sense of pastoral as well as academic responsibility. They watched you, talked about you in the staff room, thought about your best future.

The headmaster's sense of vocation was the most evident of all. I suspect he was not what would today be called an 'administrative high-flyer'. He was said to have forgotten one year to send off to the

Examinations Board the completed School Certificate papers. Even if he did not forget, the story captures some of his scatty idiosyncrasy. He was not hearty or jollying; nor was he bullying or unkind. He did not look for a special place for Cockburn in some race to get better results than the other grammar schools. He knew what grammar-school education, in the old solid sense, should be and he meant to encourage it in his school, by gentlemanly example rather than by 'management skills' and carrot-dangling. In the late Thirties he resigned to go to a school in Sussex and later, we believed, became a Church of England monk.

The small second, or in-between group, were the traditional schoolteachers whose clear professional marks of identity in that role were more important than their marks of class. Whether they had come from generations of schoolteaching families I do not know but they gave that impression; like sons who go into doctoring and look and sound like doctors' sons and grandsons; pedigree sheepdogs. They were conscientious and earnest in seeking good results from the mixed material in front of them, but their missionary spirit, though I think it existed, was concealed behind the pedantic mask. Nor did they have the slightly surprised, nervous and new air of people who are the first in their families to gain degrees and wear gowns. They wore their tattered gowns with a difference, like hospital consultants, moving from one important appointment to another. They were certainly true professionals in their own well-honed ways – in the teaching of Latin or maths or, strangely enough, English.

They set the standards for the younger teachers and assumed a duty to help those willing to learn from them. Less responsible teachers knew they were being silently judged. From one angle the lives of the old hands seemed dull, and some younger teachers decided they would never settle into such a routine; but it was a routine which cut no corners professionally and expressed a strong and undeviating sense of where duty lay.

I, for one, owe to such people much more than a respectable grounding in maths and Latin, though I did get both and from a standing start. I owe also the example of unspectacular daily attention to detail, given because that is what you were appointed to give, to fulfil the demands of your job, and to do less would have been irresponsible. The most characteristic and impressive of this group were the senior Latin master and the senior English master.

The English master was not far from retirement, grave and reserved; he did not establish a special acquaintance even with some of the boys best in English, as his younger colleagues did. His views on language and literature were conventional but not derisory – good logical attention to grammar and a Palgravesque approach to poetry are not bad foundations.

That senior English master tended to come in five or ten minutes late for the first session after the midday break. One day – I expect I wanted to show I could be a bit of a devil – I threw a stink bomb across the classroom eight or nine minutes before he was normally due, not realising that the smell would still be there when he did arrive; in fact, he came in earlier than usual and the rotten eggs were at their most potent. He sniffed and asked, more magisterially than angrily: 'Which boy is responsible for this?' There was a pause and then I stood up and said: 'Sir, it was I.' 'At least your admission is grammatical, Hoggart. You will be in detention for the whole of this week, for one hour.' It being Monday, I arrived home an hour late each night and deserved at least that. Whether I lied to cover my lateness I do not remember; certainly, no one at Newport Street guessed what had happened; they would have been unduly distressed if they had.

A silly little story but I suppose I tell it because the peculiar dignity and decisiveness of the master impressed me. He neither raged nor purported to be amused. He did what he had to do and forgot it and I do not imagine he told anyone except the master on detention duty; certainly he never held it against me. My impulse to throw the stink bomb would have come as much as anything from reading Frank Richards in the *Magnet* and *Gem*; those magazines had a more powerful hold on our grammar-school imaginations than the *Wizard* or *Hotspur*. Pseudo-public-school culture had overhauled street culture.

The third group of teachers were the 'in-comed 'uns', the new entrants, the first in their families ever to reach this foothold area in the – just – professional classes. From them also one could meet thoughtful pastoral care. As I write, I wonder whether I am overstressing the good professional side of Cockburn. I can remember scrappy teachers: the PT people in particular were not impressive. Some of the men played bridge obsessively each lunchtime in their own staff room. Women were not allowed in. But all in all I find myself impressed by the attitudes and acts of most of these people, by the fact that most of them had lights which shone steadily if not with a piercing glow and that they tried to follow them. For several good reasons I support the comprehensive idea and have seen it working well in other countries and sometimes here. That it is so difficult to get right here is due chiefly to our usual knotted-up cultural contradictions, inhibitions, lazinesses, inability to change. One major casualty, except in the more fortunate comprehensives, can be the academic idea itself, the difficulty even the most devoted staff have in clearing a space, creating a climate in which clever and bookish children can thrive. Cockburn became a comprehensive. I called in there a few years ago: movements in skilled industry, the flight of many of those who could get out, rehousing to other districts, had left the school with a recruitment area which had more than the average number of problem families, of the 'underclass'. No matter how committed the staff are it must be even more difficult to create an academic sixth form than it was in my day. Asbestos contamination caused the school to move a few years ago, though not very far away. The eighty-odd-year-old building has been knocked down.

It would be wrong to try to reconstitute the grammar schools for eleven- to eighteen-year-olds. But a tribute is due to those who in their day kept the local authority grammar schools going, who had some sense of learning and some feeling of responsibility both academically and socially towards the girls and boys who passed through their hands; especially towards the clever children from homes which have never before held a grammar-school pupil.

Such a master, having decided that I could 'have a future', took me aside one day after class and waved out of the window towards the north, over the centre towards the better-off parts of the city. 'If you play your cards right, Hoggart,' he said (the image is adequate to what he was saying, and an unintended revelation of the inadequacy of the thought itself), 'you could end up with a house in Roundhay.' 'Ever remember, my dear Dan, that you should look forward to being some day manager of that concern' . . . Victorian industrialist's aspiration translated into 1930s working-class Leeds. I did not at the time realise how thin that teacher's own professional and social experience had been. Presumably he had a degree, probably from Leeds University; he was one of the 'in-comed 'uns'. He did not sound like a Leeds loiner or native, so probably came from a township outside; now he had a house in Roundhay or at least on its cheaper fringes. The air there, the air of his whole working and domestic life, would be mild, kind but not intellectually bracing.

Another such master, one of the English Literature group, stopped me in the corridor during the second term of my fifth year. There was an annual school camp at Stratford-upon-Avon, in bell tents on a field owned by Flowers the brewers, with several visits to the theatre on the river bank. This teacher had decided that I would benefit from Stratford (since I had not, at sixteen, seen more than one or at the most two plays by Shakespeare and hardly any other plays, he was right); but he knew we could not find the £6 the camp cost. He announced in a conspiratorial way that he and some colleagues had had a whip-round. The whole operation, he stressed, had to be kept 'sub rosa'. I had not heard the phrase before but whenever I have since read it or, even more, heard it, it has sounded like the echo from long ago of an unforeseen kindness; a beautiful, brief, musical phrase.

Once again, the action had been prompted by essays they thought very promising. That is less important than the evidence the incident gives of, yet again, a sense of responsibility beyond the measurable, formal and written down, and in particular of people – many of whom had themselves climbed up with more or less difficulty – on the lookout for those children who might need and make good use of a special push. The reverse of that attitude is that such people had little time for the lazy or even the relaxed; pupils like those were harder to accommodate psychologically, given the teachers' and all our backgrounds.

The 'new' theatre had just opened and showed off its technical capabilities with a magnificent storm for the first scene of *The Tempest*. In the bus on the way down to Stratford one of the younger masters said to another that the building looked like a biscuit factory. I had not before thought it possible to have views on architecture, least of all critical views. Buildings – a new pub, a public library, a bank – simply appeared and one simply accepted them.

I enjoyed the week and all the plays very much. The atmosphere of the camp was not bad as such things go. We prowled around the masters' tent when they were not looking and discovered they had tomato ketchup with their meals, a sybaritic addition we did not share but did not resent: this wasn't Ripon. There was the almost inevitable bully, a bigger boy, perhaps a year older than our class, who took to letting down the guy-ropes of the younger boys' tents. He gave me, quite against my instincts and I am sure against his, a good lesson. After the third such mucking-up of our tent, I felt a surge of rage at the stupidly unnecessary act of malice so I went outside and, not knowing where the decision came from and aware of his superior size and strength, hit him full in the face. It did not at that moment matter what happened after. He turned and went and did not come back. I don't expect it always works out that way but the incident brought a curious relief, as if 'the only thing we have to fear is fear itself' had been validated.

There was a prize for the best essay about the Stratford camp and it was made clear I would be expected to enter. I won. The issue of the school magazine, *The Cockburnian*, in which the essay appeared was found among Aunt Ethel's papers. I must have been reading some of those people who made a living from wandering through Britain with staff and pen noting the beauties and writing fey, half-timbered prose about them:

> The joy of lazy afternoons on a smooth and navigable river like the Avon is a thing to cherish. The bathing parades ran no mean second to boating in the matter of popularity. The courage of some brave spirits, who arose at 6-30 a.m. to go for a bathe is sufficient to make lesser mortals mutely admire without attempting to emulate . . .
>
> A group of seniors decided to taste the delights of the plutocrat, and to that end enjoyed an hour eating ices on the terrace of the Royal Pump Room [at Leamington Spa], whilst languidly listening to the orchestra . . .
>
> How dreary is the business of striking camp! It has none of the bright hope, the lively, joyous anticipation of pitching. Yet let us not be ungrateful. We have gathered this week memories and experiences which will cheer us in the days to come and give us 'Roses in December'.

The teachers should have warned me off but presumably admired such awful pastiche. That prize, the pleasure of writing the essay and of playing with one way to invent the immediate past, the routing of the bully and, above all, the plays themselves made the Stratford week a landmark and a gateway.

Most of the teachers in that third group at Cockburn seem to have accepted entirely a permanent place in the tiny circle of society in which they now found themselves. I remember many kindnesses, much professional care but not a single subversive or radical thought from any of them. They were well within the system and the system had in some respects done well by them. Would they have behaved in much the same way if they had been born into, for example, the Soviet Union? I rather think so. Whatever they may have grumbled about in or out of school they never gave the impression that they questioned the over-arching rightness of the system as a whole. They were effectively corralled in their life-styles and modes of thinking. But they were not bloody-minded – perhaps they should have been. They seemed content with the middling shelf of comfort and respectability on to which they had clambered – perhaps they should not have been. But there was a unity and coherence in their lives, and for some of us they were helpful and encouraging until the point at which we cut the tow line because our own engines were by then running. No need to take the mickey out of them. I feel more quizzical towards some university academics I have known since, ideologically of the far left in the lecture room and senior common room, who go home each day for forty years to a comfortable middle-class existence in one of the better parts of the city.

It would be easy to label many of the Cockburn teachers' attitudes 'conformist' and so fit them into a prescribed analytical box. This would indicate that they were exhibiting no more than what might be expected of people who have risen a little, are not anxious to drop down again and so are keeping their noses clean. That elides the complexity of the attitudes here, is thinly caricaturish. Certainly these people were conventionally minded. Little in their training had disposed them to question, to test things for themselves in the mind and on the pulses. But they were not conformist in the sense that, having taken crafty stock, they had decided on which side their bread was buttered. They were conformist in that they accepted too easily the frames of reference handed to them. Their teaching of history, for example, was much as it had been at Jack Lane though fuller and more qualified. They were not without some criticisms of the English colonial record, but that record from the first exploratory voyages onwards did seem to them overwhelmingly the single most important thread in the history of this island, and on the whole a sound thread.

Just as some friends talk about the one master or mistress who set them thinking politically for themselves, so others speak of teachers who influenced them more generally, urged them to believe that a good democracy works by constant criticism, individual and social;

that dissidence, plain error and some wounds are necessary on the way to freedom. With slight exceptions, and a large exception which concerns the headmaster, that was not true for me until I reached university. The English master who had the whip-round so that I could go to Stratford was a great help and support and I remain very grateful to him. But he did not, he could not, open new areas of the mind or new, more inventive and exciting ways of using the mind. He saw me as a bright individual in a situation which might not let me use those talents as well as they might and should be used; but his sense of what those perspectives could be was very limited.

Whatever the classroom friendships and the tacit agreement not to compete openly, the class – and we moved up the school together for years – was a cluster of individuals, a collection of solipsist worlds. We were at bottom extremely competitive but did not like to admit it. I was not the cleverest but had plenty of application and knew how to make a little go a long way and so stayed among the top half-dozen or so up to School Certificate at sixteen. It all took its price until you built up a carapace, learned better how to pace yourself and take your own measure. That took me two years from entering Cockburn and was marked, I think about the end of the second year, by what I learned to call a 'nervous breakdown'. Grandmother must have wondered what on earth was going on. I was clearly by that time getting no joy from life, sitting at the living-room table frozen into nervous inability to put pen to paper, and quite unable to say what was the matter. I didn't know myself.

They sent me to Dr Cooke for 'a tonic', expecting a bottle of that medicine-of-all-work, Parrish's Chemical Food. He it was who said 'nervous breakdown' and that, though frightening, made it more understandable for Grandmother and aunts and so to some slight degree more manageable. They had heard of people who had had nervous breakdowns – small shopkeepers who found themselves being squeezed out of existence by a newly arrived chain-store; the occasional shop assistant with a beastly demanding boss – but in a boy a nervous breakdown was something new and bizarre. Still, hardly surprising given all the school work I had to do – 'all that brainwork' – and the earnest way I went about it – 'always lost in a book', they concluded. Small wonder that 'doing my homework' has remained a private metaphor; as has 'Ah well, better get on,' meaning get back to the work which is always there, not 'better advance myself'.

I was sent to a convalescent home in Bridlington for one or two weeks, another example of the provision which could be made by the city's Board of Guardians for those it had to look after. It was a large house, probably built as a hotel in the first place; and the food was not bad. We were taken on long health-giving walks and spent much time in a large bare common room with huge windows looking over the sea. If the nurses were not in the room some of the boys, who seemed to be having a resilient convalescence, played sadistic tricks such as locking the smaller ones in a large chest with a top lid; they soon discovered those who were claustrophobic. There was a nurse of exceptional sweetness. Not a bad set of memories all in all and much happier than those of the Ripon camp, in spite of the reason for being at Bridlington. The break seemed to do the trick and though, in the final year at university when I was straining for a first, I got near the edge, I did not slide over again. I did see, in the elegant Park Square near the Town Hall, a psychiatrist; just once, for about five minutes. He told me my best medicine was my girl-friend, that I was simply under examination strain and would soon be all right; and to hand £5 to his receptionist.

Back to Cockburn and the long process of pulling out and away. That route was overwhelmingly via print. No television; and radio, which we only got at Newport Street quite late, was not expected to connect much with the interests and drives being encouraged in us. Nor did the practice of the arts much engage us, music and the visual arts hardly at all, drama in performance a very little. So it was books, overwhelmingly. There was little interest in the intellectual life in itself and as a stimulation for its own sake; we were tenaciously utilitarian. Indeed, intellectual enquiry could worry us since it could disturb our conviction that the steady application of intelligence was entirely adequate for us to find our way successfully. When many years later I read Hofstadter's elegant comparisons between intelligent and intellectual personalities I knew at once what he meant. There were of course some intellectuals at university but it was in the army that I first came to know closely someone with a strong intelligence, a lively sense of intellectual enquiry and, most surprisingly of all, the capacity to be playful with those gifts. That capacity for playfulness still eludes me. It would be unjust to blame the lack on Cockburn: much more likely, it comes from natural disposition and the intertwining of that with the stresses of the route; not much time for pirouettes just for the hell of it, on the way.

Not long after Bridlington I did find part of a way out, a support. It was necessary to discover something for yourself, in some way to branch off the track, to make your own discoveries, find your own area of enthusiasms outside what the schoolmasters offered and beyond what all but a very few of the other boys talked about. My way was through the new Hunslet Public Library. A great many people from poor backgrounds have paid tribute to the place of the public libraries in their unofficial education. For many people what the public libraries gave was as near as they had come until then to a revelation of the possible size and depth and variety of life, knowledge and understanding. This needs stressing today when some politicians, even some members of governments, do not see very well the justification for a free library service and certainly would not set one up if we did not have one already. What! a warm room in every neighbourhood where people can read, and borrow books without charge! Surely it should be cost-effective; and wouldn't it be more appreciated if people had to pay for it? Doubtful. It is certain that many of those who most need it, who could most benefit from it, would be frozen out if the service were no longer free. Here as with most new social benefits the 'To him that hath shall be given' law would operate. Those who knew in advance its value would most use, get most benefit from, the service.

That library was a home from home for people like me. It had open access shelves, which could not be taken for granted in all areas. It even had a small study room. I could not, did not wish to, go there every night. But on certain evenings, especially when references had to be looked up or when there were visitors, it was an indispensable extension of the space, quiet, warmth and facilities of school. Homework apart, I roamed the shelves of the main library like a jackdaw not sure what it was after but sure it would eventually find it.

Within the library service itself there is nowadays a running debate about purposes. Four or five decades ago most librarians saw themselves as offering, no matter what else they made available, a good selection of the best that has been thought and said, especially for young people who were unlikely to have that access. They made sure they had well-stocked shelves of the classics, good fiction, poetry and drama. At a librarians' conference nowadays you are likely to hear an argument between those who still put first this traditional idea of the library's role and the 'democrats' who challenge the librarians' right to choose between books by their own scales of judgment, to be – in the jargon – 'judgmental', to promote some books because they think them better than others, part of the great tradition. The 'democrats' are putting a common populist argument.

Their form of it is that since libraries are paid for from the rates they must be primarily reactive rather than initiatory, must provide what the majority already know they like: shoals of romantic fiction, mounds of thrillers, forests of undemanding travel books and, increasingly, great showers of guides to information-processing and the handling of those forms of modern communications technology which are made for the home and office.

For me the great private discovery from Hunslet library was poetry. Neither Jack Lane nor Cockburn were strong on reading poetry aloud or giving a sense of its excitement and richness, so it was an area open to the treasure-hunter. The catalyst, come upon by chance, was Swinburne. I found a volume – the Chatto edition, I think – and lighted on:

> Before the beginning of years
>   There came to the making of man
> Time, with a gift of tears;
>   Grief, with a glass that ran;

Just like the Prelude to Act I of *Traviata*, my first record; music that makes you want to give all your money away. I did not notice until years later the transposition of Time and Grief. Even more, the Chorus from *Atalanta in Calydon* caught me:

> When the hounds of Spring are on winter's traces,
> The mother of months on mead or plain
> Fills the shadows and windy places
> With lisp of leaves and ripple of rain;
> And the brown bright nightingale amorous
> Is half assuaged for Itylus,
> For the Thracian ships and the foreign faces,
> The tongueless vigil, and all the pain.

I have not read that poem for about fifty years but the lines came straight from memory almost word-perfect; not difficult, since they are that kind of memorable speech which deploys a great many obvious mnemonic devices for hooking you and carrying you along in its slipstream. Later I learned to call lines such as those self-indulgent, as they are; I would like to be able to express my own self-indulgences with such rhetorical skill.

At Jack Lane our acquaintance with poetry was virtually limited to Robert Service, a sort of non-literary person's Kipling, and this was an accident; he was a favourite of one of our older teachers who filled spare or boring moments with loud renditions; that too had its value as an introduction to intoxication with language and a vigorous engagement through language with personal moral dilemmas. To a child with not much more than that by way of acquaintance with poetry, Swinburne exhibited one of the simple, strong impulses behind its making, that passion for playing with words for their own sakes, for what they can do, and be made to do without which, as Auden said, you may make a politician or a parson or a responsible citizen, but you had best not try to be a poet.

The rhyme, the alliteration, the assonance, the vowel play, the vivid imagery, the interplay of vowels and consonants, the surge up and then down in a dying fall, the whole run of the thing, all carried you along. On first reading Swinburne's lines I knew nothing of the Greek legend; I knew it was sad from the way it swung along and then glided down to that still point of pathos. I did not know and still do not know why the nightingale should be 'bright' as well as 'brown'; it is not a particularly bright bird in either looks or sound. But I knew instinctively why Swinburne put those two words together. Later I met that exceptional range of more complex and dazzling uses of 'bright': 'So quick bright things come to confusion' (the fact that 'quick' can be either an adjective attached to 'things' or, more likely, an adverb, creates an ambiguity which intensifies the effect by the shimmer between the two possible meanings); 'Brightness falls from the air, Queens have died young and fair . . .'; 'A bracelet of bright hair about the bone' (by contrast, that usage we lived with . . . 'he/she is a bright kid' sounds as though someone has switched off the light). And there is the related line, related in the nature of its effect: 'Cover her face; Mine eyes dazzle; She died young'.

Similarly, I responded to the contrast between the grand double syllables of 'tongueless vigil' and the single-syllabled dead beat of 'and all the pain'. The force of those monosyllables recalls, again, the power of Wordsworth's: 'Heavy as frost, and deep almost as life!', and of Eliot's: 'Oh dark dark dark. They all go into the dark'. All this I had found out for myself, not from a teacher; and had to respond to alone since I could not then have explained the way these things have their effects nor found anyone to discuss them with; that was the beauty of it all. By the time we had been made ready for matriculation I knew that, whatever else I learned at school, literature and above all poetry would be my main love.

I did not know until quite late that I would be staying on at school to go into the sixth form; not until Miss Jubb's intervention on seeing my report at the end of that fourth year. I still, as I have said, wonder what happened to those clever ones who could not stay on, who had no Miss Jubb to intervene, whose parents could not or felt they could not or had been inclined by the pressures of their neighbourhood to believe there was no point in continuing to have this near grown-up in the house who brought in no wages.

This was, after all, 1934 and Britain was still hardly out of the great slump. Nor was she yet creating jobs as she moved towards rearmament. We knew about the reality of unemployment as we knew about chicken-pox and consumption and scarlet fever and early widowhood and heads in gas ovens and many other apparently inescapable and inalienable ills. The pressures from outside and from the scantiness of a family's own household purse to get a child working at last, at sixteen, could only be resisted if the school insisted not only that he would go far but that he would go very far indeed. The school reacted by suggesting staying on to only the very cleverest among the children they knew to be poor. In circumstances such as those, parents could not easily be relaxed and say: 'Well, he might as well have the two extra years. You never know what might come of it.' You did know what you were failing to have added to the household income, small though that amount would be. For girls the case for staying on would have to be even more strongly made ('She'll only get married before long, anyway'). Add the unintellectual and unartistic nature of working-class experience, and in most instances pleas to stay on were likely to fail. Lucky the child one of whose parents kept enough of the old-style respect for knowledge.

After the mid-Sixties children from lower-middle-class homes and sometimes from the 'respectable' working class came to assume not only that they would stay on till eighteen but that they would then go to a university, polytechnic or college of higher education. Yet this huge expansion in higher education has inevitably benefited much more those who already knew its value for their children, rather than families of the sort I grew up among. Still, allow for these differences and the contrast in attitudes remains striking and telling; and indicates yet again that, whatever the increases in prosperity, some attitudes and actions shift more easily than others, than the more deep-seated. Cultural change is more like unconscious genetic engineering than simple grafting.

There has long been an odd contrast even within the attitudes of working-class families, and sometimes within the same families. On the one hand, the wish to get children out to work, away from school. On the other hand, the common refusal to take more than a small amount of their wages once they have started work, on the ground that they won't be so flush and free for long and had best have a good time while they can; reality – marriage, children, increasing expenses but perhaps not increasing wages – will soon enough clip their wings. It is the first high phase of the Joseph Rowntree cycle. The attitude survives, with some curious results. I had a student at Birmingham who was the only child of a Black Country manual worker and so entitled to a full, home-based maintenance grant. Most of his colleagues had parents with better incomes to whom the Means Test was applied, so that they did not receive a full grant from the State and the parents were expected to make up the rest. Many, probably most, did not fully meet the difference, and their children were quite hard up. The parents of the boy from the Black Country refused to take any of his maintenance grant from him – after all, it cost them no more to go on keeping him at home – but they let him buy his own clothes and provide his own pocket money. He was one of the best-lined students in his year and came to classes in his own fourth-hand car.

Still, in the Thirties if a sixteen-year-old put only five shillings into the family's weekly income that could make a big difference. Such a child if he or she had done reasonably well in the School Certificate Examination would have qualified for a white-collar job, and surely that was step up enough (step up enough for one generation, was the implication, though they would not have put it like that). I do not remember any classmate expressing resentment that the idea of his or her staying on was not pursued, though some of them must have realised that their ability to make use of such an opportunity was at the least as great as that of some who were to stay on. They went, and I hardly saw them again except for an occasional chance encounter in the centre of the city, slightly uneasy on both sides. Most would become clerks; some would get on well, others remain trapped where or very near where they had first landed.

They come to mind whenever I see someone thus trapped, just as much trapped as a manual worker; or perhaps more so, since there is more likely in the white-collar worker to be a sense of what might have been, as he has seen others go past him. I mean the sort of clerk in a public institution who glares out of the cage, aware that he is going nowhere, that he can predict where he will be, what he will be doing, and almost what his salary will be, from one year to the next, and the next and the next; and perhaps comparing himself with the younger brother who went to Canada or Australia and did well.

Once, getting a ticket at Birmingham's New Street Station, I found a cap on the shelf in front of the issuing-window. I tried to hand it to the booking-clerk. He gave me that baleful, trapped look. He did not respond rudely; he simply assumed I shared his views. 'It belongs to one of those filthy Pakis who are taking all the jobs,' he said. 'Just throw it on the floor.' Vistas of resentment, depression, worry in a cheap house on a difficult mortgage, opened. One of the harshest forms of regret – not remorse, since that suggests you brought about your own condition – comes from the sense that you could have done better or been better done by, that life dealt you a poor and unfair hand, one which didn't allow you to reach the level you should have reached; and that it is too late now.

That I stayed on into the sixth form is due, as I have told, to a half-sentence scribbled on my report by the headmaster and to Miss Jubb's quick sizing-up of the implications and possibilities, and her subsequent mediation with Grandmother. A small thread for so much to hang on. So I joined the small Arts Group; others went into the Sciences. Our specialist subjects became clear and were now formally identified. We began to be expected to work more on our own in school hours, to start exercising for ourselves those muscles we would need for the next leap, two years on. About that we had at first only a vague understanding.

Here, for me, the headmaster's second decisive intervention occurred. The English master was off sick for a week or two. The headmaster walked into the classroom, talked speculatively and freely in a way we were not used to, told us to choose our own subjects for an essay, to hand them in in a week's time; and left. We were already beginning to read Hardy towards the Higher School Certificate. I found the experience engrossing and puzzling. Something in Hardy's whole manner of facing experience spoke to me in ways I hardly understood. I had just registered the importance, at least sometimes, of a short and arresting opening sentence and decided to try it on. The essay therefore began: 'Thomas Hardy was a truly cultured man.'

It was the earliest instance of an interest which grew to dominate my approach to literature, that is, in the relations of particular works and authors to the general culture rather than only to those other books and authors which together make up the body and company of 'good literature'. I had been intrigued by the fact that Hardy had had little formal higher education, was not in the usual sense a sophisticated literary man, remained a countryman, and in a fashionable and snob sense could have been described as 'uncultured'. Listen to Edmund Gosse's recorded lecture on the death of Hardy and you hear the effort of someone who was in his time regarded as 'a real man of letters' to make sure that his admired but to many people rather uncultivated Hardy got into the Pantheon. Gosse's voice – fluting, terribly cultivated – and the involutions of his elaborate prose, meant to be read rather than spoken, and to be appreciated for its fine sentiments and fine style, all these underline and body out the point I was hoping to introduce in that cocky opening sentence. For the first time in my life I was trying, though I did it confusedly, to question received notions about 'culture' and 'cultivation'. Perhaps sixteen and a half was a bit late to have got only that far, but so it was; I could not at the time take the theme much further.

I must have done enough to make the headmaster think that here was a boy who was trying to work things out for himself, to see into the connections of books with life, to question an accepted abstraction rather than taking conventional opinion at its face value. I would have been startled and largely uncomprehending if he had said all that to me, and he was too shrewd to do so. What he did was call out as I passed the door of his study, in that agreeable lobby, a day or two after the essays had been handed in. He got up from the desk, came over, leaned against the door-frame, looked down and said: 'Thomas Hardy a truly cultured man . . . Maybe. I'm not sure what that means. Still . . . You must write down for me the characteristics of the truly cultured man, Hoggart. I sometimes wonder: am I truly cultured? Or have I merely learned certain ways of behaving which give that impression in our kind of society? . . .' And so on.

It was a small revelation. How could the headmaster not be a cultured man? How could he thus seriously question himself, and in front of a sixteen-year-old? It must be a game, of sorts. But as I walked away I knew that, though it was playful, it wasn't a game. I felt, for the first time powerfully and consciously, the heady shock of realising that one could and should challenge fashionable labels not only from ordinary social life but from intellectual life, not take words at face value; that one can, it follows, resist being put in a box oneself, labelled. The surprise was similar to that felt by Lydgate in the brilliant revelatory passage in *Middlemarch* where, taking down one of his father's encyclopaedias, he reads about the valves of the heart, realises for the first time that the body is a machine, and is thenceforth destined to be a doctor:

> The moment of vocation had come, and before he got down from his chair, the world was made new to him by a presentiment of endless processes . . . From that hour Lydgate felt the growth of an intellectual passion.

George Eliot's scene is too lofty for what happened in the lobby at Cockburn but my experience was part of the same universe.

Higher School Certificate came along and still we were most of us vague about what happened next. There was a girl, the daughter of a master, who was being given special coaching for Oxbridge. I recall no suggestion that others might have that. It was probably a sensible but certainly a drear decision: scholarships were few and not comprehensive; it was practical to think that most of us could not find the extra money needed for Oxbridge and we might have been miserable in one of those colleges as a result.

Miss Jubb's inspired illustration – that 'professional life' could mean training to be a doctor or parson – had stayed in Grandmother's mind and I may have been told to ask about prospects. They were of course limited. Work for a medical degree, for example, was long and required considerable financial topping-up from the family. One very gifted girl, who seemed easily the cleverest of us, found that two years at teacher training college were her only outlet. I expect her own children went to university in the early Sixties, if she had anything to do with it.

At Cockburn in the last weeks before the HSC examinations the word had gone round that if you did very well indeed you might 'go to university'; which meant to Leeds University. The City gave Senior City scholarships to university each year; Leeds University records 47 in 1936. The population of Leeds was then about 490,000. Assume that 7,000 to 8,000 of those were eighteen years old in 1936; then between one in 150 and one in 170 got scholarships. Add the disparities in opportunities by social class, the number of extra hoops working-class children had to jump through, the increasing height and decreasing diameter of those hoops at each stage, the loading against our kind of people by geography as well as by class. It is at this point that someone always says: 'There we go again, relating everything to class. Most of these inequalities have been eradicated today.' That is not true. Much has been done, many big efforts made, and there have been more breakings-through. But the main correlations of family, district, money, class and early education with intellectual, academic and professional opportunities remain very strong.

I did well in HSC and soon after had a letter saying I had been accepted by the Department of English at Leeds University. I do not remember having been interviewed for a place. I suppose my helpful English master had said at some point: 'You look like getting to university, Hoggart. You want to do' (not 'read') 'English, don't you?', and that I said: 'Yes, sir' and it went down on a form somewhere.

So the gateways opened further, the ways out progressively unrolled. One more individual, like a more than usually tenacious tadpole heading for the surface, tail working like mad, driven by a mixture of social and personal pressures, had worked his way up the system to this next point of entry. Nothing very grand, only Leeds University in the mid-Thirties; but to Hunslet as strange as if the Great Auk had broken out of its shell there. When I think of all those of good intelligence left behind stage by stage I feel like echoing Granville-Barker: 'Oh, the waste of [them] . . . oh, the waste . . . the waste!' Or even more strongly, Empson: 'The waste remains, the waste remains and kills.' Still today we should say that, far more than we wish to recognise.

Cockburn gave me, along with much else, the beginning of this basic insight: that the great majority of us carry round in our heads for good our three-dimensional pattern and picture, our slightly individual but largely socially given sense, of time and space and possibility – virtually untouched from when they first took shape. A thousand television series about different worlds and different ways of seeing the world apparently hardly penetrate; the cohesive power of the lived-into and the day-by-day is too great. I am not a strong intellectual, but what Cockburn started in me was the habit of questioning the world I had been previously offered, and that in turn reflected on my willingness or unwillingness to accept the world which Cockburn itself was offering. After a break like that you never again sit entirely or wholly at ease in your local culture, whatever the level of that culture may be – slum, semi, detached Tudor, Great House. You can make your peace with your native culture, can learn to be to some degree easy with it, may come to respect it; but you cannot again be an integral part of it, and that is not to be regretted; you have bitten the fruit.

Without feeling superior or scornful, listen directly and carefully to the conversations of men on a building site: the limited enthusiasms and dismissals, the endless repetitive arguments about the latest TV give-away show, or scandalous revelation in their newspaper – about royalty or sport or show biz – which assume they matter to more than the shallower reaches of experience, the equally endless and conventional sexual chit-chat, the routine bad language itself largely sexual in origin, the blinkered reactions to simplified political positions as presented by most of the popular press and peddled around the group. From all this you have been galvanised into breaking away. But those who have stayed there deserve better than that and are at bottom certainly not as daft as their daily commercial pabulum might suggest; nor are their conversations in themselves more conventional and repetitive than those in many a golf club. Chekhov's noble and respectful admonition to his countrymen is apt but unavailable to us: 'You live badly, my friends. It is shameful to live like that.' And still in both these locations and others like them you may find some whom the endless macaroni of fragmented and foolish information stewed in a tepid broth of received opinions has not prevented from arriving at their own kind of wisdom.

That was the last of Cockburn. When I think of the place I see first the classrooms of the sixth form, with a teacher glad to have a small group of clever children and doing his or her best to introduce them to a wider world. I think second of walking home at about 4.15 or so in the middle of winter, when the street-lights have already begun to come on. I would look round as I finished crossing the clinkered 'Moor' and still see over the house-tops half a mile away the pale yellow glow of its classrooms and corridors and its cupolas standing up half silvery-grey in the near-darkness. It exercised as powerful a pull on my imagination as Oxford's dreaming spires on Matthew Arnold's or Christminster on Jude the Obscure's.

CHAPTER 8

UNIVERSITY

Leeds University developed from the Yorkshire College of Science which was founded in 1874. One of the main impulses behind the establishment at Leeds was the realisation by local manufacturers in the textile industry that in that industry and its associates Germany was going ahead faster. It is a familiar nineteenth-century story.

When I went up in the autumn of 1936, aged eighteen, there were just over seventeen hundred students (two women to every seven men), the majority local. Thirteen hundred came from nearby and of those three hundred and twenty-four from Leeds. There were three easily identifiable, locally drawn groups. First, those whose presence recalled the origins of the University: such as the sons of West Riding mill owners studying textiles so as to take over the businesses, the gilded youth of West Yorks coming in from the hills each day in two-seater sports coupés, living at home for the time being now that they had finished with Giggleswick or Rossall or St Peter's. With that group were men and a few women, often the children of doctors, studying to be doctors themselves (over six hundred, one in six of them women), and technologists. Naturally, this group tended to have a large share of hearty types. With those locals there was in each discipline an admixture of foreign students: well-to-do Egyptians taking first degrees or doing postgraduate work in textiles, graduate technologists from India and the like.

The middle group were less well-to-do but their parents were able to pay the whole or part of the fees, or find charities which would pay: parsons' children from the Yorkshire Wolds; or such as the parson's son from a village near York with whom I shared a room for a year; and the children of teachers in grammar schools spread around the North. 'Locally drawn' can mean here a circle up to where the Durham-with-Newcastle University's catchment area began, west to the Pennines and into Manchester and Liverpool Universities' territories, east to the sea (the University College of Hull being minute then) and south to Sheffield's bailiwick; but the great majority came from very close to Leeds. There were no boundary rights; but there was an attraction to the local place if only because it was cheaper to go there, with a willingness to look more widely if there were money for residence.

The third group were the really local and the poorest, lower-middle class with some working class, and most in the Arts subjects. They were sometimes on scholarships or, much more numerous in the Humanities, recipients of government grants for intending teachers (RSTs, they were called – Recognised Students in Training) who took a first degree in their chosen subject and then a year of specific teacher training, usually in the University's own Department of Education. Heading for the most available of the soft professions, they had to sign a document agreeing to do 'x' years of teaching after their training or pay back some of the grant; but that was not always invoked in the Thirties since jobs were scarce. It is easy to see why those with scholarships, with no such strings, were regarded as in a more favoured league.

Members of this third group came to the University each day on the tram from parts of Leeds itself or from as far afield as Bradford, all of nine miles away. We tended to carry pressed cardboard attaché cases from Woolworth's or a Market stall, to wear sports jackets, flannels and pullovers; and to be clean-shaven. Anoraks, rucksacks and beards were a quarter of a century away.

The University thought very well of itself and with some justification. At a time when Professorships were rare right across the country even a provincial university could appoint people of considerable distinction. That would go without saying in the technological and scientific fields for which Leeds had become celebrated; it was also true in the Arts or Humanities: the Professors of English were a line of heavyweights, often more linguistic than literary, who usually went on or back to Oxbridge. They developed eccentricities consonant with their professional *personae*. The History professor, Alexander Hamilton-Thompson, had a high international reputation for scholarship, and local fame for oddities of delivery and corny repeated stories; his wife acted as foil on social occasions; that sort of thing was typical not only of Leeds, but of all such universities. The Professor of Philosophy, John Harvey, was a gentle Quaker who enjoyed dressing up to be a Special Policeman in his spare time. He was so bumbling in delivery that I fell asleep in one of his afternoon tutorials as he rambled on about Berkeley and perception. That allowed him to illustrate and develop his point by tapping me on the head so that I perceived again. There were only two of us reading subsidiary Philosophy that year; it would have been difficult to fail.

The public summit of the University's grandeur was the figure of the Vice-Chancellor, who lived in a large 'Lodge', with servants, a mile or two out and was driven in each day in a Rolls-Royce. One of his successors, Edward Boyle, decided to dispense with the Vice-Chancellor's car (not by that time a Rolls or anything approaching one in splendour and cost), and used public transport, or taxis at a pinch; but that was in the late Seventies. Carried in anything less grand than a Rolls, Sir James Baillie would have looked as though he was by chance hitching a lift with a lesser member of staff. He was full-faced, broadcloth-garbed, silver-haired. And silver-tongued. He paid an annual visit for dinner to the Hall of Residence I joined. He addressed us after the meal and always in the same vein. He told us that he could not have eaten better at the Athenaeum . . . or perhaps it was the Savoy. I don't know how accurate the claim was though on the few occasions I have been there the food at the Athenaeum hasn't been much to write home about. We did wonder whether the rubicund Sir James ever realised that we got a very special dinner when he was coming. His wife struck the female equivalent of his range of chords and interested herself particularly in the young ladies, none of whom were allowed to live in external lodgings, at least during their first-degree courses. Above all, she concerned herself with the propriety of the girls' manners and behaviour; she occasionally appeared on the sports field to admonish those who had bare legs there. It was one of her maids who copulated in the cellars of the Lodge, during her tea-break, with a painter-and-decorator acquaintance of mine from Hunslet. 'Ooh! What would Lady Baillie think!' the girl cried with nervous glee as they reached the climax among the wine and coal.

The sense of the importance of their *alma mater* stayed with graduates who had made good at Leeds, as it did in similar provincial places. The Parkinson building which has by now dominated that part of the Leeds skyline for about fifty years testifies to the piety and gratitude of one such graduate, Frank Parkinson, who became – his firm was Crompton Parkinson, the electrics people – a great industrialist with a world-wide reputation.

The University took such things as no more than was due to it. Its sense of consequence was copper-bottomed; and still is. When being interviewed for the Vice-Chancellorship Sir Edward Boyle was grilled in a way which suggested that he might be merely wanting a perch from which to swan off to London two or three days a week. He was reminded of the importance of Leeds University and the need for the Vice-Chancellor to give it all his time and attention. Boyle had been a distinguished Under Secretary of State for Education and Science, but in his characteristically modest and charitable way mused later that he fully understood why they felt the need to make that point. Given his professional record, I thought such a warning misjudged; but it was typical of Leeds University and Yorkshire in its directness and sensitivity to the possibility of being upstaged or taken for a ride by Southerners.

The years from my time up to the full establishment of maintenance grants for students, after the war, were the final years of the truly local universities and we have seen their passing with little recognition of what they were, at their best. I am thinking here of their relationship to the local communities. The fact that many of the Leeds students went back each night to the streets of the city or to townships around, or slipped at weekends to their homes in the Ridings, ensured that the University was felt to be part of the area in a way not easy to bring about today; its affairs and events were talked about in homes all around and became part of the folklore and fabric of day-by-day life. Local bigwigs might also think these universities their institutions, and those expectations had to some extent to be catered for in deference accorded; but the fact that the Local Authority did not, to more than a minor extent, provide the funds, meant that each university had its independence. At its best this situation – it was not a system in a deliberately planned overall sense – did give the University an organic relationship with its city and its area which inspired loyalty and made people feel they too could have, already had, an international-class educational institution; not just house one within their boundaries but *have* one. That needs saying even though one believes, as I do, that the introduction of maintenance grants was all in all an inspired invention.

The most important effect of the maintenance grants was that, as university entrance expanded, tens of thousands of young people left home, from areas whose members had rarely moved before, who did not send their children away to public school and Oxbridge. Before that they had been, in a neutral sense of the word, parochial in their habits and expectations. Some liked their new towns so well they sought jobs there after graduation. Much more important, the process created inter-region marrying on a large scale and in parts of society where it had previously been rare. This was the greatest social effect and, on balance, gain. But since working-class adolescents were still, even after the great increase in university places, under-represented, the increased movement affected them less than other groups.

All that was after the war. Before the war, skilled workmen would sometimes be sent on jobs further afield, find digs and, when they got back, talk about those areas as though they were inhabited by quite different kinds of people: 'Down there, yer know, they only drink Mild. An' they don't know what 'igh tea is. The women are smart, though.' Historically the main agent in pushing working-class people, predominantly the men, to movement around the country and abroad had long been war. Gossips would go on registering for many years afterwards that so-and-so's wife was an outsider since he had met her when he was in camp many miles away. Just as our own father and mother had met.

After some months at home with Aunt Ethel I managed, as I have said, to find a grant to enter a Hall of Residence. That transformed the business of day-by-day living: a warm room, no constant watchfulness and ever-present threat of nagging, a short walk to the University. At the start managing was hard but I did manage, as no doubt others just as hard up did.

The atmosphere at Devonshire Hall was above all amiable. Not socially sophisticated in the ways some Vice-Chancellors might have wished, in no way genteel; but not brutish or hearty either; civil and friendly, rather. Frank Smith, the Johnsonian plump Professor of Education who ran it, must have been largely responsible for establishing that atmosphere. He ate with us at the High Table of the large Dining Hall each weekday evening; I do not remember his ever treating us to disquisitions and admonitions on the nature of the civilised life; he seemed in his quiet way to exhibit aspects of such a life himself. He knew his residents more closely than we always guessed. At supper one night in 1940 I told him that I didn't yet know whether I would be drafted into the armed forces or into the pits. Smith said, with his usual dry mildness: 'If it's the pits, heaven help the miners. He'll talk their heads off.'

He did not seek to subvert the system so that when, early in 1939, a senior student whom he was known to like and respect was found in bed in his room with a girl, Smith knew the incident could not be ignored. But he was a humane man and offered the culprit the choice of being sent down or going into the Militia, and coming back to the Hall to finish his course after his six months' service (presuming no war) – our equivalent of 'go out and govern New South Wales.' And then come back to the fold.

At an early tea-party for freshers I had noticed a girl in a brown silk dress who looked very attractive; but I was entirely incapable of going up and introducing myself. I had never taken a girl out. She proved to be reading English also so we were in the same group day after day. It took me until the middle of the second term to find the nerve to ask her out and that was clumsily done on the steps of the Brotherton Library (another gift from a grateful graduate). We went to the Paramount cinema to see *Green Pastures* and, I think, each paid for our own seat. Somewhat hesitantly, because of shyness on both sides, the relationship took root and had soon transformed our lives at university; and for ever after. For me, it provided a focus of affection from and for one person; and incidentally broadened the capacity to make other friends, to become more sociable. I find it hard to imagine what university life would have been like without that relationship.

It was a modest enough way of going on: no pubs, no wine, cheap or otherwise; but occasional visits to the cinema and occasional fish-and-chips or just chips before we set off for the women's Hall of Residence at Weetwood, a couple of miles up the road past mine; then, for me, back on the tram or on foot. That was an evening routine after working quite late in the library.

Sometime in the third term I was taken home. That was in Stalybridge, thirty-odd miles away in alien Lancashire territory over the Pennines. I hitch-hiked on one of the wool-waggons which constantly crossed those hills on the old A635 over Saddleworth Moor. Mary was an only child so only Mum and Dad were waiting, as nervous as I was. It was a Sunday so we were all in our best; Dad played with the watch-chain draped across his waistcoat until he settled down. It was a neat and well-kept house as befitted the headmaster of an elementary school with a wife who had also been a schoolteacher.

Doris and Harry France were quiet people, not adventurous, a little timid before life, but honest and unmalicious, steady church-goers, acting according to very decent principles. I soon respected and loved them and so did our children. For them, quite late in life, to have three loving grandchildren, and a daughter and son-in-law living lives of much greater variety and movement, was to have horizons open which they had not known or imagined; and they took quiet pleasure in it all without giving the slightest sign of feeling either envious or boastful; in that part of Lancashire to have a son-in-law who taught at university would have been thought grounds for crowing by some people.

Father had been a poor boy from a largish family. He worked his way up through pupil-teaching to Chester Church of England Teacher Training College in the middle of Edward VII's reign, went back to his old school and slowly rose to be head of it. His one great excursion was to the 1914–18 War where, in the trenches on the Somme as an infantryman with the Lancashire Fusiliers, he was hit in the foot by shrapnel and invalided out. He never wished to go abroad again; for him, as for so many like him, foreign parts were dreary pock-marked fields. Until Mary was able to go on holidays without them, they went each summer to the same boarding-house at Cleveleys for several weeks and, they always said, felt much better for it. It was in many respects a 'who sweeps a room as for thy laws' life.

Once when we were staying there during the Christmas vacation, I asked if I could borrow one of Father's non-fiction library tickets (he read one travel book after another, sitting by the fire after an economically thought out but very palatable tea) so as to get out a book on Shakespeare which I needed for some lectures I was preparing. He was startled. He told me he would support me in an application for temporary membership of the library but that since his tickets said 'Non-transferable' it would be wrong to lend me one of them. Most people today would think that an over-rigid, letter-of-the-law or timid reaction and in some ways it was. But it came straight from the grain of his being, from his kind of uprightness and probity.

Until he died, we went there for Christmas; after that, our home became the Christmas HQ. At Stalybridge's Christmas dinner there were, as drinks for six adults (an uncle and aunt were always there), two bottles of beer and a large lemonade, to make shandy. Towards the end of the meal one year there was a little of each left and my wife suggested we drink them. 'Now Mary,' said her father, 'don't you go haphazard at that liquor.' He always steered straight and undeviating. So much so that having taught his original kind of maths with great success for forty years and ignored all fashions, he saw his type come into favour again not long before he retired.

The atmosphere in our 'year' (the group of twenty-odd studying English) was like that in the Halls of Residence, friendly but not intellectually very bracing. Most of us assumed we would become teachers, preferably in a pleasant part of Yorkshire; and tended to leave the competitive fighting to the few high-flyers. Enthusiasm for literature was more evident and powerful than a disposition to acquire sharp intellectual critical tools. We did talk a lot; and drank hardly any alcohol.

We went hiking as a group at weekends in those of the Dales which were easily reachable by tram or bus; we sometimes went to the theatre in a group. We enjoyed the English Society's 'readings' of plays. At those the lecturer who was helping might come along with sandwiches for all prepared by his wife. Perhaps banana-and-walnut sandwiches; rather different from tinned sardines, so we began to see that there were more than three possible fillings for a sandwich or teacake. Or a tutor who had decided to keep a helpful eye on us would, on special occasions, open the cupboard below a bookcase in his room and offer us a sherry.

Obviously, Leeds did not have as large a range of interesting intellectuals and eccentrics as Oxford or Cambridge. It was much smaller and more geographically recruited. Herbert Read had enrolled just before the First World War. I saw him one day in 1937, peering like a shy crane round the door of Professor Bonamy Dobrée's study; he retreated quickly when he saw our small seminar group. Storm Jameson also read English a decade later. Like other provincial English departments, Leeds clung tenaciously to the memory of those who had gone on to great things. In our day the brightest became newspaper editors, academics, writers, actors and actresses. They were the ones who could, if you chose to attach yourself to them, take you from the warm embrace of your 'year' and point to a more tonic and demanding world, much larger than Leeds and Yorkshire and right outside the particular time.

Of them all, our favourite was Tom Hodgson, a slender, good-looking, smiling, quiet and courteous student two or three years ahead of us, rightly much loved by the staff. He never showed off but his intelligence could be called luminous if that means it shone clearly but not aggressively from him. He fell in love with a beautiful red-head from our group, went to Cambridge on the best post-graduate scholarship of the year and began a study of Nathaniel Lee. The war came and he was killed in a bomber over Germany, leaving behind a volume of poems, *This Life, This Death*, which his widow saw through the press.

Only a few years ago someone told us she had long since remarried, a businessman in London; and a year or so afterwards someone else told us she had died. A whole life – a first love, great grief, a remaking, and a death – all seen as a handful of snapshots and seeming so brief in retrospect as to require no more than that; not for any of us.

Another more flamboyant personality threw into relief the official political idiocies of the time. He was a socialist and may have been a communist. He had a great shock of hair, large horn-rimmed glasses and a mouth which looked built to orate against the wind. The Spanish Civil War was being fought and some of us spent time collecting in aid of Milk for Spain or trying to help the trickle of, mainly Basque, refugees. The orator was suddenly arrested by the Special Branch and charged with seeking to persuade an airman to desert by flying his plane to Spain to help the Republican cause.

The prosecution claimed the proposal had been made in the buffet at Leeds City Station, of which the Queen's Hotel and its famous tea-lounge are part; presumably one was meant to think that the student hung around the place looking for servicemen in transit. (That buffet was used for the prospect of chance meetings – by homosexuals – and for odd assignations. I once met a man there who had just come up from London and was going back on the next train. He wanted me to join the International Brigade and go out with the next batch.) The airman pretended to fall in with the student's proposal, went back to base and reported it.

What were the rights and wrongs? Was the student an agent for the Republicans, someone the Special Branch had been watching for months? Was the airman set up as bait? We thought the student might have made a proposal, though on his own initiative; he had a scattily romantic revolutionary mind. I doubt if he did so on more than that one occasion; but once was enough. The government of the day was extremely nervous about attitudes to the Spanish Civil War, nervous and double-thinking. So they over-reacted and set in motion the full heavy machinery of the law; the student was brought up at Leeds Assizes.

We demonstrated outside the Town Hall and wrote to George Bernard Shaw asking for a statement of support. He wrote back that the student deserved all he would get for being so inept in his radicalism and that a period in gaol might help him sort things out better. The sentence was nine months, lenient if it had been felt that there was a real case of incitement to high treason, so I guess they didn't think that; but they presumably meant to deter other student hotheads. As kack-handed a public exercise as that sending of half a dozen bombers over the main urban centres. I believe the victim then passed his working life in the Civil Service; four decades afterwards he wrote to me asking how his son might become a late entrant to university.

My closest acquaintance among the university's budding intellectuals and artists was a vicar's son from a great grimy church in Holbeck. He was bent on being a poet and so, like me but more frequently, put poems in the students' magazine, *The Gryphon.* I wrote one about Christ, I suspect the result of reading Lawrence's 'The Man Who Died'. (In the Seventies an academic critic enquiring into the New Left went through back numbers of the magazine, came upon that poem, deduced the initials were mine and decided it showed that at that time I was moving from a Marxist to a Christian phase; or the reverse.) Jocelyn, the vicar's son, and I decided to write a poem jointly. 'Torpid Python' owed a lot to Blake's *Songs of Innocence and of Experience* and to Dylan Thomas, in its style rather than its substance. Symbolically, it included some lines on ejaculation, though I'm not sure either of us realised that:

> Then it bedded the snake,
> Couched spotted in its cerements, that coughed and spat
> And jerked itself to rest

The celebrated and eccentric History professor, who acted as a sort of Lord Chamberlain to the journal, banned our poem; or perhaps his wife did. On quality, it deserved banning; but I expect they had sex in mind.

Jocelyn's father, the vicar, must have been a fellow-seeker with our headmaster at Cockburn, for he too decided to go into a monastery; his wife was dead and the poet his only child. He gave his son a blessing and about thirty bob or two pounds a week (just adequate) and left. Jocelyn hired a handcart and we trundled his possessions from the south through the centre to Blenheim Road up near the University. He claimed that the best way to carry his dressing-gown was to wear it, but I knew and he knew and he knew I knew, so we both enjoyed it, that his object was to stimulate the citizens of Leeds and especially the young ladies who worked in town. He wrote and occasionally ate and entertained, but did not attend to his studies, in a seedy attic set up to suggest *La Vie bohème* done into a Yorkshire idiom. He claimed he left a few French letters hanging up as if to dry on a small line in the room, so that his girl visitors would be under no illusions.

He was determined and full of initiative and got himself down to London from time to time to make contact with those ex-Leeds literati, such as Rayner Heppenstall, who might be able to help him float on literary waters. Most of the staff thought he was an unsaveable exhibitionist but a few stood by him including, inevitably, Bonamy Dobrée. His determination and initiative were fully engaged in the war. He had a distinguished war career fighting with the Partisans in Yugoslavia and came home with a beautiful Yugoslav wife and a decoration; I believe she died early; I have long since lost touch with him.

My own emerging intellectual life had three main focusses: politics, documentary and poetry. The politics were socialist, as they still are, and the chief agents were: the *New Statesman*, to every budding intellectual from the working-class the key *vade mecum*; the Left Book Club, which had conveniently begun in 1936 – we borrowed the monthly volumes from better-off students; and the University Socialist Society. Plus lectures at the University and in town from famous figures anxious to warn us about the coming conflict; most memorably, Norman Angell, sponsored by Montague Burton, speaking to a crowded Town Hall.

Penguins and Pelicans were a main, perhaps the main force. I bought my first Penguin at sixteen; it was the first novel too. Never before had it seemed possible to buy a new copy of a novel and these were novels which excited us: *A Farewell to Arms, Chrome Yellow, Fontamara*. Sixpence. Pelicans were at least as exciting as novels, especially since they had a non-Establishment feel: Tawney's *Religion and the Rise of Capitalism*, Freud's *Psychopathology of*

Everyday Life, Mowrer's *Germany Puts the Clock Back*. These are simply the first that come to mind.

That reading, and a growing interest in social observation, led to the documentary in film or prose. Week after week I and others like me read, in little magazines, usually as we leant against a pillar in a long-suffering bookshop, accounts of life down the pit by coalface workers, on the army by dissident recruits, or on the farm by underpaid labourers in tied cottages. We followed John Grierson's films around and were particularly taken by *Night Mail* and Auden's commentary. We devoured anything *Mass Observation* put out.

Poetry was for me the main love. More than one of our tutors introduced us to T. S. Eliot, especially 'The Waste Land'. It was already a decade and a half old, but we liked to repeat the story that over in Manchester the Head of the English Department still asked students who brought Eliot into a discussion: 'Who is this man?' The short-lived *Twentieth Century Verse*, at sixpence rising to a shilling by 1939, was a bargain even for those days and brought our first Dylan Thomas. The political poets around Auden – or so we saw them – were like the First Eleven of a team we would have loved to join but doubted we could. It was important to find our own favourites in addition to the obvious names of Auden, Spender, Day Lewis and the powerful outsider MacNeice. I therefore frequently quoted Kenneth Allott:

> From this wet island of birds and chimneys
> who can watch suffering Europe and not be angry?
> for death can hardly be ridiculous,
> and the busking hysteria of our rulers,
> which seemed so funny to our fathers,
> dirties the newsreels for us.

On the day in September 1938 when Neville Chamberlain came back from Munich waving his piece of paper and saying this meant 'peace in our time', I had cycled to Aunt Ethel's. I said, as all around at the University did, that we'd been deceived and war or more appeasement would come. It was all plain to a twenty-year-old but not to her. I pedalled out of the storm. It wasn't something you could sweetly reason away.

So the months passed, the months of 'crisis and dismay'. Auden's 'September 1, 1939', later the victim of one of his characteristic and, many of them, regrettable excisions, seemed at the time to speak with peculiar power:

> I sit in one of the dives
> On Fifty-Second Street
> Uncertain and afraid
> As the clever hopes expire
> Of a low dishonest decade;
> Waves of anger and fear
> Circulate over the bright
> And darkened lands of the earth,
> Obsessing our private lives;

There was something fashionable about many of the interests I've mentioned and I do not think they were of the first importance in developing such intellectual grasp as I may have. I eventually left the University with a First Class degree but was still intellectually and imaginatively half-baked. I could jump the fences as required and give a passable imitation of understanding. Yet I stood in a field in North Africa in 1942, reading *Macbeth* from a tattered edition found in some barracks, and felt for the first time the impact of Shakespeare. I told my colleagues as of a revelation; they knew I had a degree in literature and must at the least have wondered why it had taken until then and that unlikely place for me to discover the power of a work by one of the few great literary names they knew. It was as though, to get through to the point at university at which you sat those eight or nine papers on different periods and genres, you could not allow the force of the works to flood into you; you might have been pushed off course. Or as though someone writing about many varieties of physical love had suffered powerful but temporary inhibitions in the practice of it. You did not for those three years dare to release yourself to the power of the works; you controlled your responses to them, almost unconsciously.

For me, the intellectual shocks which prompted new directions came chiefly from personal contacts such as the one with the headmaster of Cockburn over the Hardy essay. At Leeds University the main agent, the direct successor of the headmaster of Cockburn, was the Head of Department, Bonamy Dobrée. He deliberately set out to disturb your preconceptions by time and again putting little spokes into your mental bicycle wheels as you tried to make them go grinding steadily along. More important, he had a rare capacity for seeing what particular students of promise might need at particular moments in their lives. Thus he directed me in my second year to *The Education of Henry Adams*. I read it at first with little interest; until I came to passages such as this (Adams is speaking of his own university education, at Harvard):

In effect, the school created a type but not a will. Four years of Harvard College, if not successful, resulted in an autobiographical blank, a mind on which only a water-mark had been stamped.

The stamp, as such things went, was a good one. The chief wonder of education is that it does not ruin everybody concerned in it, teachers and taught. Sometimes in after-life, Adams debated whether in fact it had not ruined him and most of his companions, but, disappointment apart, Harvard College was probably less hurtful than any other university then in existence. It taught little, and that little ill, but it left the mind open, free from bias, ignorant of facts, but docile.

The graduate had few strong prejudices. He knew little, but his mind remained supple, ready to receive knowledge.

A New England Brahmin, the descendant of two American Presidents, writing towards the end of the previous century, Adams spoke with a rare directness and relevance. I was drawn to the soft-shoe precisions and dry pawkiness of his prose and the way he distanced himself from himself. An odd, withdrawn, pursed-up book, it worked at levels I hardly knew and in three main ways. Its themes, especially the stresses of cultural change, appealed to some still inchoate interests. Its wrestlings with the problems of form in this kind of writing – how to handle the interplay of personal experience and public meanings – helped on a similar search because it reinforced the feeling that it was worth doing. Its stances and tones before life – a narrow but subtle range of voices – were notes from the New World which chimed with some in native writers, such as Arnold and Hardy, to whom I was already attached. Adams had a tonic scepticism towards Europe, particularly Britain: 'The British mind is the slowest of all minds; in the brain of a typical Englishman of the Establishment there is a thick cortex of fixed ideas.'

He was, and made me realise that in our own less superior way people like myself were, between two worlds, among Matthew Arnold's wanderers. That was much of his attraction, a distanced attraction but always readable and often unforgettable. Whilst re-reading Adams, not long ago, I was also reading Bertrand Russell's autobiography. In comparison, Russell, for all his dialectical brilliance, seemed brittle, and a brittle observer of his own life and the life around him. Adams had a painful honesty towards himself; he held himself up as if with tongs from a distance, not all that enchanted with what he held; he was self-conscious and self-aware to a degree which sometimes seems masochistic and recalls T. S.

Eliot, who was in some ways a fellow-spirit. Adams was also very clever, acutely analytical and very tough in the pursuit of the kind of truth which most preoccupied him.

I did not understand all this at a first reading and Dobrée knew I would not: he guessed I would take something from the book which would bring into use yet another corner of the mind, and he was right. I still wonder at the perceptiveness which made him guess that that book might be right for me at that time, and at the assumption that it was part of his job to look out for such things on behalf of individual students.

University vacations were a problem since I did not have enough money simply to study then. I did go to one conference, in the Christmas vacation of my first year, of Christian Socialist students, held at Birmingham University; Leeds University Socialist Society paid for me as their representative. I did not justify their expenditure since I kept silent in the meetings, being surrounded by articulate students many of whom already had the lineaments of budding bishops; much as, in reverse, Head Boys tend to continue looking like Head Boys for years and years afterwards, sometimes into retirement.

The only other aspect of that conference I now remember was my first encounter with the fully-fledged. Oxford intellectual style of the time, though I do not think it has greatly changed. The 'keynote' speaker was Richard Crossman, then coming up to thirty and a star public performer among Oxford philosophy dons. I do not know if he was a Christian then; if so, he should have been billed as a muscular Christian since he was certainly an intellectual bruiser, full of aggressive confidence, sharp-edged. This came over from his platform manner. I did not meet him then, but a quarter of a century later, when he was one of Labour's Shadow Ministers, he was the only one of that Shadow Cabinet to suggest a meeting to discuss the Pilkington Report on Broadcasting. I met him gladly. His manner had not changed: the same air of total confidence, the same enjoyment in a dialectics which worked so easily because it ignored, elided, was not prepared to consider, the cultural complexities which Pilkington had at least tried to get a hold on.

More often at university, vacations were the time for getting paid work. I began, in the first long vacation, by being taken on as a dispatch-clerk to a long-distance haulage firm which did a nightly run from Newcastle to London with a stop at Leeds; and the reverse. The depot was a windy, dingy little place under the railway arches near the centre of town but it had a big old stove so, with an overcoat, you could be quite comfortable. The pay was low but there wasn't much work. You came on at nine, sometime later the down-truck pulled in, the driver unloaded stuff and took on other – and tried to fiddle by hurrying you up so that you signed for more than he had dropped off; in the early hours the up-lorry arrived and the procedures were repeated. You cleared off about six. Otherwise you were, with one exception, alone, so I read most of *The Iliad*.

The exception was that the local tarts, especially one called Irene whom I mentioned in *The Uses of Literacy*, had long had the habit of coming in when trade was slack, for a warm:

> And the whores dropping in for a word or two in passing,
> For a flip word, and to tidy their hair a bit.

Ezra Pound's were idealised whores, or perhaps he met a better class. Most of the Leeds whores were well over thirty, not what you could call fresh-looking, and grumpy. Hardly a word; this white-faced youth reading a book, this temporary clerk, was of no interest. Maybe they had struck up a talkative relationship with the regular man but I doubt if they had much 'flip' speech at any time and with anyone; you don't if your feet are hurting and you are wondering whether there's enough chance of another customer that night to make it worthwhile hanging on at draughty corners. Still, mine was quite an enjoyable job or at least not positively unpleasant; and the isolation was a boon.

Summer camps always needed helpers so I had a succession of those. There was a hilarious one at Herne Bay, set up to provide a free holiday to poor boys from the East End. The camp leader was a hearty, casual, plump man of about thirty; one wondered if he was homosexual. He was not: he went alone to the local pubs each night, picked up a girl and took her on the beach; or so he said as he checked that he had a supply of French letters before he left the other two of us to look after things. He regaled us on his return. As with the story of a girl whose knickers were held up by a large safety-pin; and dropped straight on to the sand the moment he embraced her.

The boys in his charge were not obstreperous though I don't know why they weren't. The food was ample and full of flavour, especially the local butcher's sausages, which surpassed any I have since tasted. The boys slept in bell tents, feet towards the centre pole. I asked the leader why we couldn't let them sleep longer instead of getting them up and out on a pre-breakfast run at 6.30. 'What!' he roared, 'have them wake up with their bloody great piss-proud knobs and leave them to it? They'd be tossing themselves off every morning; and each other.' Herne Bay for me is a tapestry of tales of pubs full of willing girls with large, quick-release safety-pins, magnificent sausages and little Cockney lads being taken on runs through the early morning Kentish mist so as to prevent masturbation.

Work for that Christian body, the YMCA, at a Territorial Army camp in Northumberland during another long vacation, had no such charms. Helpers were extremely poorly paid, expected to work very long hours without extra pay or time off in lieu, and the food was indifferent. The man in charge was a pious pompous fellow with an obsequious attitude towards the soldiery. We served cheap tea, sandwiches and cakes to the amateur soldiers who had all been sent up there to do their annual summer training. No booze in a YMCA canteen. But the men were well in pocket and most got a skinful each night at the camp bar. For some the fortnight was a succession of such binges and picking up members of the ATS, the women's service, and local girls. They then rolled over to us for the cheap food, and we stayed open late to serve them.

I do not know whether the YMCA's organisers ever examined the confused thinking which made them believe it worthwhile to provide such a service by exploiting student labour. I told the man in charge that I thought they should pay better wages, if necessary by charging the soldiers more since they had so much to spend on beer, give us time off when we had worked very late and probably shut earlier anyway since there were no good grounds for staying open to serve drunks just before they fell into bed. Mercifully, he did not remind me that the labourer is worthy of his hire; but he was outraged, muttered something angrily about Christian Service to men themselves serving their King and Country, and shot back to the counter and his obsequious relations with the customers. After two such challenges he suggested, much in the manner of an abbot telling a postulant that he seemed to lack vocation and should leave, that if I felt like that perhaps I had best go. Which I did, glad to be clear of the slimy situation. The fat fornicator of Herne Bay was greatly preferable to the pompous Holy Roller.

There was a complex little cameo of Yorkshire styles – some of the less attractive ones – when I applied for work on a farm a mile or two beyond Harewood and its Great House. An advertisement in the *Yorkshire Evening News* or *Post* said simply that the farmer was looking for student help. His reply to my letter told me to go at 5.30 on a certain evening to a printing works in Armley, near Aunt Ethel's where I was living at the time. The elderly owner and his son of about thirty came out and invited me to get into the back of a Riley, one of the swisher cars of the day. They talked all the way to the farm and offered not a word to me; I might as well have been a packet, or a dog they had been asked to pick up as a favour to the farmer. Insensitive but interesting since their blindness to my presence also included the assumption that I was deaf or not worth considering as an eavesdropper. So I heard about how they conducted their business (sharpish), how enchanted they were with the new car ('Did seventy all the way from the boundary, Dad') and what splendid meals the farmer's wife provided. The owner was a widower and he and his son had set up some time before as long-stay paying guests at the farm we were bound for.

We arrived; with the minimum of words they directed me to the kitchen, and disappeared to prepare to do justice to whatever was filling that kitchen with a most appetising smell. The farmer's wife looked like someone who would be kind if her husband let her; but from her hesitant manner he plainly did not. He entered and was immediately recognisable as Mr Squeers' half-brother gone into farming. Mean farmers all look mean, but mean Yorkshire farmers look as though they have come from Central Casting. If you gave them a guinea out of pure love they would bite it in front of you. He began to cross-examine me on my knowledge of farming, which was almost nil; I would have been just a pair of willing hands. After a short time he said brusquely: 'Eh, th'art no good to me. Ah wanted one o' them students 'oo'se studying agriculture and knows t' new methods.' He wanted cheap brain-picking, but meanness or cunning had led him not to make that clear, even in cosmetic prose, in his advertisement. He turned on his heel, but his wife irresolutely followed him and I heard her suggest that a bite might be offered and my bus fare back to Leeds. The bite was ruled out but he finally and grudgingly coughed up a bus fare, and I set off down the long track to the road to wait for the Harrogate to Leeds bus.

The most educative of all the vacation labours came in 1939, just before war broke out. I had finished the degree examinations, was waiting for results, knew I might soon be called up into the Militia, that Fred Karno's army which was to deter Hitler, but meanwhile had to have money. I found work helping to build blast walls, against bombing, at a hospital on the outskirts. The wards were long, narrow, single blocks with French windows at each of the ends. The blast walls were built a yard or so from the end windows. The men were a cheerful group and accepted easily this queer chap from the University who spoke so differently. Their own conversation was repetitive, boring and largely scatological; but I expected that.

It soon became clear that the bluff, hail-fellow-well-met boss who visited us every day or two in his Rover was fiddling. The right proportion of sand to cement to make a good mortar is known to any bricklayer. If you put in more sand you save money but the wall is less sturdy. The foreman, who no doubt got a back-hander, made sure we put in too much sand. Did the Local Authority Inspector know? He should have. Had he been framed by the boss? The men told me the practice was widespread, especially on Corporation jobs.

None of this was as revealing as the behaviour and role of the boss's son; that gave a first insight into what might be called the Lady Docker Syndrome, which runs through British life like a geological fault – the combination of show-biz, high-life vulgarity with popular newspaper exploitation which is known to titillate their readers. The son was supposed to be preparing to take over from his dad but in fact did virtually nothing. He appeared every few days in a nifty red two-seater sports car, sporting too a little moustache and brilliantined hair, a Don Ameche of the Leeds small-business world. He started to chat to the men and – this was the point at which the syndrome or fault revealed its strength – they lapped it up. They laid down tools and gathered round whilst he told of his latest sexual exploit. 'Eh 'eck,' they would say as the latest story unfolded, ''e's a right lad at getting 'is leg over, i'n't 'e.'

One story he liked enough, and so did they, to keep it as a running serial. He had, he said, struck up an affair with a dark-haired girl who worked on the ticket-desk at the Paramount cinema in the Headrow. She shared a flat with a friend and to that quite soon they repaired, and there had sexual intercourse on the rug in front of the electric fire, with the friend in the room. But, and this was the point which really excited the brickies, she was a bold girl and insisted on getting on top of him. A strange and wanton practice to most Leeds working-men and one they obviously found erotically very stimulating.

Before starting work at the road haulage firm that first long vacation I was required to ask permission to work instead of study from the Local Education Authority because I held one of their scholarships. A clerk passed me on to a more senior official who seemed surprised that anyone had read the terms and conditions of the grant. He disappeared, came back in three or four minutes and said the Director of Education – I think his name was George Guest – would see me. He put me through a very large and highly polished door and I faced an acre of carpet at the far end of which was a large shiny desk with a man, who seemed by comparison little, writing at it. I saw it all again five or six years ago, unchanged, and still looking big enough for the Prime Minister of a modest-sized country.

I was told, not asked, to come nearer by the grizzled and very short-cropped figure. My progress across the carpet was accompanied by his second utterance, question with injunction this time: 'Who do you think you are . . . a poet? Get your hair cut.' I ignored that, so he asked me about the work I proposed taking. 'Road haulage clerk! You won't last a week. Not with your build.' I told him I would and longer than a week. 'I tell you what', he said. 'Come back in a week and let me know how you've gone on. Off you go, lad.' The Director of Education as bluff Yorkshire mill-owner; another one from Central Casting.

I was back there a week later and swore the job was easy. He looked up from his blotter and asked as abruptly as always: 'Ever gone abroad?' No. 'Would you like to?' Yes. 'Well, come back in another couple of days, and tell me where, if I gave you thirty pounds, you'd go, how you'd travel and how long you'd be able to manage. Every detail, mind.' I was back next day with a plan to cycle to Harwich, leave the bike, cross to the Hook, take a train to Cologne and walk down the Rhine, with a side-trip to the Eifel. Youth hostelling, I could manage a month. He seemed as reasonably satisfied as he was ever likely to be, quizzed me about the Eifel, was amused that I wanted to see whether what the British chauvinist press was saying was true – that Nazi tanks there were of heavy-duty cardboard meant only to frighten the French; and told me to call in once back and tell him how I had gone on and, finally, to go there and then to the cashier's office next door. I was given thirty pounds.

I don't imagine he paid the £30 himself. Did he ask his committee chairman in advance? Or get himself whitewashed afterwards? Or had he freedom to spend amounts such as that on what seemed to him worthwhile initiatives, without asking anyone for approval before or after? He gave off a sense of decisiveness and freedom to manoeuvre, one of the Major-Generals in the Leeds Public Service.

The bike ride to Harwich was broken by a night in Ipswich. The boarding-house I found charged something like 1/6 a night bed and breakfast and wasn't worth a penny more. I shared a double bed with a large long-distance lorry driver, a mild man who went to sleep instantly. I was kept awake by itchings and bites. My torch showed the bed crawling with large black creatures, the first bed bugs I'd seen. I killed a few which spread their blood – my blood, I suppose – over the dirty-greyish flannelette sheets. The lorry driver woke, said he didn't mind, they always left him alone, and went to sleep again; I passed the rest of the night on a broken-down easy-chair in the bedroom.

I had met only the husband of the house on arrival, a wizened man who looked as if he kept ferrets; or should. The breakfast table was presided over by his lady, a huge dirty creature who did not move from her chair-of-state at the end. After we had washed at a tap in the yard, her husband served cheap bacon which seemed to have been cooked in rancid fat, and stewed tea; meanwhile she carried on a skin-creeping drip of what she imagined was polite conversation. Where on earth had she picked that up? Perhaps before she became fat and dirty she had been a servant in a well-to-do establishment. The whole bizarre scene was crowned by the grubby breakfast table setting: it held twenty-three cruets.

Cologne Station at about nine in the evening might have been bewildering. But as I cleared the barrier a young man appeared and asked in excellent English if he could help me. Within a very short time I was settled in a cheap but respectable room and he promised to appear in the morning to give what further help he could. It was clear from the questions he then asked about my proposed movements, from his concern that I should go only where he suggested and should keep in touch, as well as by indications that he knew something about me, that he had been waiting for me at the station. That the Nazis should get a university student to tail another just because the visiting student was an officer of his university's Socialist Society showed the obsessive and excessive conspiracy-theory-driven expenditure of time and effort on watching those who might be not of their persuasion which is typical of such régimes.

I shook him off and next morning started the walk down the Rhine. It began with a tiny but telling incident with a twin brother and sister which I will come to presently, and was, all in all, an interesting but lonely month. I did see the Eifel but no tanks, cardboard or steel. At the end, I cycled up England again and called on Aunt Annie in her council house; she at once rustled up my first substantial meal since I had left. The Director of Education seemed dryly pleased to hear about the trip and went so far as to say that I appeared to have 'done all right'. I don't know if he was a Yorkshireman; if not, he had totally taken over the rather stagey public *persona* which Yorkshiremen with a suitable platform like to affect: 'Ah'm a plain, blunt-spoken man but me word's as good as me bond, and me 'eart's in the right place, and if you live up to yer promises I'll see yer right . . .' – all of which was true of that Director of Education; he was a kind man.

He continued to be so, to me. Almost two years later, just before the Easter vacation of the final year, he sat next to Bonamy Dobrée at some official dinner. How's that young man going on who has to fend for himself, he asked. Dobrée told him I looked as though I would get a First but was overworking and tired and needed a break. Send him in, said the Director. So next day there I was again on the big carpet, with him asking what I would do if I had thirty or it may by then have been forty pounds. Go to Venice, I said, being anxious to see both that city and something of Italian Fascism in action. I got the money and two or three days later stepped out of the station in Venice to see headlines announcing Mussolini's invasion of Albania.

I had somewhere picked up the tip that the way to find a cheap room was to ask a porter at the station. I was led to the first narrow street on the left-hand side, to a bar at which the porter I had found used to drink away his tips between trains. I slept that week in a back bedroom, my bed curtained off from a double bed in which the proprietor's two mid-teens daughters slept. We exchanged not a word.

Venice was all I had hoped and even more. I lived on such things as a tin of sardines at sixpence and a bit of fruit; but I managed to save enough to go to opera at the Fenice. Back via Paris with a few hours' wait there for the London train, I had the equivalent of ninepence in French money, kept to buy a small sandwich and a coffee to see me through to Leeds. I went into a downstairs urinal but came out through the 'cabinet' exit and was asked for payment by the keeper of the gate. That would have spelt hunger for twenty-four hours so I summoned what I hoped was accurate French and said: 'Mais Madame, j'ai seulement pissé.' She glowered at me, hesitated as though she was checking for credibility this new excuse for not paying and then said both imperiously and contemptuously: 'Passez!'

Interesting how the business of looking into the memory is like turning over stones and being surprised by what scurries out, and also like making jigsaws out of at first apparently disparate items from remembered time and space. I have, I now realise, a strong memory for unsolicited acts of kindness and I hope my holding on to such things will count on Judgment Day, as Dostoevsky's Grushenka hoped the gift of an onion to a soul in Hell's lake of fire would stand her in good stead; a counterweight – for me – to that equally tenacious memory for unkindness, cuttings off, rejectings. No doubt that is due in part to self-pride; it doesn't have to emerge, no matter how difficult your particular circumstances may be, and has not in some people I know. I imagine an inherent quality can be fed by particular circumstances so that a naturally thin-skinned individual takes more than usually badly to being orphaned and separated from siblings. I am not complaining, just musing, paddling in uncomprehended waters. I have been very lucky since. A pity the skin remained so thin for so long, though; at an age when I should have been mentally robust enough to ignore it I could still find myself thrown into anger or even unhappiness by a careless act of rejection, even a trivial one. I may be part-exorcising that grip from the past by this account of the small incident at the Cologne hostel. I had talked a long time on the first evening with a young middle-class Englishman and his twin sister. They were a good-looking pair and their grooming made them even more physically attractive. They were friendly though they hadn't much wit in conversation; they seemed to find me good talkative company. The thought of going on with them next day did not occur to me.

The following morning we stood at the same time, though by chance, at the door of the Youth Hostel. 'Which side of the Rhine do you propose going down?' the brother immediately and crisply asked. It had the air of a prepared question and I realised he was staving off a non-existent risk. If I had been a pusher I would have responded: 'Which side are you going down?' so that he would have had to show his hand and risk my tagging on, or been plain rude and replied: 'Whichever side you aren't taking.' What I said was something like: 'I'd thought of the left' (or the right). Quick, like a door closing, he said: 'We are taking the other' and off they set, the sister silently acquiescent.

Obviously, they wanted to be alone, not to pick up odd bods, and feared I might wish to join them. It was done brutally but cleanly, neat but chilling, an object lesson in the peculiar kind of confident decisiveness taught at English public schools; or perhaps, to use the argument I have turned towards myself, it was in his nature. But it was not, after all, 'nice', as my grandma and aunts would have said. So yes, I do blame to some extent both him and the system which nurtured him and gave him those social weapons, and which he learned to use without question.

That is another instance of the way in which some people in the more secure levels of the English middle classes, for all their good manners and even suavity as needed, can be ruthless ('decisive' is the preferred word) when their interests great or small are threatened. I say 'great or small' because some people may be tempted to shrug off so small an incident, one involving people only just out of adolescence, as inadequate to bear the weight I am giving it. That would be a mistake. I have seen an upper-middle-class Major, in the immediate rear of a battlefield, most harshly dress down a young subaltern because he thought, mistakenly, that the interests and safety of his Battery were being compromised. The subaltern was a Nottingham grammar-school youth heading after the war for a teacher training college. It was a scene from *Brideshead Revisited* except that Waugh, though he registers the usual distaste for dirty fingernails and unpolished accents, does not convey the assured brutality of the class which thinks itself superior. But that instance, though poster-size, is no more telling than the story of the walk down the Rhine.

Such behaviour is not commonly found among working-class people because they do not have a sense of a large group beneath them whom they have come to assume they are to rule or boss, and because since all are in difficult circumstances they know they must stick together and help one another. There is plenty of brutality in working-class life. But it is different from a brutality which treats you as someone not entitled to the normal courtesies of social exchange. That continues. At simple everyday levels there is still a brusqueness in many middle-class people towards those they conceive to be socially below them, and this fact should not be blurred though it is the fashion to do so. It puts in their place, shows as false, assertions that we are all classless nowadays. Some of those who react most angrily against the idea that class feeling and class behaviour are still rife in England do so with conviction because the class-styles they themselves practise are so embedded in their backgrounds and training that they quite fail to recognise them; they seem like ordinary, neutral, normal ways of going about things.

To bring our books from one house to another, in a removal some years ago, I hired a van and put on my oldest clothes for the dusty operation. We turned into the unadopted lane at the end of which our new home lay, passing several largish houses behind high hedges. Suddenly a tweeded woman shot from her gateway and called out in a camp commandant's or crystal-cracking mama's voice: 'You do realise, do you, that this is a private road?' The same kind of rhetorical question as in the Pullman car incident. Except that this was less a question than an interdiction, delivered in, beyond any doubt, the voice she had since girlhood been programmed to produce for workmen of whatever sort – dustbin men, lorry drivers, postmen, shop-assistants; it was a tone of voice which indicated a hardly credible degree of insensitivity to the reality of other human beings who were not part of her own narrow group in this country at this period, a voice which carried the enclosed assumptions of her class, time and place.

What does one best do then? I leaned out and told her I knew it was a private road, since we had just bought the end house. She retreated at once, without apology; she did not know how to cope with that voice, a more 'educated' voice than her own, coming out of that appearance and that set of clothes. Perhaps I should have answered: 'Aye lass. Ah know it's private becos me an' t' missus 'ave bought bottom 'ouse for us and t'foster kids. T'black 'uns in particular is reight looking forward to playing football in t' garden.'

One can collect such instances like cigarette cards; no – like caricatured Happy Families cards. But one remains saddened that so many styles and tones suggest that, by the accident of birth or education or probably both, those who exhibit them are not only different from but superior to most others; and that those others can be given the cold shoulder not by physical assault but by tone of voice; no less than working-class people, these too are branded on the tongue. France has a more overt recognition of status differences but in practice combines that with a more demotic day-by-day style. The USA has gross inequalities coexisting with the ritualistic, egalitarian, 'have a nice day' banalities (which tourists meet more often than residents); but still tries to hold on to the idea that we are all in some important ways equal. Both countries have freer and less restrictive airs than Britain. We do move, but grindingly slowly, like a costive hippopotamus.

The name of Bonamy Dobrée has woven in and out of this chapter. The University gave me many things. Overwhelmingly the most important was the relationship that led to a marriage which, as I write, has lasted forty-five years. Next to that was the example of Dobrée. Other tutors were consistently helpful to me and to many others; but Dobrée made me one of his special charges. 'Helping to rub off the rough edges' was a favourite phrase for one part of his pastoral duties. A paternalistic phrase, but he did point to a sense of what you might do and become, without ever being pompous in the way he gave advice.

He was new to Leeds in my time and word soon got round that the University had acquired a rather more than usually colourful professor; he must have been then about forty-five. On the opening day of each session, the registration day, the University ran what was called 'The Freshers' Bazaar'. The Great Hall did look like a parish festival or church bazaar, or a bring-and-buy; it is Victorian Gothic and could well be a large chapel interior. There were great numbers of society stalls and club stalls. More important, there were tables for each department manned by members of the academic staff, where you signed on for your Honours and Subsidiary courses and in your confusion sought all the advice you could get.

When I reached the English Department table, that first registration day, Bonamy Dobrée was doing his stint at it. I was struck straightaway by his 'style', his 'presence', though I would not have used words such as those. He was unusually upright, especially for an academic, and brought to mind words and phrases which were still just in currency then: 'a military man' who 'bears himself well', that sort of thing. He had a heavy, well-clipped moustache, like those worn by decent majors in films about the First World War; he was slightly tweedy and smelt of pipe tobacco.

That makes him sound too heavy. He also had a kind of brightness. His hair helped: it was thick, long over his ears and brushed right back, but was already almost completely silver. He had a bright, bird-like eye and a quick smile which he used freely, partly to put you at your ease and also because he did enjoy being with students. To me his voice was the most remarkable thing about him. It was light and high-pitched and when it rose with enthusiasm took on a feminine ring. It was a mannered voice and in drab old Virginia Road, where the English Department occupied a Victorian terrace-house, as exotic as a flamingo's call. It was compounded of southern upper-class, Haileybury, and the regular army, all laced with the slightly nasal sing-song characteristic of Cambridge.

To us he seemed weighty, of course, as professors used to seem to undergraduates. I was immensely impressed by the number of books he owned and had read, by the range of his other affairs – he enjoyed being mixed up in some public matters – and by the brisk speed with which he handled all that. I was fascinated by the whole person or by those elements which made up the whole I constructed. I do not remember then or later seeking to imitate his manner or be like him in style except in some precise professional particulars which I began to notice after a few months. There was a lot in his self-presentation which seemed dubious to a Yorkshire adolescent; but he was always interesting and elegant in ways I had not seen before except in films.

I think he began to notice me, as a 'promising' student, towards the end of my first year. Somewhere about that time he stopped me and said he would like a word. By now I have forgotten just what had prompted him though I seem to remember, and this would be entirely in character, that he wanted to give advice based on a knowledge of some particular need I had. I do remember a small circumstance in that meeting because it was the first example of the contrasts in social habits which were again and again to be brought out as our acquaintance developed. We had run into each other on the half-landing and after stopping me he said: 'Hang on a minute. I must go in here for a pee.' I had a double reaction. My respectable working-class mind was slightly shocked. Professors shouldn't talk like that. Then my cynical teenager's outlook took over and asked: 'What's up? Is he trying to show he's unconventional?'

In the second year he began rather more deliberately to give me attention, to include me in the cluster of students from various years and more than one department who were under his wing. Since I was at that point the junior the others seemed grand and suave and self-assured. One was already organ-voiced and magisterial and was said to have London literary connections. He was lecturing in Romania at the beginning of the war, served there with SOE, and went on to a distinguished diplomatic career. Another became a leading national journalist and a literary man-of-affairs on the side. And there was the splendid Tom Hodgson.

Each year Dobrée picked one or perhaps two students like me to keep an eye on. We were probably the brightest in both the good and the limiting senses of that word. We were intelligent but likely to be quirky and offbeat, rather than steady and reliable. At our weakest we were bright rather than deep. Other members of staff gave an eye to other students according to their own interests and the students' particular talents. Dobrée always had more time for the creatively untidy than for the steadily reliable. I was on the whole a reliably hard worker and not particularly creative; he probably did not number me among his highest flyers but thought I was clever, dogged and doing well from a poor start.

He did not encourage what others – and he too for that matter – would have called a sloppy individualism; you could dress as you wanted but you had to try to keep your mind in good trim, whether you wanted to be a critic or a poet or a journalist or a diplomat. His fellow-professors did not always see this distinction. He was consistently something of a disciplinarian. It wasn't only in his carriage that you could still see the marks of the regular army officer. He never withheld saying what he thought was the right thing for fear of hurting your feelings. His principle was that hurt feelings can recover so long as the blow has not been malicious, but bad advice or uncorrected bad habits can damage a lifetime.

I was thin-skinned, raw, uncertain and resentful of the slightest hint of patronage. Which made for some silly but painful difficulties: Dobrée was patient enough to put up with them or ticked me off if he thought the shirt-tail of my self-pride was showing; but he soldiered on with acts of unsolicited kindness as well as contributions to what he must have thought of as my social education.

At about 8.15 one morning, early in the second year, there was a knock on the door of my room in the Hall of Residence. I was still in pyjamas, unshaved and dreary from a very late night's reading. Dobrée came in, looking and smelling freshly as usual; he was on his way from their house at Collingham on the Wharfe, about a dozen miles away, to the University. He had turned off the road and sought me out to say there were hopes of an extra grant so would I call on the Registrar's Department as soon as possible. I had not known he was doing anything on my behalf.

Once, on the drive out to tea at Collingham, he abruptly stopped outside a confectioner's in a narrow, humdrum street and said he ought to get some cakes since there would be other visitors. 'Come in and help me choose,' he said. I knew at a glance that this was not 'a good shop'. I don't mean it wasn't a Fortnum and Mason among confectioners. But it is part of the dour wisdom of the respectable poor that there are good cheap shops and bad cheap shops. This was one in a chain, now long defunct, and one could tell at a glance that its stuff would be 'all show and no body'; certainly not up to Dawes's standard. All cheerful fluting politeness, Dobrée bought a garish cake and led us out with panache. I tagged along feeling altogether older and unillusioned.

One day Dobrée swept in (the theatrical verb fits here) for one of his weekly lectures, looking very angry indeed. He then upbraided us because we did not go to the public lectures which the University occasionally arranged. The previous evening Sir Ronald Storrs, former Governor of Jerusalem, of Cyprus and of Northern Rhodesia, had been talking about T. E. Lawrence's Arabian exploits, with Dobrée in the chair. The hall had been half-empty and, looking round, he had seen few if any of his own students. He was deeply riled. He admired men of action; he tried not to be a sedentary bookworm himself; he respected a man of affairs who was also an intellectual and a soldier, as Storrs was.

At that stage in the term his teacher's charity was probably wearing thin. So he saw us that day as a less generous man might have seen us for much of the time: as a bunch of rather pasty, cautious calculators, people as snide about the celebration of courage as about that of patriotism; main-chancers, insurers, play-safers. We might sneer at the public schools and professional soldiers but from what countervailing strengths within ourselves? Like the traders in *Heart of Darkness* we would not recognise the heights to which we might be called or the depths to which we might fall. We were in Dante's middle range of people, fit neither to be saved nor damned. Not that he said anything like this and I do not suppose those particular thoughts went explicitly through his mind. But something like that set of judgments was driving him at that moment and he made no bones about saying how little he thought of us for refusing to stick out our intellectual necks to feel a more challenging air.

But it was Dobrée, the only one or almost the only one among the professors, who would regularly push into the noisy Students' Union coffee bar to talk with undergraduates (later, Edward Boyle did the same). Clearly, his attitude towards his Northern students, and we were in a majority, was complex; and no doubt it changed a great deal in the twenty years he was at Leeds. I think he recognised from the start some of the strengths those students can show – an awkward, pawky pushing for the truth, a refusal – as he would say in testimonials for people of whom he approved – 'to take anything at second-hand'; and especially a refusal to join the club of the knowing intelligentsia, at the best a stubborn and unstylish search for the light which would help illuminate their condition. He saw that kind of thing, respected it, but also saw that it could be the spiritual equivalent of being purse-proud. I have the impression that much else in the grain of Northern life, admirable or regrettable, passed him by. It would have needed too much of an effort at his age and with his preoccupations to close that gap. He could often walk across the deep water of those differences by simply pretending they did not exist; as in one sense, though not in others, they for the moment did not.

He did not romanticise the North in the usual cliché-ridden way, was not one of those Southern-trained, ruminatively pipe-smoking professors whose fortune has placed them in Northern universities for a quarter of a century and who have become hammy experts on the wit and wisdom of the Lancashire man or the dry salty humour of the Geordie. Grey, dirty and damp, Leeds used to be and still to some extent is; a large, tough, shabby old tom cat whom only the family could love. The contrast with Dobrée's native Channel Islands or with London or Cairo (he had taught in both) must have been acute. Yet I do not remember him ever grumbling about living in the North, as one can hear assistant lecturers grumble at length; nor did he speak with nostalgia about Cambridge. He seemed to enjoy being in Leeds and to be happy to make the best of it.

One side of him slightly romantically saw himself bringing more sweetness and light to the benighted North. His style was consciously cosmopolitan. He was fluent in French, part of that Francophile generation which came to maturity just before the First World War. In his early days America had not arrived as the new destination for the intellectual Grand Tour. If in spite of everything Leeds seemed drab to Dobrée, he seemed a wilful, academic Scarlet Pimpernel to Leeds. *The Yorkshire Post* knew it could usually get a quotable reaction from him on North v. South issues, and he in turn enjoyed giving them a good run for their money.

He liked (again, one is inclined to use Edwardian phrases) to cut a bit of a dash, to shock the bourgeoisie. Among his many literary ancestors one of the most obvious was Lytton Strachey. He liked to be odd and uncustomary. I came into his room one day and found him smoking as usual over his work. The smell was strange, though, like something wafted over damp meadows in autumn. 'Get out your pipe,' he ordered, 'have a fill.' It was herbal smoking mixture from a firm in St Albans – 'bucketful for half a crown' – mixed with his usual Dobie's Four Square. He was pleased at both the discovery and the economy. I do not know how long he stayed with the mixture but I smoked it for years afterwards.

He could be frivolous and boyish, especially when he wanted to shake someone out of 'stuffiness'. 'Stuffy' was one of the most potent words in his dictionary of dislikes. Our English Society 'socials' usually brought this out. We had at those times no visiting speaker and tended to sit or bump around, uneasy because we were out of the context within which we had grown used to each other, the daily pattern of work within our 'year'.

On one such occasion he came in when we had reached the party-game stage. He was in evening dress; there had been an official dinner. We were then playing – we always did – a literary game. He didn't like that kind of shop. Within minutes he was introducing us to some particularly complicated, quite silly and quite unliterary game. Two or three of us brooded irritably: who did he think he was anyway, jollying people along like that; we would work our own way through our own awkwardnesses; this wasn't a Duke of York's camp for clean-nosed apprentices.

The same vivacity informed his lectures; they were exciting and stimulating rather than comprehensive or exhaustive. He deliberately moved across the usual boundaries of specialisms. A congenital cocktail-maker, he laced his lectures with side-comments, odd aperçus from other disciplines, sudden changes of level, irruptions into contemporary affairs. Some of my own less formal literary-and-social interests stem from incidental comments he threw out... for instance, on William Faulkner and types of violence in literature.

He was an immensely hard worker but would have thought it a sign of weakness to complain or even show the effects markedly or consistently. You should carry your load lightly; you have made your own choices. But to do all he did, and also pay dues to those personal values and teacher's values he so much respected, he must have imposed a hard discipline on himself so as to distinguish the light-hearted which deserves time from the trivial which wastes it, the solid work which needs steady application from the merely drudging. In my time he was in his early prime and was producing, I don't know how, two books a year on average. They varied in depth, and in subjects ranged 'dangerously' widely; but they all bore witness to his dream of literature. Inevitably, some people called him a butterfly – he was certainly bright and colourful and tended to flit around. But his characteristic manner and range of interests were fed from more steadily strong-running and deeper sources than that tag implies.

Bonamy Dobrée had a dream of the 'man of letters', widely read, a good scholar who wore his scholarship easily though not lightly. Anyone who had seen him examining critically a thesis or manuscript would think twice before invoking butterflies; he was a stickler for detail, pertinacious and severe. Yet still his ideal man of letters was expected to carry his scholarship well, not to be borne down by it, not to be musty or dusty, not to be one of the 'bald heads forgetful of their sins / Old, learned, respectable bald heads'. He believed critics should have one foot if not in the foul rag-and-bone shop of the heart at least in the untidy garrets where literature is sometimes written. He tended to let others stress the steady grind of historical or textual scholarship (though in his own academic writing he practised that); instead he stressed that literature and all the arts came out of living human beings who put their hopes and pains into it. Among those he presented for Honorary Degrees were T. S. Eliot, Edwin Muir, Wyndham Lewis, Edith Sitwell, Storm Jameson and Henry Moore. I expect this attitude caused him to prop up an unstable poet before patting a steady worker's back. The special quality of the Leeds School of English then was the sense it gave that the study of literature is different in kind from most other subjects, because its material is made out of the stresses of individual lives and the attempts to make sense of them through words. We too had to make our commitments. 'Do make some authors your own,' he would say with a bright smile but insistently.

Because of those social and personal cross-currents in our relationship I have mentioned more than once, I was always a little inhibited with him. He may have felt this underneath. Others told me of meetings with him which were jolly in a way I rarely knew. He unbuttoned himself more, dropped the stance of the teacher more, with those who approached him more uncomplicatedly. A younger protégé told me that, when they were washing up in the kitchen at Collingham one evening, Dobrée had run over his life and achievements up to that point and ended by saying: 'But you see I have to recognise that my mind is not of absolutely the first class.' I was touched to hear again the straight and honest voice but also sad that in my own early acquaintance with him he had not been able to that degree to relax his role.

Two other qualities need to be stressed or the texture will lack important threads. He was extremely courteous and very careful not to give offence when he felt someone needed special care or was not yet strong enough to take direct contradiction. In his courtesy towards women, for whom he had an appreciative eye, he was slightly old-fashioned, even gallant. He would have lived for many of the years up to his early manhood in a predominantly male society, as I had lived in a woman-centred working-class home. So I was particularly impressed by the almost-public formality and attentiveness of his courtesy towards women. Once Mary and I were walking with him in his garden. I was caught up in the conversation and did not notice that Mary had fallen back, perhaps to look at some flowers. When we did notice I made to keep on walking with him partly because the talk was absorbing but also because in my world you would expect her to catch up. He cut straight across my talk and, slightly quirky, said: 'Shall we wait for Mary?' Like so much, a tiny incident but telling: he was still educating me; but also his generation of highly groomed upper-middle-class men were all the time politely attentive to their womenfolk, to women in general.

Second, were the simple kindnesses such as the diversion up to the Hall of Residence to say he had been trying to find extra money for me and thought he had it. Smaller-seeming things too, such as the day he decided I looked strained, took me home to an empty house – his wife, Valentine, was in London with her latest paintings – and said: 'Not much in, I'm afraid, but do you like coddled eggs?' I had never heard of them but he made them well. Many of these kindnesses involved some sacrifice by him as well as a consistency, a steady keeping in mind of certain people's needs. Many young writers waiting for something to be accepted knew he was always good for five pounds; I do not suppose anyone, perhaps not even Dobrée himself for he would not keep a record, knew all the ramifications of this kind of help. I knew the variety of help he gave me; I believe he treated a good many others in something like the same way, so the total giving of himself must have been widespread and complicated.

After we had both joined the army he sent me, from the camp where he was colonel in charge, some good khaki socks saying he had more than he needed and knew that recruits in basic training were never flush. Just before that, whilst I was still at university, he overreached himself and put my always super-sensitive back up. He said suddenly one day: 'Go down to the offices of the *Yorkshire Post* at eleven tomorrow. I've arranged for you to have an interview with Arthur Mann.' Mann was the formidable editor of the *Post*. It was autocratic to decide off his own bat that I should go into journalism and even more to arrange an interview before consulting me. In any event, I wanted to be an academic not a journalist and, such was my snobbery, felt slightly downgraded. But I went – to a dead duck of an interview. I could not have done otherwise, his good intentions were so plain.

It is clear that he was in many respects an intellectual father figure for me at a difficult time. But he kept the relationship taut, well-brushed and not indulgent. This too I liked: here, working-class Nonconformist self-respect chimed in with upper-middle-class professional and military proprieties. But I am once again too quickly making the social point to the neglect of the personal. Others with his background would not necessarily have acted as he did. In spite of all the social and cultural elements I have fed into the story, the basis of our relationship was affection for each other as individuals; and on my side a great respect for him, a respect which overrode considerations of social class. He showed me in action, though I do not claim to have learned to practise them, qualities such as these: hard work and thoroughness, a detailed attention to whatever job was in hand; a complex teacher's care; a touch of the happy warrior, an attack and gaiety; a disinclination to calculate and a refusal to sentimentalise; a kind of stiff dignity on occasion, but more often courtesy, magnanimity and generosity.

All these were brought out in his bearing during Valentine's long and severe illness, which overshadowed the years of their retirement, in Blackheath. The last time I saw them together was in the interval between two of her painful operations and I again saw the care and courtesy and love that had marked their relations throughout. Valentine had insisted they get a leg of lamb and stayed up for a while. We talked over the meal, straight and relaxed; and then he took me to the station, and as we went we talked – now with an openness not snagged by only half-apprehended eddies – of his life and work in retirement. As the train moved off he gave his familiar radiant smile and, being a Dobrée protégé, I remembered lines of poetry: Yeats on 'gaiety transfiguring all that dread'. If I had known it then I would have remembered also that line of Larkin's which appeared almost at the beginning of this book: 'What will survive of us is love.'

I did not see him at all as we entered the Seventies. Others told me that after the death of Valentine he began to feel very old indeed and said he hoped it would not be long before he too was taken. But he waited: 'Men must endure their going hence even as their coming hither', was his kind of line rather than anything about making one's own quietus. We had moved to Paris in 1970 and I had become over-engrossed in work there for month after month. Then one night in 1974, as I was seeing a friend from England down the stairs of our apartment block, she said quietly: 'You must have been very sad at Bonamy Dobrée's death.' It had happened several weeks before, and we had not heard.

A couple or so months after the Venice trip, I got a First. They were not common in Literature, a little more common in Language Studies; Literature students tended to produce one every two years. At our ceremony an Honorary Degree was conferred on T. S. Eliot, an old friend of Dobrée's. At the tea party afterwards Dobrée characteristically went out of his way to introduce me to Eliot who said, gravely: 'We have both seen ourselves distinguished today.' Sitting with him in his top room at Faber's twenty-five years later, I recalled this. He courteously affected to remember.

My First carried the two-year scholarship which earlier Tom Hodgson had held; the assumption was that one went to Cambridge where Dobrée had excellent contacts, and worked for a Ph.D. But by then the war was clearly near at hand and in any event I was due to put in that six months' Militia service, war or not. Dobrée advised putting off the Cambridge entry for a year. There were therefore fifteen months to manoeuvre within, with six of those out for the army. Start a thesis on Swift for the MA here with me, he said (he was working on his *Early Eighteenth Century* volume of the *Oxford History of English Literature* and thought I might contribute), you work fast and could finish that and do your Militia service before you go up to Cambridge. It meant using one year of the post-graduate scholarship money, but that problem could be left for a while.

When the war broke out in September, I was already well into the MA and expected to be called up any day. Dobrée, a reserve colonel, soon disappeared to run a training depot. But not before he had made representations to have my call-up deferred. I finished the MA in March and was called up into the Artillery in late summer; in the interim I did various odd jobs.

Round about June and July, there was a week's holiday which proved to be one of those uncovenanted periods of almost pure joy, out of time, the sort of experience which leaves the fret and strain stilled and makes even simple and sometimes silly actions seem beautiful and new-minted. My brother Tom was waiting to be called up too, his well-founded application to be registered as a conscientious objector having been predictably and uncomprehendingly refused; and Mary had just finished her post-graduate Education year. We decided to go youth hostelling on foot in the Lake District. Viewed from outside, that holiday was an unremarkable affair; we cooked for ourselves, ate simply at lunchtime, sat in the heather and talked inconsequentially. One early evening we were caught on a scree by a violent downpour and slithered hundreds of feet clutching disintegrating paper bags full of raw liver and potatoes; it all seemed wonderful and wonderfully funny. On another occasion we found an open-air swimming-pool and Tom made like a porpoise in the water; we two on the bank fell about laughing. It was all as simple as that and it was unalloyed enjoyment. We were at ease with each other; we knew that what was coming would not be pleasant and would be protracted. But we were not anxiously clutching at such pleasures as were offered; we were separated from all but ourselves, three young people very fond of each other and in a natural world which seemed in harmony with them.

Towards the last day we came down to Hawkshead and telephoned Leeds. I had the MA. Nearby was a characteristically long, low, Lakeland hotel, catering for middle-class climbers and walkers. They offered a three-and-sixpenny set lunch, the regular price for a three-course meal at a good hotel. That was well beyond our usual reach. We turned out our pockets, found we could just manage it as a celebration and sat in, if not splendour, certainly unaccustomed comfort.

For myself, I think of that holiday as the last entirely happy occasion with two people I loved, before we parted; Tom to a long struggle with the authorities and then soldiering in several countries before he was able at last to start training as a teacher, which was his natural vocation; me to almost six years away, chiefly in North Africa and Italy; Mary to the hardest lot of all, teaching and waiting. I expect we all felt much the same about that interlude, when we looked back.

INDEX